Glaser on Health Care IT
Perspectives from the Decade that Defined Health Care Information Technology

John P. Glaser

CRC Press
Taylor & Francis Group
Boca Raton London New York

CRC Press is an imprint of the
Taylor & Francis Group, an **informa** business

A PRODUCTIVITY PRESS BOOK

CRC Press
Taylor & Francis Group
6000 Broken Sound Parkway NW, Suite 300
Boca Raton, FL 33487-2742

First issued in paperback 2022

ISBN-13: 978-1-498-76852-8 (hbk)
ISBN-13: 978-1-03-234007-4 (pbk)
DOI: 10.4324/9781315366180

Publisher's Note

The publisher has gone to great lengths to ensure the quality of this reprint but points out that some imperfections in the original copies may be apparent.

Visit the Taylor & Francis Web site at
http://www.taylorandfrancis.com

and the CRC Press Web site at
http://www.crcpress.com

Contents

Foreword

The year was 1997, the place was a Marriott just outside Ann Arbor, Michigan, and the reason was my attendance at the Information Management Executive (IME) Program sponsored by the College of Healthcare Information Management Executives (CHIME) and the University of Michigan. The military sent me to this program as part of my Information Management Fellowship and Internship. This is a where I first met John Glaser. He was serving as a faculty member, helping new and young health care executives understand health care information technology (IT).

John was far more than an excellent instructor guiding and shaping the minds of the future leaders of our country's health care IT transformation journey. He was and still is the Godfather of the role of the health care CIO—and much of what we understand about the adoption of IT to change health care can be credited to John.

He served as the Founder and initial Chairperson of CHIME. Though starting small, CHIME now represents over 1,700 CIOs and other health care IT executives in every state in the nation and 20+ countries worldwide. His vision at the time was to connect, engage, and empower these budding new leaders.

John is stricken with the same affliction that many of us in this crazy, but fun, profession have: "I Can't Say No (ICSN) disease." After successfully completing the IME program in 1998, I asked John, along with another great CIO (Ed Kopetsky), to consider mentoring and guiding me through my career. Of course, both, succumbing to ICSN, agreed. Now, nearly 20 years later, I have the privilege and honor to serve as the President/CEO of CHIME. I am pleased to report that John's vision for CHIME and the role of CIOs has remained true. In fact, we just launched our new vision statement, "Exceptional Leaders Transforming Healthcare." These four words describe John Glaser perfectly: An exceptional leader transforming our industry.

If you know John at all, you know he openly and willingly shares his thoughts, knowledge, and often strong opinions through writing and speaking. I am not sure that even John knows how many articles, blogs, presentations, and interviews he has conducted and produced over his career. Although the volume is surely impressive, it is his profound impact that truly can't be measured. As CHIME now teaches more than 100 students a year in the CHIME CIO Bootcamp program and graduates 1,000+ students per year, it is important to point out that in every single class, most, if not all, faculty reference John's work, knowledge, and the impact he has made on the next generation of HIT leaders.

This book is a collection of John's finest and most challenging work. These writings represent over a decade of self- and industry introspection and critique. Some will explore the current challenges and potential solutions we face during these transitional years; some will dissect the current policy, exploring weaknesses and errors; but all will educate and inform in a witty and thought-provoking style.

Today's challenges, just like those of the past several decades, require shared learning and understanding. These writings represent an amazing opportunity to learn and understand from one of the best. He not only helped to start us on this journey but also blazed a path of discovery and innovation.

John has always endeavored to help create great and revolutionary leaders. As we strive to enable an industry full of HIT revolutionary leaders, we are guided by several key principles learned and reinforced by John's teachings:

1. **Do Not Accept the Status Quo:** Revolutionary leaders learn from the past and present to create a new and innovative (often disruptive) future.
2. **Be Flexible:** Challenging the present for a new future often results in failure that helps guide future success. Being flexible allows us to rebound quickly and continue to move forward.
3. **Plagiarism Is a Skill, Not a Crime:** Although we do not mean this from a theft of IP or someone else's thought, we do encourage rapid sharing of best practice and knowledge in such a way that we create exponential learning and change.
4. **Revolve (revolt), Not Evolve:** The pace of change must help create a new and different environment of care that truly leads to improved quality and safety, and reduced cost for our country and the patients we serve.
5. **Make Somebody Mad Today:** If we do all of the above, we will make some (and often many) mad. So, our collective challenge is to make somebody mad today by creating a new and different environment of care through the revolutionary application of technology and process change.

John has always challenged us to be our best, question what is in front of us, and create a better future. Please enjoy these amazing writings with that mind-set. Then, use the knowledge to improve your revolutionary leadership skills and create a brighter and better tomorrow.

I am sincerely a man blessed to call John Glaser mentor, teacher, and friend.

– Russ Branzell
President and CEO
College of Healthcare Information Management Executives (CHIME)

Preface

We are in the early stages of remarkable changes in health care and the ever-evolving foundation of information technology (IT) that supports it. Indeed, a new era of health care is upon us:

An era that has seen the enactment of the Patient Protection and Affordable Care Act (commonly called the Affordable Care Act or ACA), which brought about sweeping legislation intended to reduce the numbers of uninsured and make health care accessible to all Americans. An era in which changing reimbursement models are driving care providers from a care volume to an outcomes orientation, wherein evidence-based medicine—and the ability to manage volumes of clinical evidence through sophisticated health IT systems—will mean that providers can tailor treatment for the individual and intervene earlier to keep patients well. And an era in which patient engagement will become a critical component in the care process, particularly in population health management.

Perhaps most notably, from a health care IT standpoint, this era has added two inescapable words to the health care IT lexicon, permanently shifting the industry's focus from adoption to "meaningful use" of electronic health records (EHRs). This has been a good shift—a much needed shift—and a very worthy endeavor by the federal government.

As I look in the rear view mirror of a career that has provided me with multiple vantage points from which to see the industry—including that of a provider CIO, an advisor to the national coordinator for health IT, a vendor executive and CEO, a consultant, and an academic—it's clear to me that this transformation has been building for over a decade. During this time, I have had the privilege of contributing thoughts, opinions, advice, and observations about everything from preparing for meaningful use to innovation to why it is we do what we do in this noble profession in which technology strategically intersects the practice of medicine and the business of health care.

This past decade has taught us a great deal about spurring both the adoption and the meaningful use of EHRs and the systems that surround them. It has taught us about best practices in managing large-scale organizational change, reducing the risks of a complex implementation—and the leadership characteristics required by both. We have amassed volumes of knowledge on how to ensure stakeholder engagement, about what motivates us and our teams—and what, quite frankly, annoys the heck out of the health care professionals who use these systems.

This acquisition of knowledge has served us well and has helped to foster a dialogue on some of the most pressing issues the industry is facing. It is my hope that this book—a compilation of my most widely read columns from *H&HN Daily*, *H&HN Weekly*, and *Most Wired Online* during the past 10 years (2005–2015)—will continue to offer insight and guidance as we navigate the complicated terrain that is yet to come. As such, I would like to take this opportunity to thank the American Hospital Association and Health Forum for granting permission for the articles to be repurposed in this way and for joining with HIMSS/CRC Press to co-publish this book.

The columns are dated to show their original publication, and the material is organized into four broad themes: HIT Applications and Analytics Challenges, Improving Organizational Performance through HIT, IT Management Challenges, and HIT Industry Observations. Note that we did not attempt to update historical data or examples found in the original articles.

Each section offers readers an intimate look at the myriad issues associated with getting IT "right" and the organizational performance gains that can be achieved in doing so. Moreover, we examine the power and potential of the technologies available to health care providers today, as well as the transformative nature of those we have yet to fully embrace.

Writing these columns over the years and offering my voice to the industry dialogue has been a true joy for me. This is an industry I'm passionate about and one to which I've devoted 35 years of my life. What hooked me early on is that it all comes back to patient care. There are few things more fundamental to being a human being than taking care of those who are sick, disabled, or dying.

And like all of you, I want to know that the care I and my loved ones will receive at some point in life has been made safer, more effective, and more efficient because of health care IT. Because this industry never stops evolving, it is critical that we continue to improve and share its decades of learnings with those who will carry the transformation torch even further.

Although the health care IT landscape is a competitive business environment, I believe the industry has embarked upon a very humane, moral, and deep undertaking to help providers deliver the very best care possible. Regardless of which side of the industry you sit on—vendor, provider, government, health plans, life sciences, or consultant—it's going to take all of our collective effort and hard work to ensure that the transformation we've embarked upon continues to deliver the intended results, and that we are bending the cost and quality curves, emphasizing outcomes over volume, and keeping populations of patients healthy.

In fact, it is my great hope that when I look back in that rear view mirror in another 10 years, the health care system in this country will be infinitely better off than it is today, due to the collective work that we've done.

– John Glaser, December 2015

Acknowledgments

I would like to acknowledge the superb assistance provided by Molly Grasso Shane and Maryellen Kaytrosh in putting together the columns that make up this book. I'd also like to thank Kris Mednansky, CRC Press, who made this book possible. Finally, I would like to thank my colleagues in the industry who have taught me and inspired me.

About the Author

John P. Glaser, PhD, senior vice president, is responsible for driving Cerner's technology and product strategies, interoperability, and government policy development. Glaser has devoted his career to advancing health care through innovation and is committed to helping providers maximize their investment in health care information technology (IT).

Previously, Glaser was CEO of Siemens Health Services, a company acquired by Cerner in February 2015.

Prior to that, Glaser was vice president and chief information officer at Partners HealthCare. He also previously served as vice president of information systems at Brigham and Women's Hospital.

Glaser was the founding chair of the College of Healthcare Information Management Executives (CHIME) and the past president of the Healthcare Information and Management Systems Society (HIMSS). He's served on numerous boards, including the eHealth Initiative, the American Telemedicine Association, and the American Medical Informatics Association (AMIA).

Additionally, Glaser is a fellow of CHIME, HIMSS, and the American College of Medical Informatics. He is also a former senior advisor to the Office of the National Coordinator for Health Information Technology (ONC).

Glaser has published more than 200 articles and three books on the strategic application of IT in health care, including the most widely used textbook on the topic, *Healthcare Information Systems: A Practical Approach for Health Care Management* (Wagner, Lee, and Glaser, Jossey-Bass, 2013).

Glaser is on the faculty of the Wharton School at the University of Pennsylvania, the Medical University of South Carolina, the School of Biomedical Informatics, The University of Texas Health Science Center at Houston, and the Harvard School of Public Health. He received his PhD in health care information systems from the University of Minnesota.

Section One – HIT Applications and Analytics Challenges

How the Internet of Things Will Affect Health Care

June 4, 2015
By John Glaser

Devices everywhere talking to devices anywhere could radically change health care.

Before you even fully wake in the morning, your bed has transmitted information about your sleep quality to your physician. Later in the day, your elderly mother's pill bottle alerts you and her physician's office that she hasn't taken her blood pressure med. Your refrigerator has already informed the grocery delivery service that you're running low on life's essentials of soy milk and wine.

Welcome to the Internet of Things (IoT). Anything that has the potential to have a sensor can communicate to anything else that has a sensor. Moreover, analytics that are "watching" the stream of sensor data can orchestrate activity; for example, sensors on cars that indicate a traffic gridlock can lead to analytics changing the traffic light sequence. If that sounds a little too Orwellian for you, imagine the tremendous benefits from a health and welfare perspective.

Connected devices are nothing new. But the connection to date has been largely proprietary—within the confines of a single institution. In addition, device connection usually assumed that a human being was available to read the device data and decide what to do next. The IoT raises the bar—enabling connection and communication from anywhere to anywhere—and allows analytics to replace the human decision maker. The IoT can create new and customize existing processes, allowing us to control our home systems from the office through a smartphone or by sending a message to a technician that a piece of equipment has a part on the verge of failing and that a truck with the part has been dispatched.

The Internet of Things is an ever-expanding universe of devices and technologies with equally expanding potential uses. What qualifies a device to be part of the IoT? According to Verizon, a sensor-equipped "thing" must have three qualities. It must be aware; it must be able to sense and collect data about its surroundings, such as temperature and light or, in the case of health care, blood pressure and heart rate, for example. It must be autonomous. The data collected must be communicated to another device or central location automatically or when certain conditions are met. Lastly, it must be actionable. If an individual's blood pressure or blood sugar levels are at a dangerous level, it must automatically trigger an alert and initiate clinician action.

There are four categories of medical devices that meet the IoT criteria, according to a report by the Atlantic Council. The first is consumer based; fitness tracking devices are an example. There are also wearable, external devices, such as insulin pumps, and there are internally embedded devices such as pacemakers and implantable cardioverter defibrillator devices and, more frequently, miniaturized (within the body) sensors. Lastly, there are stationary devices, such as home monitoring devices, IV pumps and fetal monitors.

The IoT has been made possible by multiple technology advances. There has been remarkable innovation across a wide range of sensor technologies; think of the GPS in your mobile phone. Microprocessors are so potent and inexpensive that they can be attached to a stunning array of things ranging from shirts to human organs to rocket engines. The wired and wireless Internet provides a nearly ubiquitous, high-speed network. And, we are beginning to see the emergence of cloud-based, very sophisticated analytics that can read, interpret and act upon the collected data. Of all of these advances, the analytics are likely to provide the most power to the value proposition of the IoT.

Health Care Applications

For health care, the possibilities are tremendously exciting. Within the next two years, there will be 80 million wearable health devices. Right now, these are largely for personal use—think of the aforementioned fitness trackers such as FitBit and smart watches. The next generation of these devices—and that next generation is very near—will be able to do more than just track steps and calories.

For example, imagine the value to a patient whose irregular heart rate triggers an alert to the cardiologist, who, in turn, can call the patient to seek care immediately. Or, imagine a miniaturized, implanted device or skin patch that monitors a diabetic's blood sugar, movement, skin temperature and more, and informs an insulin pump to adjust the dosage. Such monitoring, particularly for individuals with chronic diseases, could not only improve health status but could lower costs, enabling earlier intervention before a condition becomes more serious. Already under way is a clinical trial which equips heart failure patients with sensors to measure key indicators such as blood pressure and heart rhythm. By some estimates, there is a remarkable 64 percent drop in hospital readmissions for patients whose blood pressure and oxygen saturation levels were monitored remotely. Less patient-focused but invaluable to health care will be using the IoT to connect medical equipment, such as MRI and CTs, to remotely monitor and maintain and to replenish supplies, reducing expensive downtime.

In several industries, we see the use of the IoT to choreograph complex processes: Cities managing traffic flow. Utilities redirecting power moving through a grid. Supplies being sent and re-routed to factories based on real-time needs identified through point-of-sale data. There is a high likelihood of health care equivalents.

Patients' movement through a hospital may be made more efficient through radio-frequency identification technology and sensors on patients, caregivers, rooms and equipment, using process analytics to identify and manage optimal flow. The IoT could inform caregivers that a procedure room is available or that a patient has spent too much time waiting in the emergency department or that a therapist is needed to staff a particular room.

The IoT will also provide data that can be leveraged by the emerging notion of "the digital phenotype." (See, for example, Sachin H. Jain, Brian W. Powers, Jared B. Hawkins and John S. Brownstein, "The Digital Phenotype," in *Nature Biotechnology* 33, 462–463 [2015] doi:10.1038/nbt.3223 [published online 12 May 2015].) As we know, a person's health is influenced by a wide range of environmental and behavioral factors, such as living in a polluted city and smoking. Data on these factors, such as activity on social media sites or shopping behaviors, complement the data that is gathered during the course of care. The Internet of Things will provide data that can be used to round out our understanding of the patient and his or her life settings. This broader set of data has the potential to improve the effectiveness of population health activities and strengthen predictive analytics.

We all know, however, that health care takes a cautious approach to adopting technologies and the IoT will be no different. According to Gartner's information technology Hype Cycle, it will take between five and 10 years for full adoption of the IoT by health care. That cautious approach will serve health care well in this regard. The IoT is not without its hazards and limitations, and health care could be particularly susceptible.

Need for Oversight

Currently, there's little oversight of the IoT. In February, the Senate Commerce, Science and Transportation Committee convened its first hearing on the IoT, trying to understand the implications while the technologies and uses are still developing. Lawmakers are also increasingly sensitive about regulation stifling innovation. Nevertheless, there are many potential implications of the IoT that will require some form of regulatory oversight. Among these are ensuring that the technology infrastructure is adequate to support the traffic volume of the Internet of Things. It is estimated that there may be 20 billion things connected to the IoT by the end of the decade.

Additionally, there are privacy concerns regarding the Internet of Things, and regulators will probably focus efforts there in the near term. Recently, Samsung was widely criticized for its smart TV's voice recognition capability. In the documentation, Samsung stated that if a consumer chooses to enable the feature, "Please be aware that if your spoken words include personal or other sensitive information, that information will be among the data captured and transmitted to a third party through your use of Voice Recognition."

Health care takes the privacy and protection of personal medical information as a top priority. The Anthem breach hit home for many, as it exposed the vulnerability of such information. It wasn't an isolated case. In fact, the rate of information security breaches in health care rose 60 percent in just a one-year period. The IoT brings a new component and challenges into the protection of information.

Information collected from IoT devices will have great benefit for analytical purposes, helping us better understand disease and treatment as well as manage the health of populations. But there are red flags. If information collected even from those seemingly benign fitness devices is sold to third parties, will consumers be inundated with ads for diet supplements? That's more nuisance than harm, but there are also security professionals who fear that the IoT could open up medical devices to more sinister aims, such as interfering with function. Hackers are probably not interested in harming individuals but could do something on a larger scale, such as interfere with insulin pumps.

Currently, there aren't any standards or regulations to govern how information collected via the IoT is used. The National Institute of Standards and Technology is working on a guide to secure connected medical devices, using insulin pumps as the starting point and expanding to other devices in the future.

However, it will largely be up to the industry to adopt standards in data formats and systems as an initial step in addressing security of the devices and the information they generate—and to develop new methods of securing both devices and the information they generate. The methods we've used to date must be expanded to take into account an entire new generation of technologies, and that will require close coordination and cooperation across the industry to "secure" the Internet of Things for health care.

The Internet of Things will bring a stunning array of new capabilities to our personal and professional lives. These capabilities are embryonic in many cases but there are enough examples across a range of settings and industries that we can begin to see a future that is quite exciting. The IoT brings several challenges that will require that individuals, the industry and government collaborate to ensure the IoT's promise is fulfilled.

John Glaser, Ph.D., is a senior vice president of Cerner Corporation, headquartered in Kansas City, Mo. He is also a regular contributor to H&HN Daily.

Interoperability:
A Promise Unfulfilled

April 14, 2015

By John Glaser

© Health Forum, Inc.

Ensuring that disparate health systems can easily share data is crucial for patient safety and lower costs.

Every few years, health care, like any other industry undergoing rapid changes, adopts a rallying cry. For some time now, it's been interoperability. The clamor is reaching a fever pitch, and with good reason. Our collective efforts to significantly improve health and health care through electronic health records (EHRs), population health management and even the "empowered patient," will be largely unfulfilled without interoperability.

For health care to have a shared view on interoperability, and a shared commitment to it, industry leaders need a common definition. We'll use the elegant and simple definition used by the Office of the National Coordinator (which also happens to be the Institute for Electrical and Electronics Engineering definition): "the ability of systems to exchange and use electronic health information from other systems without special effort on the part of the user."

While there are more sophisticated definitions delving into foundational, structural and semantic approaches, what it comes down to is this: Interoperability means that data can traverse organizations, groups and technology platforms. It allows the exchange of data among providers, public health agencies, patients and researchers. That means disparate EHRs—and other systems and devices—must share information both inside and outside the walls of any single institution.

The Office of the National Coordinator (ONC) has issued a draft report, Connecting Health and Care for the Nation: A Shared Nationwide Interoperability Roadmap. (The

ONC is now accepting public comment and will issue a final report around the time this article goes to print.)

In her introduction, Karen B. DeSalvo, M.D., M.P.H., M.Sc., national coordinator for health information technology, writes, "Achieving that better care system and better health for all will, through health IT interoperability, require work in 3 critical pathways: 1) Requiring standards; 2) Motivating the use of those standards through appropriate incentives; and 3) Creating a trusted environment for the collecting, sharing and using of electronic health information." The ONC is so determined to make true interoperability a reality that it has hired its first interoperability chief, Michael James McCoy, M.D., who has extensive experience in standards development.

Why We Need Interoperability

Today's health care consumer may receive care in multiple settings from multiple providers. In addition, both payment and delivery models are rapidly changing. All of this activity leads to significant demands for data fluidity—data needed to coordinate care, manage quality and reduce costs. This information is important for the person at the center of health care: the patient. Everything we do in health care should be designed for the patient. The EHR is a wonderful thing, but if it's confined within the walls of a single institution, it falls far short of its intended value. If a clinician does not have access to a patient's complete record of care, he or she must make calculated guesses regarding what's appropriate, or begin the care process again.

A recent study found that 20 percent of patients who were transferred from one hospital to another underwent unnecessary, duplicative testing. It's a costly, flawed and avoidable route to patient care.

A patient who has multiple prescriptions from different physicians may run the risk of adverse drug interactions because the pharmacy and the physicians' systems don't "speak" to each other. Even more cause for concern is that patients dealing with a serious illness may find themselves carrying their own paper records and images from clinician to clinician during an already stressful time. Lack of interoperability is inefficient at best and, at worst, adds costs and harms patients. Without interoperability, we fail the patient.

If critical information is shared between providers and systems, it creates greater efficiency and speed in care, helps ensure the right diagnosis and treatment, and eliminates redundancy. In addition, it makes all of that care more cost effective. Interoperability ensures that the vast amounts of data generated by personal fitness and wearable monitoring devices is included in the patient's EHR. Such devices capture information about activity, heart rate, blood pressure and even medication adherence and stress levels. This technology expands the body of clinical knowledge a provider will have about the individual patient under his or her care—but only if it is available.

The Challenges of Interoperability

Over the last five years, EHRs have been adopted at an impressive rate, and HIT professionals and providers, myself included, might feel the need for a few "high fives" and pats on the back. Last year, under Stage 2 of the Meaningful Use program, there was an emphasis on interoperability, although in many ways it was relatively modest, requiring only the sharing of a summary of care records. Even this limited use highlighted glaring obstacles to true interoperability.

The differences in how EHRs were developed and implemented, and the inconsistent use of standards, means that sharing data—and ensuring it is usable—is complicated and burdensome. The lack of a nationwide patient identifier hinders providers from sharing patient data. A directed exchange (sending a specific set of information to a specific provider) may be relatively simple, but pulling together data from a wide array of sources using a mechanism such as a record locator service can be overwhelmingly complicated. A new health information exchange often requires that clinical processes be re-engineered or created, work that is always difficult.

The most personal of information about an individual makes sharing of information uniquely complex and sensitive. In a March 4 Health Affairs blog by five U.S. senators, "Where Is HITECH's $35 Billion Dollar Investment Going?" the authors point out the particular sensitivity of patient data: "Unlike a credit card number, the information contained in a patient's health record is impossible to reissue. Health records contain financial records, personal information, medical history, and family contacts—enough information to steal and build a full identity or use for valuable research purposes."

There are other major challenges. Despite the calls for interoperability, often there is insufficient motivation among providers or health information technology developers to make it happen. Providers have been reluctant to share the information they have generated, and the sheer number of different systems that must "speak" to each other is staggering. In addition, some vendors have had little incentive to play together, giving rise to a pattern of data blocking.

A Nationwide Effort to Advance Interoperability

There are several efforts under way to address these challenges. At the center is the U.S. Department of Health and Human Services, within which the ONC resides. The ONC has outlined five core components that it aims to achieve:

- core technical standards and functions;
- certification to support adoption and optimization of health IT products and services;
- privacy and security protections for health information;

- supportive business, clinical, cultural and regulatory environments; and
- rules of engagement and governance.

Other Health and Human Services agencies, most notably CMS, also have critical roles to play in advancing interoperability, as do state governments. States such as Massachusetts, New York and Delaware are advancing care delivery through state-level health information exchanges.

Increasingly, the private sector is stepping up to the challenge. There are various collaborations in the works—even among traditional health IT competitors—to create standards and promote the sharing of data. The CommonWell Health Alliance has developed and implemented critical interoperability components such as a patient identification and linking and a record locator service. Carequality, another collaborative, is developing an interoperability standards and governance framework. The Argonaut Project is defining and testing the next generation of interoperability standards. The eHealth Initiative recently released its 202 Roadmap, which outlines a path to broad interoperability. The Joint Interoperability Testing and Certification program is working to facilitate the exchange of patient information across state lines.

All these collaborations bring together industry stakeholders to accelerate interoperability. No single organization, not even the federal government, can surmount the interoperability challenges without the collaboration of all stakeholders in health care.

Where Do We Go from Here?

A wide range of industries and sectors—banking, telecommunications, supply chain, transportation and emergency services—have achieved interoperability. Think about the remarkable ease of conducting transactions at an ATM not owned by your own bank. For a nominal fee, you have access to account assets anytime, anywhere. Granted, interoperability in health care is a much more significant challenge than in any other industry, but those industries have shown us that it can be done.

We have made progress. It's been slow and, at times, maddening. But the stakes are high, and it is crucial that we continue to hammer away at the obstacles.

Collectively, we must focus on several goals:

- advancing standards development and pursuing new technical approaches to effecting standards-based interoperability;
- strengthening sanctions, perhaps through the certification process, to minimize business practices that thwart interoperability;
- increasing transparency of vendor and provider progress in achieving interoperability;
- developing a trust framework that balances the need for efficient exchange with the privacy rights of patients;

- promoting collaborative multi-stakeholder efforts, such as CommonWell Health Alliance, Carequality and eHealthInitiative;
- encouraging provider-led activities within communities to broaden the range of interconnections—ensuring stakeholders such as safety net providers are included;
- creating a governance mechanism that ensures an effective interchange across a wide range of health information exchanges;
- making reimbursement changes that emphasize care coordination and population health management, all of which must continue to evolve and be implemented.

As important as these goals are, the most important thing we need to do is to remind ourselves constantly that we are here for the patient, and we will have failed that obligation if we settle for anything less than widespread, efficient and secure interoperability.

John Glaser, Ph.D., *is a senior vice president of Cerner Corporation, headquartered in Kansas City, Mo. He is also a regular contributor to* H&HN Daily.

Solving Big Problems with Big Data

December 9, 2014

By John Glaser

Big data initiatives can solve some of the most vexing issues in health care.

Big data generates a mixture of great promise, fantastic and delusional claims, impressive misunderstanding, and several early examples that are beginning to shape our understanding of it. The Internet, open systems and mobile technologies are other, earlier examples of this kind of information technology phenomenon.

Big data conferences and articles are everywhere, and big data initiatives can be found in all industries. Online retailers such as Amazon are masters at unlocking the true power of big data analytics. By monitoring our every click they are able to infer who we are and what types of merchandise we're interested in to better identify sales opportunities and suggest other items we might want to buy. Thus, they create value by optimizing their product mix and personalizing our shopping experience. Customer loyalty and satisfaction tends to trend well, and profits typically follow suit.

Health care has also begun to pursue big data. The growing volume of health-related data, including data from electronic health records (EHRs), diagnostic imaging equipment, aggregated pharmaceutical research, and personal devices such as FitBits and other wearable technologies, presents exciting new opportunities to obtain medical insights and improve patient care. Big data is often proffered as the means to unlock this value.

The Scope of Big Data

Understanding several characteristics of big data can help health care providers harness this phenomenon.

What makes big data big? Data's "bigness" is due to what is referred to as the four Vs:

The sheer *volume* of data that can be obtained, aggregated and analyzed is often several orders of magnitude more than 10 years ago.

The *velocity* of data has greatly accelerated; i.e., more data is available in real time. For example, we can monitor people's purchasing as they purchase.

The *variety* of data has become quite broad. For example, a health care provider can bring together EHR, imaging, molecular medicine, patient search behavior and environmental data for predictive analysis.

The *veracity* of data can be much improved. For example, a retailer can observe what customers really buy as distinct from what they say they buy in a consumer survey.

Big data is broadening the range of data that may be important in caring for patients. For instance, in the case of Alzheimer's and other chronic diseases such as diabetes and cancer, online social sites such as PatientsLikeMe not only provide a support community for like-minded patients, but also contain knowledge that can be mined for public health research, medication use monitoring and other health-related activities. Moreover, popular social networks such as Facebook and Twitter can be used to engage the public and monitor public perception and response during flu epidemics and other public health threats.

Perhaps it is the analysis of these more non-traditional forms of health-related data that will yield the most potent new analytics. For instance, is it possible to extract useful information to aid in spotting potential epidemics from online search queries?

It likely took only one fatal case of enterovirus D68 in a particular community before concerned mothers rushed to Google to check its symptoms. While such search query data are no substitute for local hospital surveillance, researchers believe they can certainly be used as additional input data for estimation models used to improve detection of and response to infectious disease outbreaks.

Big data is more than data; it is also analytics. As important, perhaps more important, than the data are the novel analytics that are being developed to analyze these data. In health care we see an impressive range of analytics, such as:

- post-market surveillance of medication and device safety;
- comparative effectiveness research;

- assignment of risk, e.g., readmissions;
- novel diagnostic and therapeutic algorithms in fields such as oncology;
- real-time status and process surveillance to determine, for example, abnormal test follow-up performance and patient compliance with treatment regimens;
- identification of patterns in the data; e.g., determining if a patient is following the treatment regimen by looking at medication compliance, grocery purchases, sensor and activity data; and
- machine correction of data quality problems.

At times big data involves a combination of novel analytics and novel uses of data. For example, a team at Baylor, using IBM's Watson, identified 10 kinases that might play an important role in combatting cancer by mining over 100,000 articles. This identification was subsequently confirmed through traditional bench research efforts.

Big data is a category. Big data is applied to a wide range of uses in a wide range of industries and efforts. There is no single big data product or application or technology. In this way, big data is similar to transportation or retail, both of which encompass a wide range of activities.

Despite the hype, big data's impact may be quite profound. Overall, McKinsey & Company estimates that big data initiatives could account for $300 billion to $450 billion in reduced health care spending, or 12 percent to 17 percent of the $2.6 trillion baseline in U.S. health care costs.

There are several early examples of possibly profound impact. An analysis of the cumulative sum of monthly hospitalizations due to myocardial infarction, among other clinical and cost data, led to the discovery of arthritis drug Vioxx's adverse effects and its subsequent withdrawal from the market in 2004.

Today, Alzheimer's disease research is benefitting greatly from a range of big data approaches, from whole genome sequencing to complex analyses of the huge volumes of data associated with functional magnetic resonance imaging. Analysis of large data streams—genomic, behavioral, clinical, epigenetic and environmental—from multiple observation points can lead to a more sophisticated understanding of the causes and most effective treatments for Alzheimer's.

Much of what we need to do in health care today requires that we focus on "bigger data." As we begin to manage populations and care continuums we have to bring together data from hospitals, physician practices, long-term care facilities, the patient and so forth. These data needs are bigger than the data needs we had when we focused only on inpatient care.

The expanse of quality measures that health systems need to capture, report and use is bigger than the quality measure set of five years ago.

The range of analyses is bigger. Payer mix analysis and productivity analysis are still germane, but we have extended the analysis arsenal to include predictive algorithms, assessments of practice conformance to the evidence, and patient adoption of health behaviors.

Determining if the increase in "bigness" illustrated above is big enough to constitute big data is irrelevant. What is relevant is that providers have to tackle this increase in bigness, and this tackling is not trivial.

Significant challenges exist in acquiring and managing such large volumes of data, reconciling inconsistent data arriving from disparate sources, protecting patient privacy, and effectively analyzing big data to create value.

Capitalizing on big and bigger data requires the elevation of organizational data and analytics competency. Delivering actionable data that creates value requires significant analytics capabilities. From reporting on what happened to predicting what *will* happen, a recent McKinsey & Company report steps us through a range of big data capabilities today's providers ought to have or should be acquiring:

Reporting: At its simplest, this is looking at data to determine what happened, to evaluate performance or both. For example, with very low technological complexity, today's business intelligence tools enable managers to track and report on key operational metrics such as Healthcare Effectiveness Data and Information Set (HEDIS) measures, referral patterns, census analysis and so forth.

Monitoring: Using recent and near real-time data, monitoring activities provides insight into what is happening now. One might imagine patient safety-oriented workflows that identify the potential for inappropriate medication administration.

Data mining and evaluation: Both hypothesis-based and machine-based data mining can be used to determine why a specific event happened. This investigation of cause-and-effect relationships can help inform evaluations of drug efficacy; deliver proof of the best, most cost-effective care protocols; and identify patients with potential diseases, to name just a few uses.

Prediction/simulation: Using sophisticated analytics to crunch massive amounts of data to predict which chronic disease sufferers are most likely to be readmitted or to determine the predictive indicators of relapse, for example, is fast becoming the holy grail of this new era of accountable health care and the shift to population health management.

These capabilities will be needed to effectively address several aspects of analysis that will prove crucial as providers are held more accountable for the care delivered to a patient and a population. A recent Deloitte report identified five aspects:

Population management analytics: Produce a variety of clinical indicator/quality measure dashboards and reports to help improve the health of a whole community, as well as help identify and manage at-risk populations.

Provider profiling/physician performance analytics: Normalize (both severity and case mix adjusted profiling), evaluate and report the performance of individual providers (primary care physicians and specialists) compared with established measures and goals.

Point of care health gap analytics: Identify patient-specific health care gaps and issue a specific set of actionable recommendations and notifications either to physicians at the point of care and/or to patients via a patient portal or personal health record.

Disease management: Define best practice care protocols over multiple care settings, enhance the coordination of care, and monitor/improve adherence to best practice care protocols.

Cost modeling/performance risk management/comparative effectiveness: Manage aggregated costs and performance risk, integrating clinical information and clinical quality measures.

The adoption of big data into management and clinical practice will shift the intent of analytics. Noted analytics expert Thomas H. Davenport points out that analytics have typically focused on monitoring the performance of the organization. The data used originated from transaction systems such as the revenue cycle and were largely retrospective.

Many of the examples cited above shift the organizational intent to a more proactive and predictive orientation. Can we predict readmissions? Can the data identify more effective treatment approaches? The analysis uses transaction systems but has grown to encompass non-traditional sources of data such as medical literature and patient recording of health status.

An emerging intention is embedding the analytics into medical equipment, buildings and services. This category of analytics could range from a workflow-based EHR that drives and monitors process orchestration across the health care continuum, to the construction of smart assisted-living facilities. Such facilities could feature technologies that monitor and track residents' activity level, vital signs, sleep cycles and compliance with medication regimens to help physicians better understand variation in patient outcomes.

Final Thoughts

Health care is one of the most data-intensive and data-driven industries in the world. Vast amounts of data are generated from health care providers, public and private payers, ancillary service providers such as labs and pharmacies, and health care consumers alike. The challenge is not just in storage and access, but in making this data usable.

As we strive to deliver a more personalized experience in health care, the actions of doctors and nurses and the personal connection they have with their patients will always remain the centerpiece of providing high quality care.

However, the opportunity to more positively impact care outcomes will be broadened through ongoing investments in the solutions, infrastructure and expert knowledge needed to support and advance big data undertakings. Such initiatives will cause us to look at data that has not been studied before or simply wasn't available, thereby opening up a whole new set of analysis opportunities—opportunities to dramatically transform the practice of medicine.

John Glaser, Ph.D., is the CEO of the health services business unit of Siemens Healthcare in Malvern, Pa. He is also a regular contributor to H&HN Daily.

The Role of IT in Understanding and Managing Cost

October 14, 2014
By John Glaser

In a system that reimburses for value, it becomes ever more critical to understand exactly how much it costs to deliver patient care.

We've all heard the saying that what is not measured cannot be managed or improved. There has never been a greater emphasis on accountability in health care, so the inability to properly measure and compare health care costs with outcomes can be a significant obstacle to achieving the value—the relationship between outcomes and cost—the industry collectively seeks.

Understanding the precise costs for every encounter, procedure or episode of care is essential in managing the delivery of services. Precision allows accurate assessments of the profitability of individual service lines, provider relationships or clinical management of a subset of an organization's population. Furthermore, as providers expand service coordination to every aspect of care, costing of services will extend beyond the walls of acute care facilities and physician practices to post-acute facilities and perhaps even in-home care.

Comparable to the growth in meaningful use of electronic health records (EHRs) from a clinical perspective, advanced cost accounting tools and techniques, coupled with sophisticated revenue cycle features, are becoming critical for health care organizations to remain competitive in the future.

When "Good Enough" Just Isn't

Traditional and varied costing methods may have sufficed in a volume-driven payment environment, when decision making based on cost accuracy was not crucial. But yesterday's techniques no longer effectively portray the financial efficacy of an accountable care strategy.

Providers have focused on understanding costs of care in a particular setting such as an inpatient admission for acute myocardial infarction or for a specific surgical procedure. In the future, understanding costs for units of care will remain important. However, holistic payment necessitates understanding costs across organizations and care settings and, often, over long periods of time. For example, payments for procedure bundles require that the provider understand not only the costs of delivering the procedure, but also the wraparound costs such as rehabilitation after the procedure and outpatient testing beforehand.

As such, providers may need to obtain cost data from a wide range of information technology (IT) platforms. Aggregating cost data has often required drawing from multiple systems, but the challenge becomes more pronounced with the need to perform broad cost analyses across several organizations for holistic payment methods.

Processes for costing are also changing. Providers have relied on diverse approaches to estimate and allocate costs. These approaches often result in analyses that have been "good enough" for general purposes. However, with holistic payment and the introduction of payment rewards and penalties, relying on "good enough" estimations of cost becomes increasingly perilous.

When estimations for a bundle of care rely on the summation of a broad set of estimated costs, the confidence interval for the total costs of care becomes wider. Accuracy of the cost estimates becomes impaired once the range for an aggregation of a larger number of estimated cost variables is too wide. For example, a hospital will find it particularly challenging to identify costs of diabetes care accurately if it is trying to base its calculation on estimates of all costs associated with care provided for a patient with poorly managed diabetes.

Moreover, in a payment environment that pays less for poorly managed care, a lack of costing accuracy becomes dangerous. For instance, a provider may think the organization has achieved positive margin on a procedure bundle when it actually has recorded a negative margin because the cost estimates were inaccurate. When the margins on a bundle are thin, sloppy cost estimates can lead an organization to believe it can tolerate reduced payment when it cannot.

Retooling for the Future

As value-based business models are adopted, consider more modern approaches and tools for costing and cost reporting. For example, activity-based costing and microcosting, which consists of identifying and costing every resource consumed in rendering a "unit of care," appear to be on the rise; they are paving the way for deeper, truer representation of the cost for a unit of care.

In addition to scrutinizing cost details, providers will need to examine their definitions of populations and services. Attempting to set a standard cost to care for a diabetic, for example, can be dangerous if the organization assumes that all diabetics are the same. They are not. The cost to treat a poorly managed diabetic is different from that for a well-managed diabetic. Depending on the mix of diabetics, the average cost can be lucrative or disastrous.

Moreover, the payment changes in the years ahead will require not only advanced approaches to cost accounting, but also new capabilities for revenue cycle, EHR and costing system applications, as well as a much tighter and real-time integration among these systems.

As providers transition from traditional cost accounting methods and solutions and retool their approach for costing across the continuum of care, they should consider several key technology and process questions:

Is your EHR truly an enterprise health record? To effectively participate in bundled or capitated contracts, providers must be able to share data throughout the enterprise. Every billable and nonbillable care-related activity should be accounted for in the EHR. Even if a care-related activity has little or no value to the clinical workflow, it should still be possible to account for it within the EHR in a way that does not intrude on the clinical workflow. Having this capability allows a multitude of EHRs to supply the information to revenue cycle management and cost management systems for more accurate and timely costing.

Is your revenue cycle management (RCM) system up to the challenge? They may not be able to leap tall buildings in a single bound, but today's RCM systems are expected to be the super hero—or perhaps super glue—of an organization's IT infrastructure. Indeed, much is expected of these systems when providers are increasingly accountable for the efficiency, cost, quality and safety of the care they deliver.

With regard to advances in costing approaches, the RCM system should function as the keeper of all activities, which is possible only if it is fully integrated with the organization's costing systems and EHR. For example, it should be able to aggregate care data from disparate sources and feed the data into the EHR to help guide clinical care decisions. The RCM system should also support drill-down activities at the patient level with discrete time stamps. It should provide more detailed, timely and accurate information into costing systems and provide feedback into the EHR to support greater efficiency of clinical operations.

Do you know where to cut costs? Health care providers have spent decades strengthening their revenue identification and charge capture tools and systems. Now, with an agenda that focuses not only on managing the top line, but also on improving the bottom line, providers must hone their skills in removing waste from the system. Thus, they need to understand cost at a deeper and truer level to identify cost reduction opportunities or determine more cost-effective care alternatives, such as shifting care delivery from a physician to a nurse practitioner. Indeed, the ability to conduct variation analyses across the continuum and through different lenses, as well as being able to drill down into cost drivers, is becoming critical for all providers.

Do common definitions prevail? Speaking the same language goes a long way toward avoiding confusion. For example, is the definition of "unit of care" consistent among all the providers that are collectively assuming risk? Similarly, are your definitions of fixed, variable, incremental, direct and indirect costs common among the contracted players? Additionally, from a process standpoint, will costing take place at the episode level, clinical service level, encounter level, charge code level or elsewhere? The importance of being precise in both terms and processes cannot be underestimated.

How current and accurate are your data? The old cost accounting systems were notorious for data access and quality issues, rendering them somewhat ineffective; their use was infrequent at best. New demands require timely analysis of cost and margins across services lines and along the continuum of care, so data must be current and instantly accessible. In fact, providers should transition from cost computation models that use the previous fiscal year's data as standard cost for the current fiscal year to computation models that refresh data at least monthly. In a rapidly changing environment, last year's data are no longer good proxy for making decisions.

Are your interfaces up to snuff? As mentioned earlier, some providers are achieving even higher levels of variable cost accuracy using the microcosting model. The type of cost elements that will be subject to microcosting will have an impact on the complexity of cost system implementation. For instance, if labor, materials and pharmaceutical costs are within the scope of microcosting, existing interfaces to key feeder enterprise resource planning and revenue cycle systems may need to be reviewed or rebuilt. Similarly, the capture of staffing and utilization data by shift and the measurement of labor costs require tweaks to the payroll, human resources, and revenue cycle systems and interfaces.

Can leaders act on your data? Most organizations generate far too many reports, many of which simply go unread. Today's more advanced revenue cycle and cost accounting solutions provide user-friendly executive dashboards that improve transparency and facilitate proactive management of key performance metrics. The same way an organization cannot improve what it cannot measure, it cannot act on data that shows no clear direction.

In addition, the time frame for action will shrink. Finding out that you are losing money on a population 60 days after the fact is too late. This is particularly true as margin pressure increases. The reporting must be done in real time so that problems can be corrected before too much financial damage has occurred.

The Age of Transparency

Making a healthy margin and demonstrating value to purchasers of care are critical success factors for health care organizations. Research highlighted by the Robert Wood Johnson Foundation and others has shown there is almost a complete lack of understanding of how much it costs to deliver patient care—and little is known about how prices are derived.

As the conversation in health care eventually turns to price, spurred by the Centers for Medicare & Medicaid Services proposed price transparency rule, the need for an organization to understand its actual costs will only grow in importance. After all, how can a provider effectively set its procedure prices without knowing its true costs and, therefore, its margins?

A costing approach that is comprehensive, accurate and modern—and backed by technologies that enable providers to collaboratively make decisions based on cost data that were previously unavailable—is essential for success. Partial, manual, retrospective assimilation of costs does little to facilitate effective decision making. Nor does it enable detailed, timely and accurate financial reporting to internal and external stakeholders.

Furthermore, in this age of transparency, the relationship between the EHR, revenue cycle management and costing systems is of utmost importance, with data becoming an enterprise's key strategic asset.

As the industry emphasizes the identification and capture of all costs to determine the actual cost of care, the implementation of newer technologies and advanced costing methods should hold a prominent place on every provider's strategic plan. But, as with all technology implementations, use of these systems without careful consideration of the organization's needs and processes regarding their use will hamper their effectiveness.

John Glaser, Ph.D., is the CEO of the Health Services business unit of Siemens Healthcare in Malvern, Pa. He is also a regular contributor to H&HN Daily.

Heeding the Call for Health Information Exchange

December 10, 2013
By John Glaser

Streamlined, secure information exchange for providers not only prepares health care organizations for payment reform, it is also critical to the nation's substantial investment in electronic health records.

From meaningful use requirements to participation in accountable care organizations, there is no shortage of pressure on health care providers to share information more effectively. In fact, payment reform can be considered the major stimulus behind the increase in health information exchange (HIE).

Payment arrangements that reward high-quality, cost-effective management of a patient's care over time and between various care venues will incent providers to invest more deeply in HIE. Yet, to date, the level of exchange across the country is well below our collective aspirations. According to recent industry data, 30 percent of U.S. hospitals and 10 percent of ambulatory practices send and receive data through HIE.

While the barriers to widespread HIE have been well documented—most notably, maintaining a sustainable business model and working with immature interoperability standards—the Office of the National Coordinator for Health Information Technology has defined a sound framework for both accelerating HIE and advancing standards and interoperability.

Additionally, meaningful use criteria for stages 2 and 3 will ask more of providers with regard to HIE, attempting to spur greater demand for and participation in exchange efforts while challenging providers to overcome the roadblocks.

Improving Care across the Continuum

Health information exchanges come in a variety of flavors and exist through various types of organizational arrangements. In some cases, an HIE could be provided by a regional or state organization that facilitates a public exchange among all providers in a geographic area. In other cases, the exchange is likely to be provided by a hospital or health system that wants to initiate targeted interoperability with ACO participants or to simply increase information exchange (and thereby affinity) with community physicians.

Regardless of the organizational structure or technical platform used to support the exchange, there are notable benefits for a health system participating in HIE:

- establishing, managing and expanding referral and test/procedure order patterns within the ambulatory community;
- growing physician affinity through technical connectivity and marketing activities, regardless of the physician's electronic health record (EHR) technology;
- improving physician access to clinical information, including lab results, radiology studies, discharge summaries, etc.;
- increasing connectivity between specialists, post-acute care and primary care;
- messaging across transitions of care, supporting care planning and other patient coordination activities;
- engaging patients in their own care and connecting them with providers; and
- supporting the efforts of public health agencies and purchasers of care to understand disease patterns and changes in care quality and efficiency.

A successful, sustainable HIE's economic model and business structure is often based on self-interest. While some cooperative models based on altruistic intent succeed, they are, unfortunately, the exception rather than the rule. Successful ones are usually directed by strong leaders and run by a supportive community with a passionate, patient-centric commitment that combines self-interest and benevolence in a manner that provides sustainability.

One such HIE is run by Inspira Health Network, a community health system composed of three hospitals in southern New Jersey, with more than 5,000 employees and 800 affiliated physicians.

With nearly 40 EHRs connected to the exchange and more than 600 providers using its clinical portal capabilities, Inspira's HIE has strengthened the ties of its physician community to the organization. Since Inspira competes for ambulatory practice business, the HIE makes it easier for physicians to get data into their electronic health records, providing access to the latest information on their patients from member providers practically anywhere. Whether they're in the hospital or in the office, physicians see the complete picture of the patient as aggregated among these members.

Beyond the physician community, Inspira boasts some creative connections to its HIE, including its fitness center, which may receive physician referrals and can deliver an electronic report back to the practice and even notify a physician if a patient doesn't show up as expected.

Additionally, Inspira's home health agency gets lab results delivered right to its EHR—a huge benefit when nurses go to a patient's home and have the latest patient information right at their fingertips. Inspira case managers also use the HIE to help coordinate care and identify patients who need to be placed into rehab centers or long-term care facilities. The exchange enables them to proactively provide relevant information about a patient through secure electronic transmissions to applicable facilities that service their area. This can lead to more efficient and effective discharge planning and thereby help reduce patient length of stay.

Operating a private HIE does not preclude a provider from joining other exchange services. Inspira is also a member of its regional HIE, which was formed with two other health systems in the southern part of the state. Participating in the regional network enables Inspira to share data in a broader area and jointly pursue federally funded grants to offset HIE expenses.

Key Considerations

While streamlined, secure information exchange prepares health care organizations for payment reform, it is also key to realizing the desired quality and efficiency gains to be derived from the nation's substantial investment in electronic health records.

Like Inspira Health Network, a number of providers have done some terrific work getting their exchange efforts off the ground. Key learnings from their experiences are worth sharing:

Try a phased implementation. Resist the temptation to bite off more than the exchange can chew at the launch. Cast a wide net to all care community members, concentrating on simple initial use cases (e.g., sharing clinical information originating in the hospital) and grow from there. A phased approach allows the HIE to deliver immediate value, generate support and enthusiasm, and make learn-as-you-go adjustments.

Even with simple information exchange capabilities, caregivers have easier access to more comprehensive information to improve treatment planning and optimize care transitions. With a staged feature deployment approach, the exchange can progress from simple results distribution to multidirectional communication and eventually coordination of sophisticated workflows.

Keep the patient front and center. One of the thorny parts of participating in an HIE is the myriad decisions members will need to make regarding their shared information. For example, what data need to be exchanged for an ACO to perform well? Who's ultimately responsible for data security? How much do we share and with whom?

Indeed, HIE members will need to think long and hard about whether they prize cooperation and transparency over competition and secrecy. Despite the devil living in all these details, most operational HIEs have found that if they keep a focus on what's best for the patient, many seemingly complicated decisions become much easier.

Know your community and stay connected. Designating an outreach coordinator who knows the community and its key health care stakeholders can make a huge impact on the success of the HIE.

It's also important for all members to work collaboratively to understand the data flow needs and changing requirements of other participants. As such, instituting regular HIE user group meetings for decision making, progress reporting, issue resolution and ongoing community outreach efforts will help ensure the HIE continues to meet the needs of all participants.

Get creative with connections. Facilitating secure information exchange with a broad community of health system participants will help organizations deliver more coordinated care, increase the productivity of staff members, and ultimately improve the economics of care delivery.

When you're thinking about where information gaps exist within the community—where time and money are spent on calls, faxes and postage—look beyond practices to include other members of the health care continuum whose information needs are not being met. Additionally, each time a connection is added, use the opportunity to redesign and optimize processes, especially during care transitions between providers.

Tap physicians to help with expansion. If physician response to the HIE is lukewarm, cultivate practice champions or physician liaisons to inspire their peers by discussing the benefits they're seeing from using the exchange.

Working with the HIE outreach coordinator, practice champions can serve as excellent trainers for those who need help getting up to speed.

Don't overlook non-EHR users. Health systems initiating an HIE may be hesitant to offer Web-based clinical portal capabilities, for example, to practices not using an EHR, fearing that such capabilities would delay EHR adoption in a practice that perceived its clinical IT needs were being met adequately through the HIE.

This was a key inspiration for Inspira, which does not hesitate to roll out HIE capabilities to practices that are still planning an EHR implementation. With the benefit of hindsight, Inspira leaders now know that the HIE can deliver immediate efficiencies to even paper-based physician offices—and could very well help steer them toward EHR adoption as they desire increased functionality.

Make membership turnkey. Having standardized open enrollment forms and practice sign-up sheets available at all times can enable same-day fulfillment of requests for membership. Additionally, having distributable legal and governance documents, such as data sharing agreements, terms of use, and privacy considerations available early in the process can speed deployment, adoption and return on investment.

Check your sources. Those initiating an HIE are wise to work with their vendor and participating partners to perform a thorough data analysis of all source data. This will help ensure that the exchange can consume, transform and distribute a broad range of transactions in a variety of formats.

A Critical Linchpin for Better Care

Health information exchanges, which enable disparate organizations to securely share patient data, have emerged as a core element of health care reform and the delivery of high-quality, safe and efficient care. HIEs can deliver tremendous value by facilitating more coordinated care among hospitals, physician practices and key members of the health care continuum, such as skilled nursing homes, home health agencies and durable medical equipment suppliers.

Although we've seen considerable growth in the number of HIE efforts, particularly over the past two years thanks in part to HIE-related meaningful use criteria and ample state and federal funding, substantial challenges still exist.

Overcoming technical and legal matters, addressing privacy and security concerns, and tackling the sustainability issue will continue to be a key focus for policy makers, purchasers of care and providers that engage in their own HIE efforts. Furthermore, to derive maximum improvement in care quality and efficiency, our health care organizations and public institutions will need to expand beyond local and state-level HIE efforts to achieve a more widespread adoption of HIE across state lines.

This expansion will be made possible by current and future payment reform efforts and meaningful use requirements focused on exchange and patient engagement capabilities, driving continued growth in local HIEs. When those exchanges join regional or state HIEs, the result will be a larger system of providers to pull data from, and therefore, greater benefits for patients. For example, with such expansion, we open possibilities to use the data aggregated and generated by HIEs to facilitate comparative effectiveness research or to enable syndromic surveillance reporting in support of a more rapid response to public health threats.

But, as we know, there is no running without first walking. And when it comes to truly overhauling the nation's health care system, there is no such thing as a sprint.

As such, we should applaud all those health care communities across the country—communities like southern New Jersey—as well as state-sponsored HIEs that have already achieved some potent gains in improving care coordination and efficiency. Indeed, with the industry's collective goal of becoming *meaningful* users of health information technology, now is the time to heed the call for HIE.

John Glaser, Ph.D., is the CEO of the Health Services business unit of Siemens Healthcare in Malvern, Pa. He is also a regular contributor to H&HN Daily.

Reprinted from H&HN Hospitals & Health Networks, by permission, December 2013, ©2013 by Health Forum, Inc.

The Growing Role of Analytics and Business Intelligence

October 9, 2012
By John Glaser

© Health Forum, Inc.

Preparation is the key as analytics and business intelligence take on greater importance in health care.

In the coming years, federal, state and private sector purchasers will implement a wide range of new and resurrected reimbursement schemes to effect improvements in care. These schemes include:

- penalties for poor care (e.g., high levels of hospital readmissions);
- bundles and episode payments that provide fixed reimbursement for all care required for a surgical procedure, such as a hip replacement, or all care needed by a diabetic in the course of a year;
- reimbursement reward for care above or below national averages (e.g., value-based purchasing); and
- financial rewards for efficient care (e.g., shared savings programs).

These schemes vary in their maturity and will be introduced over the course of the decade.

To respond to these payment pressures, providers will increase their efforts to establish care processes such as care coordination and population management. And they will participate in widely discussed new care models such as patient-centered medical homes and accountable care organizations (ACOs).

Providers will need to enhance their measurement and reporting so they can implement these new care models at the individual patient and population levels and so they can manage the diverse payment arrangements. For example, ACOs will want to measure the effectiveness of care protocols, such as exercise compliance, for a population of diabetic patients. Surgical service providers will need to understand the costs and quality of proposed procedure bundles. Understanding what works and what does not is key to ensuring reimbursements, controlling costs and, most importantly, providing the best care for the patient.

As such, business intelligence and analytics will become essential in this new care delivery environment. These tools will enable providers to assess, for example, risk factors of a defined population in relation to a care protocol, the measurement of the effectiveness and efficiency of a program, and data mining to develop clinical evidence for best care practices.

The Focus and Nature of Business Intelligence and Analytics

The various payment reform alternatives (and the associated new care models) have several common themes. They all encourage the following:

- a view of care as longitudinal rather than a series of disconnected encounters;
- patient risk prediction and stratification models;
- funding of lower cost services that substitute for higher cost admissions, emergency department visits or face-to-face physician encounters;
- using lower cost providers for tasks they are competent to perform;
- patient self management; and
- systems of care where information flows within and between provider organizations.

Health care reform will force significant changes in the data needs and strategies of provider organizations. Providers will need to link patient encounters by disease and to assess the care activities that occur over lengthy periods of time in different care settings. The data must allow providers to determine the specific care activities, e.g., medications prescribed, laboratory test results and the costs of care delivered. The finance analytics databases will need to include a much broader and deeper set of longitudinal clinical data.

Providers may also need to incorporate encounter data from outside the organization (enabled by health information exchanges) and eventually data that patients enter through personal health records. And the provider's analysis capabilities should include software that allows analysts to identify patients who are at greater risk of needing care, enabling the organization to strengthen support for those patients.

Moreover, providers will need to assess the costs and quality of alternative care settings and to model the implications of moving patient care to settings other than the hospital or physician's office. The analytics software should support an organization's intent to optimize performance, control key processes and decisions, and react to changes in the environment as well as deviations from performance.

Overall, providers will need to be more focused and aggressive in managing the organization and their patients. Changes in reimbursement will require providers to predict which patients will need extra care, determine the financial implications of changes in quality scores, assess the performance of core organizational processes such as transitions of care, determine conformance to medical evidence, and report quality measures to purchasers. Business intelligence and analytics will also need to be more real-time and accessible at the point of care.

In addition to the need for enhanced business intelligence capabilities, the "context" of business intelligence will change due to the technology, shifts in the provider business model, and the fact that administrators and clinicians are growing increasingly comfortable with information technology.

For example, consider the following:

- Analytics from the data warehouse are going to be expressed in much more of a real-time and distributed fashion, pushing information as close to the point of decision as possible.
- Traditional command and control structures to monitor adherence, track performance variances, and take corrective action through retrospective quality improvement and training initiatives will no longer be the only way to align an organization's goals. Information will be pushed to the front lines, guiding decisions at the point of highest possible impact.
- Relationships and meanings can be inferred from available data, some of which is structured and some of which is unstructured, and all of which is expanding rapidly as new technologies become available to capture information. What information means, its relationships and potential combinations, will become less reliant on exactly how it is captured, extracted and stored. This diminishes the burden on clinical processes and resources.
- As new relationships are discovered, predictive models can emerge from the data as a byproduct of machine learning capabilities, rather than as an exclusive derivative of the human investigative process and statistical analysis. Analysis technology will become more "invisible" to the end users even as they take greater advantage of analytical applications in their day-to-day workflow.

Ramifications for the BI and Analytics Management Ecosystem

To respond to the business intelligence needs that result from payment reform, providers will need to implement next-generation analytics and address the changes in the data context and in its use. As is always the case, effective use of technology requires implementing a sound ecosystem of management practices and policies, as described below.

Establishing BI governance. Data governance is the most critical contributor to the effective day-to-day use of BI. Good quality data is of greater organizational value than state-of-the-art analysis software. Data governance involves creating and continually managing the organization structures, policies and processes needed to define, control and ensure the quality of the data. Moreover, the governance function helps providers determine what types of analyses are the next focus of BI efforts.

The form and organizational location of the governance function will vary, largely driven by the scope and intent of the BI effort. If the organization is focused on using BI to improve the revenue cycle, then the governance structure may report through the finance department, and the governance steering committee will be composed of stakeholders who manage operations that are key components of the revenue cycle. The governance body may spearhead changes in process and information systems to ensure the accuracy of insurance information acquired at registration and to develop a single definition of the data element "visit."

If, on the other hand, the organization is focused on using BI to measure care quality, then the chief medical officer might oversee the governance structure, and the steering committee could be composed of a large number of clinicians and managers of ancillary departments. The governance body may commission system changes to improve data capture on medical error events and to define clinical best practices for treating patients with a chronic disease based on data derived from the electronic health record (EHR).

Developing data use policies. Data exchange among health care entities raises data management questions for both the senders and recipients of data. For example, under what conditions can data from one organization be used by another organization, e.g., for care operations assessment or clinical research? And if one organization needs to amend data it has exchanged with others, how is that amendment propagated to the various recipients?

Broad EHR adoption will open the door to secondary uses of clinical data: clinical research, care improvement, population health and post-market medication surveillance. Early efforts to use EHR-based data in these fields show promise but have also exposed data quality issues. Providers may also be approached by data aggregators who are interested in pooling data from multiple organizations in order to pursue these secondary uses. The contributing organizations will need to establish policies and agreements that enable them to benefit from these arrangements but also protect themselves.

Defining data management practices. Data management refers to the steps an organization takes to ensure that its data has a well understood meaning, is of good quality, is appropriately used, is protected and has potent analyses tools. Data management is very difficult. The work is not sexy—it can involve slogging through process changes, cajoling clinicians, engaging in difficult discussions on data meaning and edits, reducing multiple data silos, and fixing application software with insufficient edits.

Enhancing the quality of data will become more complex and daunting. For example, steps to improve data capture often hinder operational efficiency. This challenge will spread from registration areas to the exam room. In addition, managers are often uncertain about the quality of data in their reports and are unsure of the "source of truth." As the organization's data encompass sources beyond the organization, confidence and truth become difficult to assert.

Determining business needs and value. Managers should discuss why they want to make the investments required to establish and maintain an effective BI effort. The rationale must be more compelling than a statement such as "we need better data." It can focus on reasons such as organizational imperatives to understand cost structure, care quality or revenue cycle performance. Regardless of rationale chosen, the case should be clear to managers.

The value of having better analysis capabilities can be very difficult to measure. It may not be obvious if an investment of several hundred thousands of dollars to understand care quality will be "worth it." BI investments very often rest on the strength of management judgment that this investment is necessary if the organization is to achieve its goals and objectives. This should not preclude efforts to measure the return on investment of BI investments. Rather, managers should understand that ROI alone will not be a good assessment of BI value.

Developing an end-to-end vision. The organization will need to develop an overall vision and road map that defines the scope of the BI effort and the plan to achieve that scope. This vision often starts with efforts to improve data collection practices at the front end, e.g., the processes used in identifying referring physicians in the specialty clinics. The vision moves all the way through definitions of the composition and organizational location of the BI analysis staff. The vision will describe the types of analysis desired and the classes of users who will authorize the analyses and receive the results.

Defining target areas for BI implementation. It is not practical to implement BI technologies and disciplines throughout the organization all at once. Rather, managers should target areas for initial implementation based on business needs and value. As leaders learn from these pilot efforts, they can make decisions about the breadth and pace of BI implementation.

The Learning Years

Health care providers in the United States are entering a decade of profound change driven by reimbursement changes and care models that are intended to elevate quality and reduce costs. While there have been attempts to use reimbursement to drive change, the decade before us has no parallel in terms of the complexity, significance and potency of these efforts. They will alter the structure of health care provision, and providers will need to make investments in a comprehensive portfolio of information technology.

A critical investment will be in BI, analytics and ensuring that a sound management ecosystem is in place for successfully using the technology.

In the next few years, we will all be challenged to develop a more comprehensive understanding of analytics and BI in health care. As we rely on techniques like data normalization and consolidation, we will learn to exploit other data types and analytical techniques to provide the answers we need to deliver optimal care to the communities we serve.

The choice will not be between retrospective or predictive analytics, consolidated or distributed data, and human or machine-driven decision-making. We must do all of these.

Indeed, there will be much to learn and new knowledge to share as we move boldly into this data-rich future—a future we ought to be preparing for now.

John Glaser, Ph.D., is the CEO, health services, at Siemens Healthcare in Malvern, Pa. He is also a regular contributor to H&HN Daily.

From the Transaction-Based EHR to the Intelligence-Based EHR

August 14, 2012
By John Glaser

As our smart phones become even smarter, our EHRs will likely need to follow suit, especially with a health care system in transformation.

Health care information technology adoption has taken a relatively sharp jump, last year in particular. According to a recent Office of the National Coordinator for Health Information Technology (ONC)/American Hospital Association (AHA) study, the number of U.S. providers using either a basic or a comprehensive electronic health record (EHR) system is on the rise. The substantial increase between 2010 and 2011 is probably due in no small part to the federal incentives for meaningful use.

Still, the percent of hospitals and physician practices with very sophisticated electronic health records remains relatively modest. Additionally, while the industry emphasizes the need to lessen the gap between the haves and the have-nots, small, rural providers still show a much lower rate of technology adoption than their larger counterparts.

As we encourage EHR use, shift the balance from basic to comprehensive EHRs, raise the bar on the definition of meaningful use, and narrow the gap between provider haves and have-nots, we must also focus on the shifting nature of EHRs—a shift that will be necessary if EHRs are to effectively support accountable care.

The Transaction-Based EHR

If you look back at the electronic health records implemented over the years, you'll see that the focus has been on transactions such as writing a prescription, retrieving a result or documenting a visit. In automating these transactions, we had to address several different challenges.

For example, in the outpatient arena, every 15 minutes, there's another patient to see, so transactions must be performed in a fairly narrow window of time—about five or seven minutes. In the inpatient arena, the core challenge is the coordination of care: ensuring that those responsible for a patient's care are aware of the care tasks that need to be performed and the results of tests and procedures. In both inpatient and outpatient situations, the EHR has to support care in very diverse settings such as obstetrics, primary care, neurology, cardiology and the ICU.

As the early EHRs came on the market, we emphasized speed, efficiency, ease of use, and the ability to cover the spectrum of inpatient and outpatient settings. We talked about the ROI of these systems in terms of the improvement over paper-based transactions. There were fewer legibility problems and fewer medication errors, documentation was more complete, data was more accessible, and transcription costs dropped. A variety of studies illustrated the strides we made as an industry in improving the clinical transactions associated with care delivery.

To be fair, the focus of these EHRs was not strictly on supporting transactions. We built in clinical decision support that provides health maintenance reminders and ensures order appropriateness. We added some basic analytics to assess provider performance, care costs and quality. We also ventured into patient engagement via personal health records and disease-specific monitoring. While these advances provided key stepping stones, the core focus of today's EHR remains the transaction and making it as efficient and as effective as possible.

Tackling the Accountable Care Challenge

There are several cross-cutting problems we have to solve if we are to provide the type of care that we expect and, frankly, need to deliver under this new era of reimbursement and of patient and consumer expectations:

Failure to follow the evidence. Any number of studies during the past decade have shown that U.S. health system performance continues to fall far short of what is attainable, especially given the enormous resources devoted to improvement efforts. For example, in 2003, Elizabeth McGlynn, Ph.D., and her colleagues at the RAND Corporation looked at some well-established treatment guidelines.

They attempted to determine to what degree patients receive care according to the protocol. They found that only a little over 50 percent did, indicating a massive failure to follow the evidence for a good amount of the care. Now, obviously, given reimbursement pressures and expectations, this type of failure is going to be less and less tolerable.

The care delivery system has begun to respond to those dismal findings. More recent studies, such as The Commonwealth Fund's 2011 National Scorecard on U.S. Health System Performance, show that adherence to treatment standards for heart attack, heart failure and pneumonia, for example, has experienced notable improvement. This is likely due to federal policy linking Medicare payment updates to hospitals' agreement to publicly report their results. Nonetheless, a significant gap remains between leading and lagging hospitals.

There's simply too much to know. The second problem we face is that there's too much information for physicians to master. If you had leukemia 100 years ago, they called it blood disease and you likely died. Sixty years ago, five different forms of leukemia or a lymphoma had been identified; today there are upward of 90 leukemia types or lymphomas combined. Last year, 700,000 articles were added to the referring biomedical literature. Ten years ago, it was 400,000. It is anticipated that in the coming years it'll be 1 million. There's just too much to know.

Increasingly, we have to help those who deliver care be up to date on what the most current (and rapidly growing) knowledge or practice is in terms of both diagnosis and treatment.

A lot of care processes just don't work very well. We've all heard stories, or perhaps experienced, a problem with care in which we can't help but wonder what went wrong to cause such poor communication, how a key piece of information could have been overlooked, or why something fell through the cracks.

Extrapolated data from various studies of outpatient care clinical processes show that for every 1,000 women with a marginally abnormal mammogram, there appear to be 360 women who will not receive appropriate follow-up care. Similarly, for every 1,000 patients who qualified for secondary prevention of high cholesterol, 380 will not have an LDL-C screening within three years on record. As there's no argument about what constitutes an appropriate next step, the question is: Why is there such a remarkable failure of a process?

The answer varies. In the case of the mammogram, at times the patient refused. Or she went to a different organization and the care provider wasn't made aware. Or she received follow-up care, but it wasn't recorded. Or perhaps, with approximately 150 test results crossing the desk of the average primary care provider every day, a particular patient may have fallen through the cracks.

These cross-cutting challenges—failure to follow the evidence, too much to know and inadequate care processes—indicate a need to surround the transaction with intelligence. At a minimum this intelligence will need to suggest steps required to ensure that care follows the evidence, to identify treatment options that result from the dazzling pace of medical discovery, and to alert providers that care processes have deviated from acceptable levels of performance. This intelligence must detect acts of commission (choosing an outdated treatment approach) and of omission (a patient has failed to keep an appointment to see a specialist).

Toward the Intelligence-Based EHR

The above scenarios illustrate that while we've made some impressive gains in automating core health care transactions, much work remains to address both the process and knowledge issues that plague care delivery and to ensure the best evidence is routinely followed. To accomplish this, we must make the shift from a transaction-oriented record to an intelligence-oriented record, capable of achieving the following core objectives:

- guide clinical diagnostic and therapeutic decisions;
- ensure the sequence of care activities conforms to the evidence and performance contract requirements;
- monitor the execution of core clinical processes;
- capture, report and integrate quality and performance measures into EHRs;
- expand the scope of clinical data gathered about a patient, including data from other providers in the region, data provided by patients and data that is captured from one's genome; and
- support the interactions of the care team, as all intelligence is not necessarily machine intelligence focused on specific transactions. Often the intelligence is the care team working together (perhaps using social network tools) to come to a conclusion and a consensus about how best to treat the patient.

In order to achieve these core objectives, the EHRs we provide must have several key capabilities, including:

- foundational sets of templates, guidelines and order sets that reflect the best evidence or established best practice;
- a process management infrastructure that supports basic transaction checking such as drug-drug interactions, as well as asynchronous alerting like panic lab reporting and process monitoring and guidance;
- team-based care support such as shared work lists, as well as tools for patient engagement and health information exchange;
- novel decision aids like predictive models that can tell us if a particular patient is likely to be readmitted because he or she is fragile or has a sub-standard social situation at home that may negatively impact healing;
- context-aware order sets and documentation templates that guide the physician and help infer what types of orders should be placed and what types of documentation should be done; and

- intelligent displays of data, intelligent correction and identification of data, and extraction of structure by going through free text and pulling out quality measures or problems that were not previously in a patient's problem list, for example.

Lastly, there will be a new generation of real-time analytics that will measure quality and process performance and assess guideline adherence, financial performance, and provider treatment and outcome variations.

Smarter Tools to Manage Big Data

The shift to intelligent EHRs will require incorporating the capabilities described above. In addition, tomorrow's EHRs will be shaped by work, still early, that applies "big data" techniques and methods to health care data. The "big" part of big data will be the result of the growth in patient data captured in EHRs coupled with data from imaging, molecular medicine, patient-provided data and insurance claims.

Consider hypertension, which can be managed with diet and lifestyle modifications and with medication in some cases. Also consider that improperly managed hypertension can often lead to more significant issues such as heart disease, stroke or even heart failure.

Through a combination of advanced in vitro diagnostics, diagnostic imaging, and the data archiving and extraction capabilities afforded by an intelligence-based EHR, we can identify the individuals most at risk and start them on a regimen modifying diet and behavior—well in advance of the onset of hypertension, and certainly well before more serious issues develop.

Bringing together the clinical evidence and drawing meaningful conclusions will require sophisticated and refined IT tools to extract valuable information from volumes of data. These same tools will also enable us to refine our processes and significantly reduce the variation in care that has long plagued our health care system. Big data approaches will be used to support post-market surveillance, comparative effectiveness and clinical trial hypothesis framing.

While we must not lose sight of our nation's goals of increasing the adoption and meaningful use of EHRs by all providers, we must also understand that the transition from the transaction-based EHR to the intelligence-based EHR may become one of the most critical undertakings in our journey toward more accountable, cost-effective care.

John Glaser, Ph.D., is the CEO, Health Services, at Siemens Healthcare in Malvern, Pa. He is also a regular contributor to H&HN Daily.

Surviving a Revenue Cycle System Conversion

June 12, 2012
By John Glaser and Veronica Ziac

Many providers are realizing they'll need to invest in new financial and billing systems.

The Affordable Care Act (ACA), despite the uncertainty of many of its specifics, is sure to significantly alter reimbursement structures and the delivery of care. Because of performance pressures, health care organizations need a consolidated view of care delivery and revenue management among multiple providers to ensure optimal revenue cycle performance.

Some organizations, as in the case of Ellis Medicine in Schenectady, N.Y., will encounter factors beyond their control that lead to a system conversion as the industry continues to consolidate.

In 2008, Ellis fell victim to the New York State's Commission on Health Care Facilities in the 21st Century, also known as the Berger Commission, and was required to merge three hospitals into one entity. This resulted in a significant financial system conversion. Ellis successfully merged three hospitals and cultures (the former Ellis Hospital, St. Clare's Hospital and Bellevue Hospital), improved the cash flow of the new organization, and realized an $8 million gain post-merger. The organization also re-engineered and standardized the revenue cycle processes of its three facilities while completing a big bang conversion of all three hospitals to a next-generation revenue cycle system (RCS) in 2010.

Preparing for the Unknown

Regardless of the reasons an organization undertakes an RCS conversion, the journey can be a daunting one. In fact, few events trigger more anxiety than bringing a new financial system live. With a very small margin for error, no organization wants lost claims or disruptions in cash flow.

While careful planning and thorough testing and training can help alleviate some of the anxiety, the unexpected will occur during some component of the installation.

Ensuring that a revenue cycle conversion goes as smoothly as possible and results in the desired performance gains depends largely on three factors: maintaining a positive working relationship between the provider and vendor; maintaining a positive working relationship between the revenue cycle and IT departments; and having ongoing, visible support from top managers. In addition to these factors, several lessons learned by Ellis can aid others faced with introducing a new revenue cycle system and making related changes in revenue cycle processes.

Charting a Course for Success

As Ellis embarked on its conversion journey, the team had an overarching goal of doing what's right for its patients. Having multiple systems was not only very inefficient for staff; it was also painful for patients. So, an objective right from the start was to create a more patient-friendly billing and registration system. Helping staff see the direct benefit to patients throughout the project kept the level of engagement high.

The following insights and best practices can help other providers plan for a successful RCS conversion and more readily achieve desired financial performance goals:

Realize the significance of the culture change that accompanies a large system conversion; staff the project and coach users accordingly. Success can come only through organizational buy-in. In messaging the project to your organization, be careful not to minimize the importance by referring to it as simply an "IT project" or "new billing system upgrade." Staff members will struggle to feel a personal connection to the project unless they understand the direct impact on their work as well as the big picture impact—that every single patient visit will be affected by the system change.

With a new system install, you want key departments to understand how they fit into the overall revenue cycle. For example, Ellis' conversion to a next-generation system moved charge capture management from the back-end or business office to the departments where charges are generated. While some revenue producing areas may not have appreciated the importance of charge capture and reconciliation, Ellis' project leaders didn't hesitate to pull in C-level people to work with selected ancillary departments to more clearly explain their stake in ownership.

Finally, you'll want to ensure your implementation team is made up of people who are change agents, who are comfortable with change, who are natural leaders and who can bring the right attitude to a project of this scale.

Develop a comprehensive plan that covers all the nuances of report generation and management within your organization. A core task is to inventory all report users from your legacy system and ensure they're covered on the new system. When Ellis underwent its conversion, the obvious report users such as patient admitting areas, the business office and the finance department were covered. However, other departments, such as the information desk, pastoral care and the foundation office, were missed during the analysis phase. As such, phone calls came into the command center during go live week with staff assuming their printers were broken. Of course, it wasn't the printer that was broken; the legacy system was simply no longer generating a particular report and no arrangements for new reports had been made. Be sure to think outside the box on this issue because there are users you may not think of right away who are relying on admitting or charge data to manage their responsibilities.

You'll also want to establish a reporting team or infrastructure before going live. Prior to Ellis' conversion, reporting was very much decentralized. The process was boiled down to users e-mailing or calling particular people they knew who could create reports for them, but there was no general coordination. During its conversion Ellis was able to develop a dedicated team of report writers, as well as a systematic way to handle and prioritize report requests. This meant ensuring that the ownership of reports was clear and enforced.

It's also essential to have your must-have reports ready for day one, not three months after going live. Furthermore, ensure there is daily monitoring of key operational reports. Ellis had several inpatient accounts get stuck in the system; because a particular report was not designated for daily review, it took a week to identify the issue, which resulted in a brief cash crunch.

Monitor operational performance throughout the conversion. To develop a meaningful dashboard or metric report while going through a conversion, it's important first to develop some comparative metrics. Ellis did this by using two comparative metrics, one being baseline metrics which consisted of an average of its six months pre-live metrics, then incorporating several of the Healthcare Financial Management Association benchmarks.

Post-live metrics monitoring should include daily as well as weekly monitoring, such as DNFB (discharge not final billed), claims submitted and even cash. You may want to review these metrics again monthly with year-to-date averages as well as some percentage trends compared with your baseline figures.

Assess policies and procedures prior to implementation. A thorough assessment of the currency, awareness of, and adherence to the organization's policies and procedures is key. One thing you don't want to do is build your new system around old processes. Even the best systems cannot make up for poor workflows, processes and communication. Since you'll be determining newer, more effective workflows, they will likely require new policies and procedures. One effective means to accomplish this task is to use small groups to work right in the new system, determine what kind of a workflow is most appropriate, then develop and test the new policies and procedures with those workflows.

Implement a solid formal change management structure. Change management is important when you're going through a conversion. One of the lessons Ellis learned is that changes to an enterprisewide solution such as a new RCS can affect many systems and users. As such, you need to very carefully consider any change to the system and how that may affect other systems and other users. Ellis' change management program is led by its IT department, and the team meets weekly to review proposed changes and decide to approve, deny or postpone. Every proposal is subject to a waiting period of at least five days prior to a vote. The organization also has key leaders sign off on changes, so decisions are well documented.

Avoid other conversions during the same time, or at least carefully consider the risks and impacts. Some things may be under your control and some may not be. Ellis' fiscal intermediary underwent a conversion that didn't go very smoothly about two months after Ellis' conversion, resulting in delayed payment from the intermediary. Ellis also implemented a new payroll system around the same time and brought some outsourced functions (its self-pay function in particular) in house with the conversion. All of these changes going on simultaneously caused a bit of a struggle. While the organization got through them, it learned a valuable risk management lesson.

Begin risk management discussions with payers early. An RCS conversion can involve high risk process change, so it's essential that all issues affecting these processes are considered up front. Explore all options concerning cash flow issues with payers and partners. For example, Ellis worked with a payer who was willing to do a claims push to expedite processing. You'll also want to work closely with your accounts payable department and vendors to keep them all informed of any changes and assess any impact of fluctuations in cash outflows during the initial post-live period. It's equally important to be aware of anything outside the conversion that may affect cash; physician incentives, vacations and payouts fall into this category.

Continue weekly meetings post live. Although it's been over a year since Ellis went live with its new system, the implementation team, which consists of vendor and hospital resources, continues to have weekly status meetings to review any system or process issues. This management technique works especially well for those issues that might require a multi-departmental approach. For example, Ellis has people from patient access, revenue management, IT and medical records on the implementation team—the ongoing face-to-face dialogue among all stakeholders has been effective in issue resolution.

RCS conversions are typically complex and stressful. Ellis Medicine's system conversion experience emphasizes that with the right planning, staff engagement and executive support, the intended gains can be achieved with minimal disruption to the revenue cycle.

John Glaser, Ph.D., is the CEO of Siemens Health Services in Malvern, Pa. He is also a regular contributor to H&HN Daily. *Veronica Ziac, M.B.A, C.H.C., is the revenue cycle systems director at Ellis Medicine in Schenectady, N.Y.*

Six Key Technologies to Support Accountable Care

April 10, 2012
By John Glaser

Fundamental accountable care processes will require a range of information technology components and capabilities—some of which will introduce new competencies for many providers.

Health care is the most complex, knowledge-driven industry in the world, representing one of our most significant economic challenges. While the transition to a system of more accountable care will be evolutionary, real challenges exist in building successful accountable care organizations or supporting ACO-like operations. One core challenge will be the diversity of forms of ACOs; the Centers for Medicare & Medicaid Services definition will be one of many.

What lies ahead is the re-orientation of decades of organizational processes and structures that have long supported fee-for-service payments, competition among providers and strained relationships with payers. We are embarking on a transformation of epic proportions, one that requires the industry to come together with a common purpose. We need a laser focus on care coordination, quality improvement and cost reduction.

A key tenet of accountable care is to improve integration. ACOs are expected to implement a wide range of managerial, legal, clinical and other leadership structures. The goal is to ensure that the health and wellness of the population is managed, the most cost-effective care is provided, clinical processes are streamlined and follow the best evidence, the necessary reporting is in place, and the payments and reimbursement are appropriate.

Last but not least, the ACO must demonstrate, in a variety of ways, its commitment to being patient centered and to engaging patients in managing their care and overall health.

Shifting Perspectives and New Competencies

Accountable care will require industry perspectives and health care delivery practices to shift

- from care providers working independently to collaborative teams of providers;
- from treating individuals when they get sick to keeping groups of people healthy;
- from emphasizing volumes to emphasizing outcomes;
- from maximizing the use of resources and assets to applying appropriate levels of care at the right place;
- from offering care at centralized facilities to providing care at sites convenient to patients;
- from treating all patients the same to customizing health care for each patient;
- from avoiding the sickest chronically ill patients to providing special chronic care services;
- from being responsible for those who seek services to being responsible for the needs of the community; and
- from putting forth best efforts to becoming high-reliability organizations.

Additionally, accountability will bring new performance and utilization risks to providers, as the focus shifts from optimizing business unit performance to optimizing network performance. At the same time, instead of maximizing the profitability of care, organizations will increase the volume of desired bundled episodes while controlling costs.

As providers assess their risk tolerance, they must also strengthen their ability to manage several core processes in an accountable care environment. These core processes include:

Identifying, assessing, stratifying and selecting target populations. It will become imperative for providers to store, access, maintain, derive and update population data and categories (stratification) from multiple sources. Additionally, within target populations, providers will select cohorts for specific programs based on predefined metrics (cost, utilization, outcomes).

Providing care management interventions for individuals and populations. This includes patient-centered management and coordination of care events and activities in multiple care settings by one or more providers (e.g., identifying care gaps and situations requiring additional interventions, as well as managing care transitions). The aim is to manage the most complex patients through the health care system, taking their preferences and overall situation into consideration. In addition, managing the overall health of a select population (diabetics, elderly, well, etc.) will require proactive care, communication, education and outreach.

Providing high-quality care across the continuum. While this is an obvious goal for all providers, ACOs must facilitate cross-continuum medical management for active episodes and acute disease processes or for any patient outside of the defined goals of a target population. It also includes fine-tuning coordination among care team members, transition of care planning, targeting venues of care, establishing patient and family engagement initiatives, and monitoring and improving clinical performance.

Managing contracts and financial performance. With new payment models (bundled, shared savings) emerging, proactively understanding patient coverage and financial responsibility will be critical. Financial teams must have a solid handle on estimating reimbursement and associated payment distributions, carrying out predictive modeling for reimbursement contracts, measuring performance against contracts and predicting profitability, as well as integrating with other key processes to share information.

Monitoring, predicting and improving performance. With payment so tightly linked to quality and outcomes, tracking and measuring system performance in key areas become paramount in an accountable care environment. Under value-based purchasing (VBP) programs, there will be real ramifications for poor care and rewards for improved care. Providers can work with their quality and clinical staff to adapt processes accordingly. In a VBP model, even low-performing areas can qualify for high payments if they demonstrate year-over-year improvement.

Across the risk spectrum, these accountable care processes will require a range of IT components and capabilities—some of which will introduce new competencies for many providers.

IT Building Blocks to Support Accountable Care

Several application systems will be essential for responding effectively to accountable care and new payment models. In addition to an electronic health record that spans the continuum of care, the following six key technologies will enable the core accountable care processes:

1. **A revenue cycle and contracts management application that evolves to span the continuum of care.** One could argue that the revenue cycle system forms the foundation of a provider's response to accountable care and payment reform. As the reimbursement

environment becomes more complex, revenue cycle systems must evolve to support payments based on quality and performance, requiring new capabilities such as:

- aggregating charges to form bundles and episodes, with the aggregation logic enabling different groupings for different payers;
- managing the distribution of payment for a bundle to the physicians, hospitals and non-acute facilities that delivered the care;
- streamlining transitions between disparate reimbursement methodologies and contracts when billing and collecting; and
- providing tools for retrospective analysis of clinical and administrative data to identify areas for improving the quality of care and reducing the cost of care delivered.

These new capabilities must complement routine activities such as registering patients, scheduling appointments and administering patient billing.

2. Care management systems that span the continuum for individuals and populations. Care management systems support proactive, preventive and cost-effective care for individuals and populations. Specific capabilities include care venue transition management, care coordination (utilization and case management), disease management, population management and wellness management.

These care approaches focus on preventing unwarranted emergency department visits and avoiding acute episodes. Additionally, disease registries will enable providers to identify cohorts of patients with focused care needs, review summary data sets and make necessary interventions when care is not up to standard.

3. Rules engines, workflow engines and intelligent displays of data that enable intelligent processes across the continuum, defined by best practices. Processes that are efficient, predictable and robust enable an organization to thrive in an accountable care environment. Workflow and rules engines can monitor process performance, alerting staff to missed steps, sequence issues or delays.

Workflow engines specialize in executing a business process, not just decisions made at a discrete point in time. The technology can greatly assist in clinical decision making by not only presenting clinicians with alerts and reminders, like a rules engine, but also by encouraging teamwork in clinical decisions, assisting with the time management and task allocation in process delivery, stating changes in patient or operational conditions, and creating behind-the-scenes automation of process steps.

4. Sophisticated business intelligence and analytics. Analytics will facilitate proactive management of key performance metrics. For example, there will be a greater need to assess care quality and costs, examine variations in practice, and compare outcomes. As such, the application of business intelligence in health care will become the platform upon which the organization not only monitors performance, but also makes critical decisions to uncover new revenue opportunities, reduce costs, reallocate resources, and improve care quality and operational efficiency.

However, the industry lacks experience with the tools and techniques associated with advanced data analysis. Thus, enhancing an organization's competency in data management and business intelligence will become an essential requirement for internal purposes as well as for external reporting requirements.

5. **Systems that enable interoperability between affiliated providers.** Having information available is critical to the success of accountable care. A health information exchange (HIE) platform will become increasingly important to enable the secure flow of data about patients and can, for example, facilitate access to information needed for:

- performance metrics, such as care cost and quality;
- patient events monitoring, such as a visit to the emergency room or a failure to show up for an appointment;
- patient status, as in a hospitalization in a member hospital with a specific discharge destination; and
- ensuring that the care team has a comprehensive view of a patient's status and the care delivered by all members of the patient's care team.

While there has been some success in the regional HIE movement, much of the focus now is on HIE capabilities at the integrated delivery system or ACO level. This enables providers to obtain a composite clinical picture of the patient regardless of where that patient was seen. In time, a provider will be able to request data about a patient from any other provider in the region, perhaps even in the country.

6. **Technologies that support the engagement of patients.** In addition to providing high-quality, effective care at the best possible cost, providers need to engage patients in staying well and managing their health. A system that allows patients to communicate with caregivers, perform self-care activities and participate in health screenings, for example, can improve quality of care and outcomes, especially for patients with chronic diseases.

While few are taking advantage of patient portals and personal health records, organizations are using other approaches to engage patients in their care, including texting and social media channels. Such engagement efforts will increase over time, and we will use these technologies in a variety of ways, such as:

- providing patients with access to their data so they understand their current health status;
- allowing patients to communicate with their care providers (ask questions, discuss symptoms, renew medications, requests appointments, and so forth);

- enabling patients to enter their own data (ranging from correcting a medication list to entering data about their symptoms, particularly if there's been a change in treatment pattern); and
- providing patients access to health information and management tools (education, discussion forums with other patients who have conditions similar to theirs, and so forth).

Aligned, Focused and Moving Forward

A more accountable system of care supported by aligned incentives is long overdue in this country. Such a system creates shared accountability and incentives for managing a patient's health—a much different health care system than the one in place today. Accountability will require that care be accessible to the community and that providers deliver a high-quality experience focused on keeping patients healthy and engaged in their own care.

New payment models will be disruptive, and parts of the journey will be chaotic. Additionally, the long-term success of this transformation relies largely on building the robust, secure IT infrastructure to support the far-reaching goals of accountable care. However, thanks to a well-crafted federal health information technology agenda which lays the foundation for payment and structural reform—a reform that encourages widespread meaningful use of interoperable EHRs—the industry is aligned, focused and moving forward.

Savvy providers will use the meaningful use mandates to help prioritize and plan for IT investments that also enable the core processes associated with accountable care. Even for providers that may not be participating in an ACO, building the organizational and IT competencies to support accountable care is critical to staying competitive. Organizations that fail to develop and demonstrate accountable care capabilities may not fulfill their obligations to the community they serve—in fact, they may not survive.

John Glaser, Ph.D., is the CEO, health services, at Siemens Healthcare in Malvern, Pa. He is also a regular contributor to H&HN Daily.

Accountability and the Revenue Cycle

October 11, 2011
By John Glaser

Revenue cycle systems will likely undergo significant changes as providers respond to a vastly more complex reimbursement process.

The U.S. health care industry is about to undergo one of the most dramatic periods of change it has ever seen—perhaps since the advent of Medicare and Medicaid in the 1960s.

The economic crisis of 2008 led to a significant growth in federal deficits, underwater budgets in many states, and a more aggressive business community. Against this economic backdrop, purchasers of care are taking new, far-reaching steps to tackle care cost and quality issues.

These steps are taking many forms, such as financial penalties for high readmission rates, incentives for prescribing generic medication, and denial of payment for never events. At the center of this shift is the Affordable Care Act and its many programs designed to hold providers more accountable for the care they deliver.

Although we are not yet able to map out all of the nuances of the transformation, we should acknowledge that three significant realities await us:

- The absolute amount hospitals and care providers are paid will be lower relative to inflation. Margin pressures will increase.
- Providers and health care facilities will have to prove the quality of their outcomes as well as their processes under requirements with higher risk relative to performance.

- Health care providers will move toward more holistic care, focusing not solely on the instance of care, but also on the total care provided.

Certainly, success within the various payment reforms will build on the meaningful use of certified and interoperable EHR systems—and the country is making good progress implementing the required technology. But it's the revenue cycle system that will form the foundation of an organization's response to payment reform.

Ramifications of Accountability on Revenue Cycle Systems

An organization's revenue cycle system (RCS) will need to support a provider's management of financial, administrative and clinical processes. It will require software that groups charges into bundles and episodes and supports definitions of bundles and episodes that vary among purchasers. The RCS must allow an organization to disburse a single capitated payment to the various providers that treated a patient with multiple chronic diseases.

While these capabilities are critical, the RCS will also take on several fundamental features:

- supporting revenue diversity and complexity;
- enabling greater process efficiency;
- serving the full continuum of care;
- acknowledging the ascendance of data;
- interoperating within a larger ecosystem; and
- improving organizational agility.

Support of revenue diversity and complexity. Fee-for-service payments will continue to exist in the era of accountability. Not all encounters can be neatly packaged into bundles or episodes that can be clearly defined by evidence-based guidelines and unambiguous measures of quality. We are unlikely to see a "trauma bundle," and it can be very difficult to define the outcomes of psychiatric care.

Different purchasers will have different definitions of bundles and episodes. These purchasers are likely to develop similar but different measures of quality and arrive at similar but different statements of care guidelines.

The RCS must manage this diversity, which encompasses both old and new payment methods, an explosion in the number of salient quality measures, and a burgeoning set of guidelines that define acceptable and non-acceptable treatment procedures, medications and tests.

The RCS must also shield, as much as possible, its complexity from the staff who perform front-line registration and the clinicians who are focused on doing what is best for the patient.

Process efficiency. With the pressure on reimbursement, revenue cycle processes must become more efficient, a particular challenge given the growing diversity and complexity of reimbursement.

Improving process efficiency requires, at its core, organizational prowess in understanding and reengineering processes. This prowess is not easy to develop and sustain. The RCS can support these process improvement efforts.

Workflow and rules engines can monitor process performance and alert staff when steps are not taken, or occur in an incorrect sequence, or take too long. These engines can ensure that communication between staff occur and can suggest subsequent steps.

Analytics for these engines can help managers understand whether the organization is doing a good job of following its re-engineered processes. These analytics can point out processes that seem to have uneven performance and can suggest additional training or further re-engineering.

Continuum of care. The health care industry already has revenue cycle applications that support the hospital and different applications for physician practices and long-term care facilities. Now, to improve accountability, the industry needs better care coordination between care settings.

The RCS will need to support the full continuum of care. In effect, the industry shifts from a portfolio of diverse RCSes to a core RCS that is extended into these different settings, with the extension possessing features unique to that setting while preserving an integrated core set of capabilities, data and engines.

Ascendance of data. The industry is fairly primitive in its ability to look at data, to understand what it means and to take actions based on that understanding. The role of data and the importance of data management will likely grow significantly after payment reform. If you don't know whether you're making or losing money on a particular bundle or episode, you could wind up in a lot of trouble quickly, even if your clinical staff is using a top-notch EHR.

Thus, organizations will need to make sure they have business intelligence technologies, including one that will assess their quality and their costs not only for internal consumption, but also for reporting purposes. There will also be a significant need to look at variations in practice and understand where providers are falling short, or whether a particular provider or set of providers has uncovered a new or better way to deliver care.

In addition to reporting, the RCS data environment will need to handle a range of modeling. For example, we might do an assessment to determine whether some of the care could be delivered by a nurse practitioner rather than a physician, or if care should be moved from one specialty group to another specialty group to improve quality while managing or lowering costs.

The RCS will need to enable predictive modeling to, for example, identify those patients who are likely to experience significant distress or additional care needs in the months and years ahead. We might also want to determine if healthy patients are at risk of becoming unhealthy.

Interoperating within a larger ecosystem. Revenue cycle systems have had to live with interfaces since their inception: Registration data flowed to clinical and departmental systems and charges flowed back. But now the RCS will need to interoperate within a larger ecosystem.

Charges may flow from EHRs and ancillary systems that are outside of the organization. An organization may contract with a group of cardiologists, for example, to provide care for a capitated population. As a result, the RCS will need to receive charges from an EHR outside of the organization's direct control.

Virtually all RCSes have a master patient index in their foundation. With accountability models, it becomes much more important to track a patient visiting different care settings. If a patient has been seen in four or five different provider organizations, we need the means to link that patient with the different medical record numbers she's been assigned by these organizations. The goal is to roll up all the clinical data, not only for the purposes of treating the patient, but also to have an estimate of the cost of her care, as well as the quality of that care.

New businesses will pop up that offer accountability functions to hospitals and health systems. These new businesses will offer to negotiate rates, assist in population management, perform predictive analyses to identify high risk patients, and assist with process re-engineering efforts. In many cases these new businesses will provide a valuable service to providers. The provider RCS must interoperate with the systems used by these businesses.

Organizational agility. While the overall emphasis on increasing accountability is clear, the mature form and effectiveness of proposed new care delivery organizational models and payment strategies is unclear. No one really knows, for example, whether an accountable care organization, based on a collection of affiliated providers, will really "bend the cost curve."

The country is in for a lengthy period of experimentation and uncertainty. It is not possible to know the mature form of these delivery models and payment approaches. Hence provider organizations and their RCSes must be able to adapt to the inevitable tuning and course correction.

Application systems can be designed to be agile. Service-oriented architecture, tools that enable adding new types of data and changes in computer-based forms and rules, and workflow engines that allow editing of workflows and rules—all of these support, albeit imperfectly, agility.

Focus on the Fundamentals

It's impossible to anticipate every detail of how the future will unfold. While a provider may decide to wait until the future becomes clearer, this is a mistake.

Whatever course reform takes, quality measures will be integral to payment reform. Focusing on quality improvement today will serve health care organizations well, as will reducing costs and streamlining processes. Improving data quality and the organization's skill at using data is always worthwhile. Organizations should keep moving forward with their EHR and quality data efforts and track the progress of their plans.

The future does not have to be fully clear in order to prepare for it. Many of these initiatives take several years to accomplish, and an organization can wait too long and be forced into a mode of hasty catch-up.

RCS Checklist

Managing the risk and financial responsibilities of more accountable care will require a significant reorientation of traditional revenue cycle activities. As the reimbursement environment becomes more complex, revenue cycle systems must evolve to support payments based on quality and performance of the clinical enterprise.

The system will need logic that groups charges into different bundles and episodes. It will need analytics that bring clinical performance and revenue cycle data together in real time so leaders can understand whether variations in clinical performance will have an immediate impact on expected reimbursement. Support for a high degree of interoperability will be paramount. Additionally, the system must be able to manage increasingly complex processes via workflow and rules engines in a setting that will have less and less tolerance for inefficient and ineffective processes. These new capabilities must complement routine activities such as registering patients, scheduling appointments and administering patient billing.

In ensuring that a fully functioning revenue cycle is in place, providers and their IT vendors will need to collaborate. The two groups must work together to manage a complex information technology infrastructure and application base and share a strategic perspective on the evolution of the technology being implemented. The partnership must work in lock step to support the provider's strategic plan, with the vendor having a broad understanding of the organization's long-term clinical, financial and administrative goals.

Health care providers will have to respond not only to changes regarding the best way to achieve efficient, high-quality care through new reimbursement strategies, but also carefully hone their own information management processes to ensure they thrive as the industry changes around them. A well thought out and carefully constructed approach to revenue cycle management is crucial to successfully navigating uncharted territory.

John Glaser, Ph.D., is the CEO of Siemens Health Services in Malvern, Pa. He is also a regular contributor to H&HN Daily.

The Next IT Revolution: Nearly Ubiquitous Computing

June 14, 2011
By John Glaser

Sensors and mobile devices will allow us to monitor a patient's condition, track movement through a hospital and conduct better effectiveness research.

Over the last 50 years, information technology (IT) has been revolutionizing the world. The impacts of IT are diverse and numerous; IT has spurred global finance, transportation, smart buildings and virtual communities—even public protests against oppressive regimes.

This revolution has come in waves. Each wave is the result of a new ecosystem of converging information technologies and business models. For example, the networked personal computer wave resulted from advances in microprocessors, the maturation of local area networks, a breakthrough application (the spreadsheet), and the openness of the Intel/DOS platform for use by many independent developers.

The Four Waves of IT Revolution

There have been four major waves of IT revolution:

The mainframe wave introduced IT to the business community and allowed diverse companies to automate routine clerical tasks such as airline reservations, bank asset management and hospital patient accounting.

The minicomputer wave fostered new software platforms such as UNIX and, in health care, facilitated applications for departments such as clinical laboratories and radiology. It also made clinical information systems more accessible to medium-sized hospitals.

The networked personal computer wave provided users with a powerful computer of their own and enabled them to share resources, such as printers and storage. This wave accelerated the growth of smart medical devices, enabled an explosion in software for small businesses and brought the computer into the home.

The Internet wave has significantly altered the retail, content publishing, and distribution and travel industries. This wave has seen the establishment of new forms of communities, powerful advances in information-seeking capabilities, and an explosion of new ways to reach customers.

The Fifth Wave

The term "nearly ubiquitous computing" can be applied to the fifth wave of IT revolution, which we are now entering. This wave has several characteristics:

- networked, powerful processors almost everywhere and on almost anything;
- a diverse array of sensitive and specific "sensors";
- massive amounts of data, and novel methods for analyzing it;
- software delivered as a service; and
- a wide variety of collaboration, community and knowledge resources.

Powerful computers can be found on people (in mobile devices such as the smart phone), buildings, automobiles, credit cards and electrical grids. In addition to their power, these computers are generally always connected to a very-high-speed, usually wireless, network. Often working in tandem with these computers are diverse arrays of sensors that can measure air quality, medical images, chemical concentrations, traffic, human physiology, building temperature and train locations.

These nearly ubiquitous computers are generating massive amounts of data. Novel methods are being developed to analyze this data to conduct post-market surveillance using electronic health record (EHR) data, determine consumer behavior by examining web search behavior, and understand traffic patterns in cities.

Increasingly, the software used by these computers is offered as a service. You pay as you "consume" the software, reducing the need to obtain a software license. The data being generated and the software application are hosted in a "cloud"—a set of servers somewhere "out there."

Nearly ubiquitous computing extends the reach and the power of the collaboration, community and knowledge resources that arrived with the Internet. These resources can be accessed from anywhere—not just from the personal computer at work or home.

The Potential of the Fifth Wave

The fifth wave will enable us to:

- develop sophisticated models and test hypotheses using large sets of data;
- orchestrate complex processes;
- deliver new services, e.g., location-aware and location-invariant services; and
- extend and enrich fundamental human activities, such as being a member of a community and searching for information.

Using the vast amount of EHR data, health care providers will be able to answer questions such as "Is drug A more effective than drug B?" by analyzing the data gathered during care delivery. Consumer product companies will be able to assess the degree to which one product is often jointly purchased with other products by analyzing point-of-sale data. We will be able to generate and test complex hypotheses using existing data, potentially avoiding expensive and lengthy analysis approaches such as clinical trials.

Using the network of sensors and powerful machines, we will be able to orchestrate complex processes. For example, a smart city will sense traffic jams and alter the timing and duration of traffic lights. Power grids can detect locations consuming more or less power than normal and re-route the grid accordingly.

These devices will cater to the user's location. For example, automobile GPS devices can provide directions and data on looming traffic problems, while mobile devices can consider the location of someone requesting restaurant suggestions.

And these services will enhance core human activities such as belonging to a community or sharing information with a family. Applications can tell you if your friends are nearby. You can take photos with a mobile device and share them instantly with grandparents.

Ramifications of the Fifth Wave

The IT of previous waves does not disappear with the advent of a new wave; many organizations are still using mainframes. However, each new wave builds on and extends the previous waves.

The fifth wave of IT revolution will affect health care. Only health record data can produce some forms of comparative effectiveness research. A powerful, networked computer can help the patient who carries it in managing his or her chronic disease. Sensors, along with technology that tracks patients' location, condition and expected course of treatment, can improve patient flow through a facility. Communities of patients and caregivers have long been central to good care; technologies that strengthen these ties strengthen care.

The impact is clearly not confined to health care. All aspects of society are affected: Witness the use of a mobile device by a fisherman off the coast of East Africa, before he heads to shore, to determine which port is offering the best price for his fish. Or the Twitter, Facebook and Skype accounts of the unrest in Northern Africa. These are a few examples of the revolution that has just arrived.

As remarkable as the fifth wave will be, we should remember that IT waves arrive about every 10 years. We will see several more revolutions in our careers.

John Glaser, Ph.D., is the CEO of Siemens Healthcare Health Services in Malvern, Pa. He is also a regular contributor to H&HN Daily.

Accountable Care Organizations and Health Information Exchange

February 15, 2011
By John Glaser

ACOs will require well-integrated networks for exchanging patient data and performance metrics.

The goal of an accountable care organization (ACO) is to improve the integration of care among providers. This integration could encompass a wide variety of provider types, such as physicians, nurse practitioners, hospitals and non-acute providers. Ultimately, this integration should result in care that is safer, of higher quality, more efficient and of better service.

The organization of ACOs will vary: In some cases the ACO will be led by an integrated medical group, but in other cases the ACO will be led by a health plan, a hospital or an integrated health system. The ACO provider members may also belong to one parent organization, such as an integrated health system.

And while the ACO provider members will, in most cases, be legally distinct organizations that are bound by contracts, ACOs will be diverse in composition, legal form and patients served. Patients may be organized by condition (diabetes, cancer or heart disease) or category (children and the underserved).

The Need for a Health Information Exchange

Despite this diversity of provider types, ACO members will have a common need to implement a health information exchange. This exchange must ensure the flow of data about patients and facilitate the exchange of the following:

- performance metrics, such as care cost and quality;
- patient events, such as a visit to the emergency room or a failure to show up for an appointment; and
- patient status, as in a hospitalization in a member hospital with a specific discharge destination.

This health information exchange could be provided by a regional or state organization that facilitates it among all providers in a geographic area. However, this exchange is more likely to be provided by an organization that is focused on interoperability targeted to the ACO participants.

Targeted Interoperability

Targeted interoperability is common in industries other than health care. A manufacturer will have a high level of interoperability with its critical suppliers, while a computer manufacturer may have supply chain product forecasting and design interoperability with the company that produces its core electronics. Extensive interoperability may also include the exchange of a wide range of data and applications shared between the manufacturer and supplier, such as circuit design software.

That same manufacturer may not have such a high level of interoperability with suppliers that provide less essential components or those that are easily replaceable. In these cases, integration may take the form of a website that lets suppliers know of its needs and supports supplier bids for business.

A health care provider will have variable interoperability needs with respect to its electronic health record, as well as variable needs for the integration of its care processes. In some cases, such as when a provider is a member of an ACO, the interoperability needs will be great between it and the other members. In other cases, such as a hospital and a provider practice that only occasionally refers a patient for admission, these needs will be less.

Extensive interoperability will be targeted to other providers for which there is a great deal of patient sharing and a joint accountability for the care delivered.

A Foundation for Targeted Interoperability

Implementing and managing targeted interoperability in health care is complex and challenging. The ACO will need to address several challenges, including governance, standards and shared processes.

Governance. ACO members will need to make decisions regarding their shared information technology (IT) infrastructure. For example, what data needs to be exchanged for the ACO to perform well? Does this data include patient no-show events? The shared infrastructure may involve more than connecting several electronic health records. Should members share internal phone and e-mail directories with each other? Should they use a common application for functions such as case management?

Identifying the boundaries of the shared infrastructure will require decisions regarding the capital and operating budgets for the shared infrastructure, the reporting relationships of the IT staff who manage this infrastructure, and the allocation of IT costs among members.

Standards. While the federal government has established an initial set of standards to support health information exchanges, ACO members may decide to exchange data for which there are no national standards. What standard should they use in this case? Organizations in other industries have developed their own standards, accepting that these standards might not be used outside of their targeted exchange and might one day be replaced by national standards.

Shared processes. Targeted interoperability might start as a discussion about connecting electronic health records, but it will quickly move to a discussion about shared or consistent processes. Consistent processes can take the form of common clinical decision support and a common workflow engine logic among all participants, even if that support and logic need to be implemented in different electronic health records. Consistent processes can also take the form of a jointly defined approach to patient education.

Shared processes could include case management, business analytics, clinical trials recruitment and shared laboratory testing facilities. ACO members will decide to share processes when the sharing reduces the costs of providing care and improves the quality. While ACO members will share processes to improve performance, they will need to be mindful that extensive sharing can make it difficult to exit an ACO or to remove an underperforming member, due to high switching costs.

Almost any process that is shared or consistent will require an IT foundation to support that process.

Differing Levels of Information Exchange

Over time, ACO members will use two overall categories of health information exchanges: an extensive exchange between themselves, and a limited exchange with providers for which there is modest patient sharing.

However, the type of exchange necessary may not be so clear-cut. For example, two providers may not belong to the same ACO but may engage in more than modest patient sharing. Hence they may decide to implement some but not all aspects of the extensive ACO exchange infrastructure. They may decide to exchange diverse types of data but not share processes, for example.

The ACO exchange capabilities are a portfolio of targeted interoperability capabilities. This portfolio includes elements that may be used in some cases but not others—and within which some set of elements will be used, outside of the ACO, with one provider. A different set will be used with another provider.

The broad adoption of health information exchanges in the United States will be facilitated by the formation of accountable care organizations. However, ACOs will require an extensive exchange that will be more diverse and complex than the movement of clinical data from one provider to another—an exchange that involves diverse data and shared processes.

John Glaser, Ph.D., is the CEO of Siemens Healthcare Health Services in Malvern, Pa. He is also a regular contributor to H&HN Daily.

Reprinted from H&HN Hospitals & Health Networks, by permission, February 2011, ©2011 by Health Forum, Inc.

Information Technology for Accountable Care Organizations

September 7, 2010
By John Glaser and Claudia Salzberg

Recent federal legislation is encouraging the formation of accountable care organizations. To be effective, these ACOs must use sophisticated information technology.

An increase in health care costs and the lack of a corresponding increase in quality has prompted the rise of new health care organizational models. These models, whose purpose is to significantly improve the coordination and efficiency of care delivery, have as their centerpiece the accountable care organization (ACO).

The Accountable Care Organization

The goal of an ACO is to improve the integration of care among physicians, nurse practitioners, hospitals and other providers. Within an ACO, one organization, such as an integrated medical group, would be accountable for care coordination, quality and efficiency.

The recently passed health care reform legislation signals a federal government interest in ACO care delivery. The government has stipulated the requirements for an ACO:

- accountability for the overall care (including its quality and cost) of assigned Medicare beneficiaries;

- implementation of legal, leadership and management structures to support necessary treatment, payments, clinical processes and administrative systems;
- adequate participation of primary care physicians to cover assigned beneficiaries;
- promotion of evidence-based medicine;
- performance reporting on quality and cost measures;
- coordination of care using tele-health, remote patient monitoring and other such enabling technologies; and
- commitment to patient-centeredness and the promotion of patient engagement.

ACOs also call for a change in payment: ACOs would receive a fixed payment, often based on patient condition (e.g., diabetes) or care episode (e.g., hip replacement). This payment would be per patient for an agreed upon interval of time (such as one year for a chronic condition) or for a set of related services (such as hip replacement surgery followed by rehabilitation services). This payment structure incentivizes providers to coordinate patient care and reduce costs, such as those stemming from a redundancy in services and tests.

In many ways, ACOs are not new. Health plans have served as ACOs, and capitation payment models put providers in the role of ACOs. Still, ACOs are emerging in a different health care context. Health care cost and quality pressures are more significant now than they were 10 years ago, so there is greater pressure to implement the model and for ACOs to perform well. In addition, the HITECH regulations will lead more organizations to adopt electronic health records, share clinical data and improve the standardization of quality measures. These HITECH outcomes will minimize some of the challenges faced by earlier ACO efforts.

Health Information Technology Ramifications

An ACO requires electronic health records, data management, personal health records and health information exchanges. Each of these elements must provide "traditional" capabilities: For example, EHRs must support the documentation of a patient's problems and e-prescribing, and health information exchanges must enable the transfer of discharge summaries and procedure reports between providers. Some of these elements also need additional features.

The electronic health record. The electronic health record captures necessary patient data; supports care-related transactions, such as e-prescribing; and provides clinical decision support that will help ensure that evidence-based medicine is delivered, and that providers are aware of ACO quality and efficiency goals. The EHR must also:

- allow the ACO to identify those patients for whom they are accountable;
- possess master patient indexes that link a patient's medical record numbers among ACO providers;

- provide registry capabilities so the ACO can track the care provided to ACO patients and assess the degree to which the ACO and its providers are appropriately managing cohorts of patients; and
- include communication tools and functions that support multi-provider, team-oriented care. These tools may range from provider discussion forums to EHR-based notification, to messages between providers seeing a patient in an emergency room.

Data management. In addition to application systems such as the electronic health record, ACOs will need to implement sophisticated systems to manage data. These data management systems will need to:

- capture and report data on care quality and efficiency (these data and analyses are necessary to ensure that the ACO is meeting its performance goals and can identify areas where care performance can be improved);
- help the CEO assess the costs of alternative care settings (for example, the ACO will want to model the implications of having a nurse practitioner, rather than a physician, treat some patients); and
- identify high-risk patients who demand greater care and focused care resources.

Data management will require the development of new data use and management procedures. As the level of EHR interoperability increases, the data repositories of an ACO will expand to include data generated by multiple-provider legal entities. Policies and procedures will need to address issues such as secondary use of data where multiple organizations are contributors, and correcting data that have spread to other organizations.

Personal health records. In their efforts to improve care performance, ACOs will have to actively engage patients in the care process. Personal health records will become more common. These records will need to provide patients with access to their EHR data and work with a range of care management, telehealth and health information tools. A patient may engage in disease and wellness management programs by tracking his vital signs and laboratory results, communicating electronically with his caregivers, accessing trustworthy health information on treatment options, and managing follow-up appointments.

Health information exchanges. ACOs will require providers to share clinical data with each other. This could involve an acute care hospital sending a discharge to a non-acute facility, or a primary care provider discussing a patient's history with the consulting physician. A health information exchange can support such data transfers.

In addition to moving clinical data, health information exchanges will need to send messages triggered by important patient events. For example, clinical staff in the ACO will need to know if a patient has been seen in an emergency room, missed an appointment for a radiology procedure or had an unplanned return to the operating room.

It's All about the Data

Relatively few health care organizations have adopted the core applications needed for an ACO. However, the HITECH incentives are likely to increase their use and to establish the regional health information technology necessary to foster ACO development and to improve performance. The HITECH provisions can be seen as laying the groundwork for the payment reform provisions of the health care reform legislation.

While applications such as the EHR and the patient health record are important, data may be the most important ACO information technology asset. For example, if payment is based on conformance to chronic disease protocols, the organization must have data that illustrate how well it conforms to those protocols. An ACO's performance may be severely hindered if its data are of poor quality—even if its clinicians are using a sophisticated EHR.

John Glaser, Ph.D., is CEO of the Siemens Health Services Division and is a former vice president and CIO at Partners HealthCare in Boston. He is a regular contributor to H&HN Weekly. *Claudia Salzberg, M.S.,* is a researcher and analyst in the Center for Patient Safety Research and Practice and the Division of General Medicine of Brigham and Women's Hospital, also in Boston.

The Variability of Patient Care

May 11, 2010
By John Glaser

© Health Forum, Inc.

Electronic health record (EHR) systems should accommodate different treatment patterns.

In discussions about using electronic health records to improve care, we often make the assumption that all care is similar. We see this in the fact that diabetes is frequently used to illustrate EHR features.

The implication is that all care is like diabetes care and has clear and measurable outcomes, well-established care guidelines, treatments that deliver reasonably consistent results, and a cookbook set of steps that patients can take. As a result, the EHR must offer protocol support, evidence-based clinical decision support and structured documentation capabilities; it must also produce quality measures to assess practice variation.

But a large portion of care is not like treating diabetes. The outcomes of a stroke are variable and difficult to measure. There are often no crisp guidelines for treating the fragile, elderly patient with multiple chronic diseases. And it would be a challenge to adequately structure the documentation of the clinician's thought process for a patient with a rare disease that is eluding diagnosis.

Iterative and Sequential Care

Richard Bohmer, author of Designing Care, notes that there are two classes of care in a hospital and in physician practice. Iterative care is a form of discovery: It addresses complex diagnoses and conditions for which the diagnosis and treatment are a repeating series of hypothesis-test/treat-revise hypothesis steps. Sequential care, on the other hand, is a form of production: It involves performing well-understood tasks in a well-understood sequence: e.g., routine heart surgery.

So what does this diversity mean for the design and implementation of an EHR?

The EHR must accommodate this diversity within an organization as well as for an individual clinician (a clinician may see this diversity daily) and for a patient (any patient may move from iterative care to sequential care and back again).

Both classes of care require some core EHR capabilities:

- the ability to retrieve test and procedure results, progress notes and history within a provider organization and from other provider organizations;
- support for transactions that initiate care activities such as ordering a medication, scheduling a surgery and initiating a referral;
- displays of work status such as a list of today's clinic patients and orders with pending results; and
- decision support that looks for gross deviations from good practice, such as a potentially fatal drug interaction, or warns of a panic condition like a rapidly falling potassium level.

For patients who are receiving sequential care, the EHR should also provide:

- pathway and guideline support that informs the provider of a recommended treatment approach through suggested orders, problem-based documentation and health maintenance reminders;
- means to efficiently capture structured data such as a patient's problem list; and
- analyses tools that enable providers and health care organizations to assess variability in care costs, outcomes and treatment patterns.

For patients who are receiving iterative care, the EHR must have capabilities such as:

- tools that enable collaboration between members of the care team, ensure that accountabilities of the team are clear and highlight relevant patient status information;
- decision support that helps narrow the potential diagnoses as well as subsequent test and treatment strategies; and
- documentation that provides some structure but also reflects nuances in the patient's condition and in the thought processes of the provider.

While there is a core set of EHR capabilities in both classes, the needs are different. Structured documentation may not be helpful for iterative care patients. Collaboration tools may be little help for patients with straightforward, acute conditions. Introducing

EHR tools that are relevant in one class into the other class may interfere with rather than assist in the delivery of care.

A Need for Agility

We have a tendency in the information technology field to re-engineer processes. But we must recognize that engineering takes different forms. With sequential care it is possible to engineer a preferred sequence of steps and have the EHR guide the care team in performing these steps. And it should be quite possible to measure the outcomes of these steps. As we do this we have the mental image of a production line in our head.

Iterative care is different. The mental image should not be the factory floor but a group of scientists in the laboratory. In this scenario we must encourage collaboration, enable an unpredictable set of actions to be taken, and provide easy access to information and other experts that might help the team form and test hypotheses. Measuring the outcome of discovery is very difficult.

The EHRs that we produce, and our approaches to their implementation, must accommodate the diversity of care characteristics. The need for this agility poses a significant challenge for EHR vendors and EHR implementation teams.

However, this agility is probably essential. The EHR and its implementation have to support both classes simultaneously. Any provider may be involved in both during short periods of time, and any care setting may have both classes simultaneously.

Because the EHR cannot know whether a patient is in the middle of iterative or sequential care, it must enable the provider to decide, and the EHR must respond to that decision. We often note that EHR implementations struggle when the systems don't "fit the workflow" or when providers note that the systems don't support "the way they think." If we introduce systems and implementations designed for one class into the other class, we are almost assured that we won't fit the workflow or support the way they think.

We may be able to learn from other settings in which iterative and sequential activities are occurring simultaneously—for example, soldiers in combat situations, pilots landing planes in the Hudson River and scientists conducting experiments. These settings must also balance the information technology needs and the implementation mind-set.

Supporting diverse classes of care may be challenging, but it may very well significantly increase our success in EHR adoption and meaningful use.

John Glaser *is a vice president and the CIO of Partners HealthCare in Boston. He is also a regular contributor to* H&HN Weekly.

Managing Clinical Decision Support

March 22, 2007
By John Glaser and Tonya Hongsermeier

Clinical decision support (CDS) is a critical contributor to efforts to improve the quality and efficiency of medical care and patient care operations. But to achieve CDS's promise, an organization must establish management structures and processes that enable it to identify priorities, develop and maintain the required content, and evaluate the technology's impact on care.

CDS management structures and processes should accomplish several objectives, many of which revolve around the technology's logic. CDS logic refers to real-time, computer-based rules and algorithms that guide a clinician's treatment of a patient, e.g., drug–drug interaction checking during the entry of a medication order into a Computerized Provider Order Entry system.

For CDS to function properly, designated teams or committees need to be in place to identify new types of CDS logic that need to be incorporated into the organization's clinical information systems. These groups also must ensure that CDS logic can be clinically defended through review of the literature or consensus-based decisions by appropriate clinical staff while ensuring that existing logic is reviewed at an appropriate frequency. Finally, these groups must provide direction on priorities for incorporating or modifying CDS logic.

The organization also must establish structures to facilitate and encourage clinician use of the system, including educating clinical staff on the rational for a CDS rule. The organization needs to assess the impact of CDS on provider decisions and practices to determine if the desired outcomes are being achieved, and review strategies to improve the effectiveness of existing CDS uses. Two other issues to explore: whether computer-based intervention impedes workflow and whether the application interface confuses rather than informs the user.

Finally, the IT staff or application vendor needs guidance to ensure that appropriate specifications have been developed and testing has been performed.

There is no best way to organize these responsibilities. However, there are several commonalities that can guide the development of CDS management structures and processes.

Leverage Existing Committees

The use of already existing care-oriented committees can help address several aspects of clinical decision support management. For example, an existing pharmacy and thera-peutics committee could be asked to manage medication-centric CDS logic, while a committee already devoted to improving cardiac care should be asked to oversee CDS logic related to hypertension and congestive heart failure guidelines.

These committees possess the expertise necessary to determine the clinical utility of a specific decision support recommendation. And because decision support must be maintained by regularly reviewing and updating content, this logic maintenance is best handled by a committee already familiar with current content. The committee also will be most effective at educating clinicians about the value of decision support.

A care-oriented committee is in the best position to prioritize CDS requests. A patient safety committee, therefore, will have the best organizational perspective on major patient safety issues and the priorities for developing and implementing CDS logic. For instance, should work on chemotherapy dosing logic be given higher priority than logic that adjusts dosing given a patient's renal function? In addition, because of their care-specific expertise and understanding of the organization's care practice defi-ciencies, these committees are most likely to "discover" new logic or new opportunities to deploy existing logic. This discovery can be based on the experiences of the organiza-tion or on review of the advances of others.

Examine Committee Composition

CDS logic often span domains, such as when medication-centric logic is relevant to a committee focusing on cardiac care. To the degree that there is likely to be a sig-nificant set of CDS logic that is relevant to several committees, there should be cross-committee representation. In general, this cross-committee representation is already in place; the boundary-spanning issues were present before the introduction of clinical information systems.

Cross-representation should not only account for clinical discipline, but overall per-spective as well. For example, it is important that clinicians representing the strategic concerns of the health system be balanced by those representing usability and efficiency concerns. Respected clinical champions can be those in management positions as well as the clinicians in a community practice who are greatly respected by their peers.

It's important to place an information technology staff member on each of these committees. This person can help the committee members focus on the most feasible and effective IT strategies to address a particular challenge, such as alerts at the time of ordering and the use of defaults and options for incorporating decision support into the workflow.

Ensure IT Review and Assessment

Because the clinical information system will have limitations—some of which may mean that certain proposals cannot be practically implemented—clinical decision support proposals must be examined from an IT perspective. Both clinical and IT staff must understand the effort required to implement a new proposal. Additionally, the IT staff that must "codify" and test the decision support will have a backlog that needs to be prioritized.

Define Oversight Group

The individual committees that manage portions of the CDS technology will require oversight, and an existing group can be tapped for this responsibility. Many organizations have committees that have broad authority over care improvement; for example, an integrated delivery system may have a chief medical officer's forum. In other cases, an oversight group has been formed to provide overall direction for the implementation and management of the organization's clinical information systems.

The actions of individual committees often will conflict. These conflicts can center on the definition of appropriate clinical decision support logic, in which committee members have different opinions on best practices. The committees also will face tradeoffs between practicing best care and working within operational realities, such as the primary care physicians who are so harried that additional health maintenance reminders will fall on deaf ears. Another common clash is the prioritization of scarce organizational resources—budget limitations mean that not all ideas can be implemented. In addition to the need for resolving conflicts, an oversight group can ensure that different committees don't independently embark on duplicative CDS strategies.

The oversight group is responsible for seeing that CDS use conforms to the organization's medical policy. At times, a decision support idea may lead to a need to alter policy. It may also indicate the need to examine organizational roles, such as who should respond to an asynchronous panic lab value alert. This committee must have members who can work with other groups, such as the compliance committee, and determine when it is appropriate to move some issues to those other forums.

Organizations need management structures and processes to ensure that clinical information system and CDS investments achieve desired organizational goals. These goals include CDS linkage to organizational strategies, prioritization of resources and determination of the impact of clinical decision support.

John Glaser *is vice president and CIO of Partners HealthCare in Boston, senior advisor, Deloitte Center for Health Solutions, and a regular contributor to Most Wired OnLine.* ***Tonya Hongsermeier, MD,*** *is the corporate manager, clinical knowledge management and decision support of Partners HealthCare.*

The Service-Oriented Solution for Health IT

November 22, 2006
By John Glaser, PhD, and Steve Flammini

From time to time, there are major shifts in information technology architecture that have significant impacts on how we construct health care application systems and the value that those systems can deliver to the organization. Networked personal computers, distributed processing, clinical decision support and the Internet are examples.

The Service-Oriented Architecture (SOA) is one such shift. This shift is in its early stages but is well on its way to materially changing the information technology industry's approaches to developing, acquiring and managing applications.

In its simplest terms, SOA enables you to view applications as composites of components or services. A service can perform discrete functions or provide access to data. Examples include services to identify patients, provide decision support, manage the problem list, retrieve data and render presentations for flowsheets and record, retrieve and detect allergies. In effect, an electronic medical record is not an application; it is a collection of integrated services.

A service orientation enables one to use the same functionality or logic across a wide range of applications—e.g., many applications use the same patient identification service. This provides the ability to achieve targeted standardization across a suite of applications. Sometimes an organization would like to standardize pieces of its applications or specific types of data but does not want to engage in whole-scale replacement of application suites.

An application can be composed of services that are common with other applications and services that are unique to that particular application. This ability to compose an application from existing services and new services should significantly reduce the time required to develop and maintain applications. A new application need not recreate functions that can be "borrowed" from other applications.

An organization may decide that advances have been made in the approach or technology behind a specific service. For example, advances have been made in rules engine or workflow engine technologies. The organization would like to leverage these advances and, through SOA, is in a position to remove and replace that technology without having to disrupt the remainder of its applications or application suite.

Services can improve interoperability across heterogeneous systems. Services have well-defined interchange protocols, known as "contracts," where the parameters between the service consumer and provider are clear and abstracted from any underlying native technology implementation. For instance, a patient identification service expects parameters such as name, date of birth, medical record number, etc., to be supplied. The service may carry out extremely sophisticated matching operations internally, but this complexity is shielded from the calling application (or consumer). The consumer only expects a list of candidate patients to be returned, in accordance with the agreed upon contract-established priority. This type of contract-based interchange dramatically lowers the barriers of interoperability, when contrasted with an API-based approach, where both consumer and provider needed to share the same underlying technology platform.

Such an approach to services enables an organization to ease the challenge of integrating third-party applications with its core application suite. In addition, it can ease the challenge of integrating with systems from other organizations—e.g., determine eligibility or retrieve clinical data from a Regional Health Information Organization (RHIO).

Overall, SOA offers the potential to achieve three critical organizational objectives:

- Targeted standardization
- Efficiency in application development and integration of third-party applications
- Agility through enabling faster application development/acquisition and effecting targeted standardization and new technology incorporation in a way that minimizes the need to engage in extensive application replacement

While having exceptional promise, health care organizations should be sober and wary of claims that SOA will fix all that ails the health care information technology industry.

Many application vendors are not able to play well in a SOA environment. Substantial investments in a sizeable base of application software that is installed in hundreds of client sites make it difficult to justify the recasting of that base using a service-oriented architecture. Moreover, vendor research and development resources are often directed to immediately pressing needs to increase functionality rather than increasing the agility of the applications. This reality is understandable.

Some vendors have done a reasonable job of "wrapping" portions of their applications such that aspects of the applications can be treated as services by other applications. For example, a wrapper may enable an IT group to retrieve data using SOA conventions layered on top of a legacy application. However, the effectiveness and extent of this wrapping is variable across the industry.

Convincing the leadership of an organization to invest in SOA technologies or replace existing applications with ones that are very effective adherents to SOA precepts can be difficult. One of the harder jobs of the CIO is to explain IT concepts, like SOA, to a bright but IT-ignorant board. While goals such as agility are very important, they are intangible. Hence, it is harder for a leadership team to justify investing in technology to improve targeted standardization when it is easier to justify investments that make physicians happy or at least happier.

Managing a SOA environment will require new skills and orientation for the organization's IT group. Viewing applications as collections of services takes some getting used to. New standards and design patterns will permeate the development process. Services must be managed with respect to security, version control, performance, auditing, metering, and monitoring, and these issues must be managed at a more fine-grained level, and not just the level of applications or network access.

SOA is an emerging technology. As a result, many vendor offerings of SOA environments are immature. SOA hype can be deafening and drown out the whimpers of a feeble offering. Most IT groups are unsure how they would evaluate the market and the SOA offerings of one infrastructure vendor over those of another.

Health care SOA standards are embryonic. However, SOA standards are emerging across all industries. And through federal efforts, health care–specific standards are likely to be seen in the near term.

SOA is not another name for Nirvana. SOA technologies and architectures are in their youth. SOA is hard to explain to a room full of physicians. However, ten years ago the same could be said of the Internet. Thirty years ago the same could be said of the personal computer. And as those technologies have matured to become a staple of health care information technology and have been applied to enable significant advances in our ability to provide IT-enabled value, so too will SOA.

John Glaser *is vice president and CIO of Partners HealthCare in Boston, senior advisor, Deloitte Center for Health Solutions, and a regular contributor to* Most Wired Online. *Steve Flammini* *is the Chief Technology Officer of Partners HealthCare.*

Applications as Foundations: Laying the Groundwork for Evolution

September 6, 2006
By John Glaser

In the health care information technology industry, we often view our task as the serial implementation of applications: Laboratory systems. Patient accounting systems. Provider order entry systems.

While the view of serial application implementation is important, we may be better off, in some cases, if we focused our thinking on implementing and then leveraging an application foundation. A foundation provides the broad ability to perform a "never-ending" series of application-leveraged small, medium-sized and occasionally large advances and improvements.

We have many examples of foundations in our day-to-day lives.

The economic, legal, political and educational systems of this country provide a market and commerce foundation that has led to a level of well being that has no equivalent in the history of the human race. Schools, religion, culture, community and family provide a moral foundation that has a significant influence over our daily behavior.

There are several examples of application foundations.

Provider order entry systems can be used as a foundation to improve physician decision making. Once implemented, the organization can, on an ongoing basis, introduce a series of decision support rules and guides. These rules can address medication safety issues, improve the appropriateness of test and procedure orders and assure that data relevant to an order are displayed to the physician. These rules and guides can be implemented over the course of many years. No single rule may turn the tide in an organization's efforts to improve care. But in aggregate they can be leveraged to effect significant improvements.

The electronic medical record can be used as a foundation to improve outpatient care processes. The organization can, on an ongoing basis, introduce modules that improve health maintenance, referrals, medication order effectiveness and the capture of billing documentation. In aggregate, these changes can provide significant improvements in outpatient care.

Software to support patient–provider communication can be used as a foundation to more closely engage the patient in their care. The software can be used to support the management of diabetes, help patients manage their medications, provide information to address health care questions and support the development of communities of people with a chronic disease.

This view of applications as foundations has several ramifications.

Implementation never stops. There may be a flurry of intense effort as the foundation is "laid." The initial introduction of provider order entry and the electronic medical record is difficult work that requires great skill and significant resources. However, once the foundation has been laid, implementation continues as the foundation is leveraged. Continues forever.

If implementation never stops, then management and clinical mechanisms must exist to manage the ongoing implementation. These mechanisms must continuously identify the next area to be leveraged, ensure that the requisite analyses are performed, install needed software modifications and enhancements and reengineer relevant processes. In effect, these processes and mechanisms must continue the tasks that one sees prior to go-live.

Architecture becomes very important. The foundation must be able to support an implementation that never ends. The foundation must be able to evolve gracefully. Tools that enable rule development, the safe addition of local modifications, the incorporation of new data types and coding conventions and the efficient interoperability with other systems become essentials. The foundation must be able to capitalize upon new technologies in a manner that is efficient and minimally disruptive.

In many ways, the architecture, technologies and tools that enable ongoing implementation may be more important than the current functionality of the application.

The RFP becomes less important. The RFP process implies that all functionality ever needed must be understood and defined. While one should try to understand up front as much as one can about the functionality that is needed, there is little likelihood that one can anticipate all that will be needed.

The view of a foundation leads one to try to implement functionality in a continuous series of modest-sized "chunks." The organization learns during and after each implementation of a chunk, and this learning makes it smarter about the nature of the following chunks. In effect, one has an ongoing incremental learning process rather than one large "cramming for a test." This learning process and iterative implementations will arrive at, over time, the implementation of a large chunk of functionality. But that large chunk is likely to be rooted in a deeper understanding of what is needed.

This learning process iteratively defines functionality requirements. The utility of the RFP that attempts to comprehensively define functionality needs is diminished. The utility of the RFP that attempts to understand the ability of the architecture and technology to enable iterative learning becomes elevated.

Determining ROI is difficult. Assessing the "return on investment" of a foundation is a more difficult exercise than determining the ROI of an application. While the ROI analysis should never conclude that "we can't assess the ROI since we don't know how we'll evolve," nonetheless, it becomes more difficult to state the outcome of a never-ending implementation. Despite the analysis challenges posed, the organization is much more likely to see a return if it views its task as the implementation of a foundation than if it views its task as the serial implementation of individual applications.

Foundation replacement ought to be rare. If the application suite is effectively evolving as the organization changes and matures in its understanding of the ways to apply the system, foundation replacement would occur under one of four unusual circumstances.

- The vendor goes out of business and the support disappears.
- A new vendor arrives with products that have dramatically superior capabilities or lower costs.
- There has been a serious failure of the foundation to incorporate new technologies.
- The care or business model upon which the foundation is based undergoes such radical change that the foundation becomes useless. For example, a foundation built for a home for a family of four would be useless if the decision was made that the structure would become an apartment building.

Our goal of applying information technology to improve organizational performance will be advanced if we view our task as implementing, and then perpetually leveraging, application foundations. This view increases the likelihood that the information technology investment will enable gains in organizational performance.

John Glaser *is vice president and CIO of Partners HealthCare in Boston, senior advisor, Deloitte Center for Health Solutions, and a regular contributor to* Most Wired Online.

Reprinted from H&HN Hospitals & Health Networks, by permission, September 2006, ©2006 by Health Forum, Inc.

Advanced Interoperability: Beyond the Exchange of Data

July 20, 2006
By John Glaser

The national health care information technology agenda is focused on furthering the adoption of interoperable electronic health records.

Much of the agenda has centered on the computer system interoperability provided by clinical data exchange technologies. Definitions of interoperability have been developed. The federal government is examining strategies for the harmonization of standards, reviewing privacy laws and initiating the creation and management of a National Health Information Network infrastructure.

The discussion of the agenda often obscures a central goal of clinical data exchange: improving the interoperability of patient care processes between organizations. There will be multiple forms of IT approaches, in addition to a clinical data exchange, to achieving this goal.

In some ways, the current clinical data exchange approach assumes passive relationships between organizations. Two organizations may need to effect a connection, ensure that they follow standards and have necessary legal agreements in place. However, once "implemented," a clinical data exchange does not require that two organizations routinely work together. The care processes within one organization can largely be ignorant of the care processes in the other. As an analogy, the presence of a global phone system that enables interoperable voice communication does not require that any two organizations that utilize this network have any process interoperability.

There are three forms of IT approaches that can support active and powerful classes of interoperable organizational processes. In fact, the decision to pursue these forms is based on a desire to have some significant level of interorganizational process interoperability. These forms may have more value potential to the participating organizations than the "simple" exchange of clinical data between them.

The first form involves one organization extending its systems into another organization. For example, a joint venture to provide cancer care may involve one organization, a cancer center, extending its oncology EMR into another organization, e.g., a community hospital, for use by clinicians at both organizations. The ongoing evolution and management of this shared application becomes a shared responsibility. This kind of collaboration is deeper than the exchange of data—e.g., it is likely to involve using common care protocols and is predicated on two organizations (or more) engaged in a substantive partnership surrounding a joint approach to delivering a clinical service.

The second form centers on two or more organizations using the exchanged data to address problems or opportunities of mutual interest. For example, a provider and payer may leverage the exchange to integrate data from medication claims with the provider's EMR data. This merged set of data enables both organizations to examine medication compliance and misuse issues and jointly develop strategies to improve care.

In the third form, two or more organizations may leverage an exchange as one tool in a joint effort to improve the effectiveness and efficiency of an interorganizational process. For example, claims submission using an insurance transaction exchange does not remove all of the issues that contribute to the inefficiency of the claims process. Misunderstandings of payment policies and rules may not be addressed by the machine-to-machine exchange of data. Nonetheless, the exchange has become a tactic for the efforts of two organizations to improve a critical process that binds them.

A clinical data exchange can leverage these advanced process interoperability opportunities in several ways.

First, several of the examples above utilize a clinical data exchange. However, the exchange is being utilized as a tool to further a significant joint undertaking to advance an aspect of care. The focus and difficult work are primarily directed to a process and secondarily to information technology.

Second, a clinical data exchange moves the industry towards commodity class data standards and exchange technologies. The federal standards harmonization efforts and the development of exchange reference implementation models enable multiple companies to address market needs. These commercial efforts will be subjected to significant price-performance pressures.

Commodity-class technologies make it easier and more efficient for an organization to engage in advanced process partnerships. As an analogy, it is very efficient for two organizations to create a design team composed of members spread across the country—they can use the phone network or the Internet. If these networks were not commodity-class technology, these two organizations would have to create their own version of the network before the design team could "meet."

Third, most advanced interoperable processes between two or more organizations are leveraged by the involvement of organizations that surround but are not necessarily part of the core collaboration.

Two organizations that are collaborating on a joint oncology service (and use a common oncology EMR) will need to send and receive data from the patient's primary care provider. The cancer patients may also be treated in a regional emergency room.

Clinical data exchange technologies can be used to extend the reach of the advanced collaboration.

Fourth, the presence of a clinical data exchange provides a form of process agility. Collaborations (and, hence, interoperable process needs) form, change and complete over the course of time as the needs of collaborators evolve. It is easier for an organization to be agile if it does not have to create a core exchange capability every time collaboration needs to be created or an existing collaboration needs to change.

Fifth, a clinical data exchange can lower the activation energy necessary to achieve interoperable processes that are valuable but may be modest in initial ambition or value. If the costs to achieve process interoperability are too high, some collaborations may never happen because "it is not worth it."

The promulgation of interoperable electronic health records will enable the country, and its stakeholder organizations, to take a major step forward in its efforts to improve the quality, safety and efficiency of care.

We should remember that care process interoperability is our real goal. Achieving that goal will lead to several forms of IT approaches to achieving interorganizational process improvement.

John Glaser is vice president and CIO of Partners HealthCare in Boston, senior advisor, Deloitte Center for Health Solutions, and a regular contributor to Most Wired Online.

Section Two – Improving Organizational Performance Through HIT

Telemedicine Hits Its Stride

December 10, 2015
By John Glaser

Telemedicine can improve the efficiency, convenience and cost-effectiveness of today's value-based health care system.

We conduct many aspects of our lives through computer-based communications. We talk to the kids on the other side of the country using Skype. We do our holiday shopping without ever leaving the couch. We avoid the bank branch and still manage our finances. We expect that these service efficiencies should be at the center of our health care experiences as well. Now, after decades of low adoption, telehealth might finally be the next big thing in health care.

Medical uses of communications technologies date back to the late 1950s; they were born out of a desire to connect remote populations to a variety of health services. One of the more novel first applications of telemedicine is credited to Massachusetts General Hospital, which established a telecommunications link with Boston's Logan Airport in 1963 to evaluate and consult with airport employees and ill travelers. Years later, the hospital added an interactive television microwave link that provided electrocardiograph, stethoscope, microscopy, voice and other capabilities.

In the decades that followed, telemedicine use grew to include demonstration projects, remote interpretation of images, care consultation for captive populations, and support for rural patients. Though effective and well received in the communities where its use was prevalent, interest in telemedicine waxed and waned.

Today, a confluence of factors is driving a renewed interest in telemedicine, including the demand for a consumer-driven health care system, a growing shortage of specialists, and cost containment strategies that shift financial risk from payers to providers and consumers.

Additionally, advancements in technology are enabling higher definition video and more robust data to be transmitted more efficiently. Patients and providers have become quite adept at incorporating technologies such as smartphones, iPads and video chat apps like FaceTime into their daily lives.

Another Access Point to Care

The American Telemedicine Association defines telemedicine or telehealth as the exchange of medical information via electronic communications to improve a patient's clinical health status.

Health care providers are embracing telemedicine because they see it as an efficient and cost-effective way to deliver quality care and improve patient satisfaction. From basic fitness tracking data shared with a primary care physician in support of health and wellness programs to virtual consults with specialists in time-critical care situations, today's telehealth framework spans the continuum of care and can include services such as:

- telepsychiatry;
- remote image interpretation (teleradiology, teledermatology);
- e-visits or televisits between providers and their patients;
- video visits for semi-urgent care;
- clinician-to-clinician consultations;
- critical care (virtual ICU, telestroke);
- remote monitoring of a patient with a chronic disease; and
- cybersurgery.

These services vary in their use of communications technology and in the information technology systems that are deployed. For example, remote patient monitoring requires devices with sensors and software that aggregates data for clinician review. Video visits must have applications that "find" available care providers, while clinician-to-clinician consultation requires electronic health record integration between health systems.

As the industry continues its collective march toward a more interoperable health care system, it further strengthens the foundation for more application of telemedicine.

According to the American Hospital Association, 52 percent of hospitals used some form of telehealth in 2013, and another 10 percent were beginning to implement such services. Its growth potential is also notable. Business information provider IHS predicts the U.S. telehealth market will grow from $240 million in revenue in 2013 to $1.9 billion in 2018—an annual growth rate of more than 50 percent.

Making the Case for Online Care

In addition to the growing demand for access and convenience, the need for telehealth is driven by other factors such as:

- a significant increase in the U.S. population;
- a shortage of licensed health care professionals;
- increasing incidence of chronic diseases;
- the need for efficient care of the elderly, homebound and physically challenged patients;
- a lack of specialists and health facilities in rural areas and in many urban areas; and
- avoiding adverse events, injuries and illnesses that can occur within the health care system.

These factors become increasingly important as new health care delivery and payment models evolve and providers are challenged to better manage chronic diseases, avoid readmissions, improve quality and remove low acuity care from high-cost venues. As we know, for example, the long-term benefits of population health programs are predicated in large part on managing high-cost, chronically ill patient populations more effectively.

Furthermore, the rapid deployment of high-deductible health plans, which make consumers more conscious and accountable for their health care consumption and spend, has added to the pressure on providers to provide low-cost, convenient options.

Against this backdrop, consider one of the biggest health system challenges today: lack of 24/7 access to physician specialists. The supply of specialists is shrinking—a substantial percentage of specialists such as pulmonologists, cardiologists, orthopedic surgeons and psychiatrists are over age 55—while medical school capacity remains flat.

When the right specialist is not available, everyone suffers. Accurate diagnosis and best practices are often missed. Patient outcomes are frequently poor. Care is prolonged, resulting in higher costs, and often times patients must be transferred at considerable cost and family disruption.

Even more troubling, studies show that upward of 20 percent of patient deaths or permanent injuries related to emergency department delays are attributed to lack of specialists' availability.

Among its many value propositions, telemedicine provides an opportunity to combat the specialist shortage by enabling more efficient use of limited expert resources who can "see" patients in multiple locations without leaving their facility. Additionally, studies of speed-to-care rates have shown that specialists at a remote location can be "at the bedside" in an average of nine minutes. Compare that with an on-site provider, who can take up to 60 minutes.

Overcoming the Barriers

Telemedicine's rebirth can be attributed to its usefulness as both a potential cost lever and an avenue to deliver expanded routine and specialty care.

However, those who are active in telemedicine can quickly discover a fairly complex playing field, muddled by the absence of consistent guidelines governing who can provide telehealth services, where they can be provided—and, most importantly, what's covered and who pays.

Medicare, Medicaid and private payers all apply different definitions, may cover different services, and have varying requirements for payment, making it a bit like the Wild West on the reimbursement front. Adding to the complexity, while a majority of states provide some form of Medicaid coverage for telehealth services, reimbursement is not standardized. On the Medicare side, coverage and payment for telehealth services still face restrictive statutes and regulatory limitations, though these problems are improving.

Disparate regulatory and reimbursement treatment of telehealth has been one of the main barriers to the expansion of services. However, updated payment policies of remote care management and coordination services on the public payer front are signaling a changing tide, eliminating restrictions and expanding the scope of covered services.

On the private payer side, telemedicine use has been bolstered by a growing number of states enacting parity laws, which require health insurers to treat telehealth services the same way they would in-person services.

In addition to reimbursement challenges, state policies limiting licensure have slowed the adoption of telehealth by U.S. providers. Once again, each state has unique laws regarding the scope of practice permissible through telehealth. Even more limiting, licensed providers who practice telehealth across state lines have needed a full, unrestricted license in the state where the patient is located, which has often been cost prohibitive.

To combat the limitations associated with licensure, a growing number of states now recognize a medical license issued by another state to treat patients via telehealth services. In fact, the creation of a multistate licensure compact model is expected to lead to the development of a national framework of telehealth providers. Additionally, though the particulars vary widely, most states maintain a consultation exception in their licensure requirements, enabling licensed physicians to consult with a licensed physician in another state.

Efforts are also underway to address other policy issues such as privacy and security, malpractice insurance, and fraud and abuse, which present their own legal and regulatory challenges.

For example, providers may need to revisit their security risk protocols and update their data privacy and security practices to combat any vulnerabilities associated with using telehealth technologies. Moreover, the AHA predicts that as utilization and coverage of telehealth services continues to ramp up, the potential for exposure to liability under various federal and state fraud and abuse laws will only grow.

A Good Prognosis

Like shopping or banking online, consumers now expect a no-hassle Amazon-like experience when they're interacting with their health care system. Telemedicine not only affords this opportunity, but also holds the potential to dramatically improve patient satisfaction and outcomes while providing an affordable alternative to traditional modes of care.

Telemedicine proponents espouse its value in making patient interactions more convenient, expanding geographic horizons particularly where needed medical specialists are few in number, and making care more accessible to those with mobility issues.

Although there are several complex and evolving issues related to its application, the barriers to widespread adoption of telemedicine are eroding under mounting pressure from all health care constituents. Licensure portability will further ease the barriers to accessing services, while regulatory and payment policy changes in support of telehealth are widely expected in the coming years. This alone will help further cement telemedicine's place in modern health care.

From the growing use of remote patient monitoring to virtual ICUs, telemedicine is well on its way to becoming a foundational technology for care delivery—as unremarkable as buying a book on the Web.

John Glaser, Ph.D., is a senior vice president with Cerner in Kansas City, Missouri. He is also a regular contributor to H&HN Daily.

From the Electronic Health Record to the Electronic Health Plan

August 11, 2015
By John Glaser

© Health Forum, Inc.

The electronic health record is evolving to become the electronic health plan. The result is better outcomes for patients.

The health care industry's focus has been, and is still, replacing the paper record with the electronic health record. HITECH accelerated the adoption of the electronic medical record. The personal health record was introduced to enable patients to become a more active participant in their care by providing them access to the record. Health information exchanges and interoperability have become more important.

These improvements are important. However, they are all centered on "the record."

Provider organizations will not thrive in an era of health reform because they have a superb and interoperable electronic health record. They will thrive because the care they deliver consistently follows a plan designed to ensure desired outcomes. The EHR must evolve so it focuses on individual patients' care plans—the steps required to maintain or create health.

Every patient's EHR should clearly display the master care plan—a long-term care plan to maintain health integrated with short-term plans for transient conditions. The EHR should be organized according to this master plan: It should highlight the steps needed to recover or maintain health, list the expectations of every caregiver the patient interacts with, and include tools such as decision support and a library of standard care plans. Interoperability is a necessity, as various providers must be able to use the plan-based EHR.

Transformation of the Care Delivery Business Model

We are witnessing a truly transformational change in the business model of health care delivery. It is evolving from one of reactive care with fragmented accountability and a dependence on full beds to a model of health management, care that extends over time and place, and rewards for efficiency and quality.

Because changes in reimbursement reinforce this new model of health care, providers are taking new approaches in organization and practice. They are uniting multiple venues of care, holding clinicians accountable for the care delivered to a specific patient, and creating patient-specific care plans that follow the evidence.

Business models are not only leading to significant changes in organization and practice, they are also leading to changes in the fundamental nature and design of the electronic health record. These EHR changes can be characterized as a transition from the electronic health record to the electronic health plan.

The Care Plan

The care health plan has attributes that need to be present to ensure health. The plan should be based on some fundamental ideas:

First, all people have a foundational plan. If the person is a healthy young man, the plan may be simple: establishing health behaviors such as exercise. If the person is a middle-aged man with high cholesterol and sleep apnea, the plan may be annual physicals, statins, a CPAP machine and a periodic colonoscopy. If a person is frail and elderly with multiple chronic diseases, the plan may be merging the care for each chronic condition, ensuring proper diet, and providing transportation for clinic visits.

Second, plans are a combination of medical care strategies with goals to maintain health (such as losing weight) along with public health campaigns such as immunizations.

Third, on top of foundational plans there may be transient plans. For the patient undergoing a hip replacement there is a time-bounded plan beginning with pre-surgery testing and ending when rehabilitation has been completed. A patient undergoing a bad case of the flu has a time-bounded plan.

Fourth, people who have a common plan are members of the same population. These populations may be all patients undergoing a coronary artery bypass graft in a hospital, all patients with a certain chronic disease, or all patients at high risk of coronary artery disease. Moreover, a particular person may be a member of multiple populations at the same time.

Fifth, risk is the likelihood that the plan will not be followed or will not result in desired outcomes. A patient motivated to manage his or her blood pressure has a lower risk than a patient who is not motivated. A frail person with multiple chronic diseases is at greater risk that the plans will not keep him or her out of the hospital than a person whose health is generally good despite having multiple chronic diseases.

Sixth, not all care will be amenable to a pre-defined patient plan. Life-threatening trauma, diseases of mysterious origin, sudden complications—all require skilled care-givers to make the best decisions possible at the moment.

Seventh, plans should be based on the evidence of best care and health practices. And the effectiveness of a plan should be measurable, either in terms of plan steps being completed or desired outcomes being achieved.

The Plan-centric EHR

The electronic health record needs to evolve into plan-centric applications. These applications will have several characteristics:

A library of plans that cover a wide range of situations. This library will include, for instance, plans for managing hypertension, removing an appendix, losing weight and treating cervical cancer. There will be variations in plans that reflect variations in patient circumstances and preferences, e.g., plans that depend on whether the patient is a well-managed diabetic, or plans that reflect the slower surgical recovery time of an elderly person.

Algorithms to form a patient's master plan. A master plan will combine, for example, the patient's asthma, hysterectomy, depression and weight reduction plans into a single plan. These algorithms will identify conflicts and redundancies among the plans and highlight the care steps that optimize a patient's health for all plans. For example, if each of the five plans has six care steps, the algorithms can determine which steps are the most important.

Team-based. The master plan will cover the steps to be carried out by a patient's pri-mary care provider, specialists, nurse practitioners, pharmacists, case managers and the patient. Each team member can see the master plan and his or her specific portion of the plan. Team members can assign tasks to each other.

Traversing care settings, geographies and different electronic health records. Health care systems will need interoperability approaches that enable individual providers to integrate their native systems with the shared plan.

Decision support and workflow logic. These tools will remind team members of upcoming and overdue activities, suggest changes in the plan should patient conditions and care needs change, and route messages to the appropriate team member regarding new test results or patient events.

A summary screen. This screen will present the status of the plan: on course or not, next steps per the plan, and key pieces of patient data that elaborate on plan status, such as active medications and recent lab values. This summary is different from a medical records–centric summary that highlights recent results, current problems and medications but does not tell providers whether the plan is on course.

Analytics to assess the degree to which a patient's care and outcomes conform to their individual and master plans. These analyses determine whether and to what extent a population's care is on plan and whether the desired outcomes are being achieved. In addition to outcomes and process assessments, the analytics enable the assessment of the costs of carrying out a plan. As we become more proficient at analyzing large volumes of clinical data, the analytics will be able to suggest steps, based on the treatment patterns of other patients, that can be taken to improve plan efficiency, simplicity and outcomes.

The Evolution of the EHR

We will still need traditional electronic health record transaction capabilities: Providers need to review a radiology report and document a patient's history and the care delivered. Problems must be recorded and medications reconciled.

However, the evolution to a plan-centric record is under way. For example, evidence-based pathways and decision support logic have been embedded into electronic health records to guide provider decisions according to a plan based on patient condition.

Also, EHRs now include population health management technologies that enable the organization to understand its aggregate performance in undertaking disease-specific plans for multiple patients. Health information exchanges help providers coordinate care at multiple venues. Personal health records improve the patients' ability to become active members of the care team. Providers are using CPOE-based decision support to help guide test orders and new prescriptions based on the evidence.

The evolution of the EHR will also blur the boundaries between population health, electronic health records, analytics and the personal health record applications. For example, logic that identifies next steps in the plan will need to be present in all of these applications.

Business Models in Other Industries

Financial services, retailers and music distributors, along with many other industries, have also experienced massive shifts in their business models.

Several decades ago, financial deregulation enabled banks to offer brokerage services. The business model of many banks shifted from banking (offering mortgages as well as checking and savings accounts) to wealth management. As banks shifted from transaction-oriented services to services that optimized a customer's financial assets, their core applications broadened to include an additional set of transactions (buying and selling stocks) and new services (financial advisory services).

Prior to the web, most retailers' business models focused on establishing a brand, offering an appropriate set of well-priced products, and building attractive stores in convenient locations. The web enabled retailers to gather significantly richer data about a customer's buying patterns and interests (and to use real-time logic to guide purchasing decisions). Retailers' core applications broadened to include well-designed e-commerce sites and analytics of customer behavior.

In both examples, even though there was a significant shift in the business model, applications necessary for the previous model continued to be necessary. Banks still had to handle savings account and mortgage payment transactions. Retailers still needed to manage inventory. And advances in these legacy applications—expanding inventory breadth and reducing inventory carrying costs—continue to be important.

In each case, a critical new set of applications were added to the legacy applications. Often, these new applications were more important than legacy applications.

The New Business Model

Major changes in an industry's business model invariably lead to major changes in the focus and form of the core applications used by that industry. The business model changes in health care will lead to a shift from applications focused on the patient's record to applications focused on the patient's plan for health.

The shift is under way. The electronic health record does not disappear as a result of this shift, but the strategic emphasis will move to technologies and applications that assist the care team (including the patient) in developing and managing the longitudinal, cross-venue health plan and assessing the outcomes of that plan.

John Glaser, Ph.D., *is a senior vice president of Cerner Corporation, headquartered in Kansas City, Missouri. He is also a regular contributor to* H&HN Daily.

Reprinted from H&HN Hospitals & Health Networks, by permission, August 2015, ©2015 by Health Forum, Inc.

The Evolution of Accountability and Collaboration

June 10, 2014
By John Glaser and Neeraj Chopra

We must innovate so that each of us is served by a health care system free of waste, duplication and error.

It appears to be an unstoppable force: providers being held more accountable for the care they deliver. Still, we have much to learn about the mature organizational forms, provider capabilities and associated reimbursement models that will ultimately lead to higher quality, less expensive and more accessible care.

For example, while not unexpected, the ability of the Pioneer accountable care organizations (ACOs) to achieve their quality and cost goals has been somewhat mixed. In fact, with nine of the 32 Pioneer ACOs opting out of the program, clearly there is not a one-size-fits-all approach to making ACO implementation work. Similarly, the 114 organizations participating in one of the two larger Medicare ACO efforts also showed uneven results in the first year, according to recently released data from the Centers for Medicare & Medicaid Services (CMS). Therefore, we are in for many more years of experimentation and learning about the ACO (and other) models.

The same holds true for population health management, with its heavy emphasis on patient engagement. While the industry has built a solid electronic health record (EHR)–based foundation to support accountable care and population health, our levels of patient engagement and community integration are simply not as deep as they ought to be. This is compounded by a host of core informatics challenges regarding population health management applications and the realization that the skills required of providers to successfully manage patient populations are still fairly immature.

These skills include improving the sophistication of data management and use practices, successfully driving large-scale organization and culture change, understanding the full gamut of factors that lead to health behavior change, and altering the composition and structure of clinicians to include more team-based care and non-physician caregivers. While many organizations are well accomplished in these areas, others have work to do.

As such, while accountability evolves, the next several years will be a Darwinian time for the industry as we determine what works and what doesn't. Perhaps it is also the right time to ask ourselves if we, as an industry, are innovating enough—and how the entire health care ecosystem might collaborate better.

Five Key Areas to Explore

Few problems are more vexing than figuring out how to transform the largest and most complex sector of the economy. Moreover, since we remain in "mid-flight," with various public and private sector payment reform efforts still emerging, it is not possible to have a complete understanding of the mature forms of the new health care system.

Collectively, we can let this quasi-chaotic transition paralyze us. Or we can embrace this transformation and seek creative ways to make effective breakthroughs.

In his stellar work *Great by Choice*, author and researcher Jim Collins and his colleague, Morten T. Hansen, remind us that, even in a chaotic and uncertain world, greatness happens by choice, not by chance. They further point out that leaders who steered their companies through the most difficult times did not have a visionary ability to predict the future. Rather, they observed what worked, figured out why it worked and built on proven foundations. Moreover, they all possessed three core behaviors:

- fanatic discipline: consistency of action and goals no matter what the conditions;
- empirical creativity: a blend of creativity and discipline that relies on direct observation, practical experimentation and tangible evidence to make bold moves from a sound empirical base; and
- productive paranoia: staying highly attuned to threats and changes in the environment, even when all is going well—essentially, channeling fear and worry into action.

One could argue that today's health care leaders might aptly apply Collins' framework to guide our efforts as accountability becomes less about theory and more about results.

In the future, we must be careful not to restrict our "solution set" to those of the past. For example, focusing on hospital-physician integration and increasing the adoption and meaningful use of EHRs have certainly been important endeavors, but they won't be enough. Hence, we should consider the following five key areas which are ripe for further exploration and innovation:

Non-traditional collaborations and business model innovation. In the years ahead, we will see shifts in the roles played by the major participants in the health care ecosystem as well as changes in the relationships between these players.

Retail pharmacies are venturing into medication management in collaboration with providers and are providing front-line primary care. Providers are assuming a risk management function traditionally held by payers. Payers are pursuing a significantly deeper relationship with patients to encourage healthy lifestyles. These changes require collaborations between players that have been antagonists or that have largely ignored each other.

In addition, these players will form relationships based on novel value propositions as a result of the benefits of the diagnostic, therapeutic or care contributions that each brings to the table. These value propositions will be more data driven, evidence based and individualized.

For example, providers, payers and pharmaceutical companies may collaborate on medication adherence and management. Providers benefit from medication discounts from a given pharmaceutical supplier and patient engagement expertise from a payer. The pharmaceutical company receives data on medication usage patterns and circumstances. The payer can achieve lower premiums due to improved management of subscribers with a chronic disease.

Most importantly, all members of the value chain will be motivated by the innovative, transparent business model that yields improvements in the patient's health and quality of life.

Use of novel information technology (IT) that goes beyond transaction-oriented IT. With the use of EHRs at an all-time high, we now have an opportunity to enhance these transactional-based systems with data and analytics to create effective, knowledge-enabling platforms and fuel the industry's innovation engine.

Think about the combination of data generated from imaging modalities, peripheral health devices such as Fitbits, Web-enabled nutritional calculators and glucoseometers, with data generated through social media, census findings, news aggregators and a patient's health record.

These connections will provide valuable information (e.g., on side effects; dosing parameters; environmental, societal and behavioral factors; and so forth) to optimize diagnostic and treatment cycles and to inform new product and service development.

The potential exists to reduce the costs of post-market surveillance and comparative effectiveness studies by an order of magnitude. We know that environmental and behavioral factors, including patient lifestyle, play a significant role in a patient's health, but we don't understand the relationship between these factors. Achieving these potentials is complex but possibly breathtaking.

The unique convergence of big data, technology innovation, lifestyle choices and economic evolution will spark endless creativity. It will drive the application of data science across disparate, vertical industries, thereby delivering broader concepts and new tools that can be applied to the care process.

Deeper relationships with patients. Providing Americans with greater access to care is a major step forward. But we must ensure that we don't provide access to a system that becomes cold and impersonal in its quest to become more accountable.

As we know, what often matters most during an illness is the human connection between patients and their caregivers. With inpatient utilization declining and care expanding into our communities and homes, each member of the value chain is responsible for protecting and enhancing the sanctity of the patient-provider relationship and improving care coordination.

Furthermore, as the Internet and social media platforms bring patients together with information, each other and a greater voice than ever before, patients now have the power to become potent change agents in how their care is managed. This is not to be taken lightly.

Deepening patient relationships is hard. It is trivial to say but it is true—each patient is different. Patients have different capabilities, goals and capacities. At times we think that education is the key to engaging patients, but engagement, as behavioral economics shows us, is much more multifaceted than education. Moreover, our attitude toward engagement is often that patients should just do what we tell them to do. That attitude is not engaging. Finally, we seem to forget that health care is a service, and service excellence goes a long way toward fostering deep relationships with patients.

The true measure of success over the long haul will be whether the nation's providers can demonstrate that, by comprehensively engaging with patients and their families, care is indeed better coordinated, outcomes are improved and costs are decreased.

Viewing government as a collaborator rather than simply a regulator. We've all heard phrases such as "the perfect storm" to describe the overwhelming amount of regulation facing the health care industry. In bracing for this seemingly insurmountable storm, it's easy to bemoan the government and question whether its abundance of policies and regulations will in fact deliver the necessary means to the right end. In this case, the end is a reformed and more accountable health care system supported by a robust and interoperable health care IT backbone.

But, despite our tendencies to view government simply as a regulator, we ought to remember that without government involvement, health care in the United States would be a very different enterprise. Notably absent would be the groundbreaking research programs and vast array of medical services benefitting millions of Americans every day.

On a very fundamental level, government is and has always been a chief collaborator: funding, guiding, providing access and offering new ways to invigorate the market—essentially establishing and expanding many of health care's core sub-sectors.

From a purely health care IT perspective, prior to the creation of the Office of the National Coordinator for Health Information Technology and the EHR incentive program, fewer than 4 percent of non-federal U.S. hospitals had EHR systems with computerized physician-order entry (CPOE). Today, 90 percent of hospitals have CPOE. Previously, less than 20 percent of office-based physicians had any kind of an EHR; today, more than 78 percent do.

These achievements alone are the direct result of collaboration—across government, private sector suppliers and providers of all kinds—and may be our greatest accomplishment as an industry.

More extensive use of a wide range of health professionals. New care delivery models require a transition from individual care providers to collaborative teams engaged in keeping patients well. Some telling professional statistics further support this shift:

- Primary care physician shortages are predicted to reach as high as 40,000 to 52,000 over the next decade.
- Nurse practitioners are the fastest growing segment of the primary care workforce.
- The American Academy of Physician Assistants reports that the number of licensed physician assistants has doubled over the last decade and could increase by another 30 percent by 2020.

As the patient-provider relationship moves from the acute-centric environment to multiple venues of care, the question becomes, Will a patient have a better medical outcome (e.g., control his diabetes better) because of these multiple touch points in the care cycle? Will primary care practices that use non-physician clinicians more extensively have lower costs compared with other primary care practices? Moreover, will the care experience be better or more personal? Will it send patient engagement levels soaring?

Care delivered by a wide range of health professionals has the potential to positively or negatively affect care outcomes and how we perceive the care experience. Only time will tell if we're innovating or collaborating enough to make a positive impact in this area, but it is surely one worthy of our continued focus and learning.

Where Do We Go from Here?

True progress very rarely comes in a straight line or on the first try. Ensuring that the accountable health care system of tomorrow delivers on our collective goal of improved quality and decreased cost at the patient and population level, we will need to continue testing new ideas and adapting as we go.

In describing the select companies in *Great by Choice* who were exceptional overall and especially in chaotic times, Collins noted, "They don't merely react; they create. They don't merely survive; they prevail. They don't merely succeed; they thrive. They build great enterprises that can endure."

Significant change in provider reimbursement represents the most potent form of "disruptive innovation" in health care. It is also an opportunity for deeper collaboration and leadership across the health care ecosystem—a renewed commitment to ensuring that our great enterprise can indeed endure.

John Glaser, Ph.D., *is the CEO of the health services business unit of Siemens Healthcare in Malvern, Pa. He is also a regular contributor to* H&HN Daily. *Neeraj Chopra* *is the director of strategic consulting, health insight and reform, for Siemens Health Services.*

Ensuring IT-Enabled Gains in Organizational Performance

April 8, 2014
By John Glaser

As electronic health records proliferate and their use becomes more meaningful, significant improvements in organizational performance ought to be the norm rather than the exception. Yet, not all providers are reaping the same benefits from their information technology investments. Two key pieces of research may tell us why

The health care industry is rapidly implementing interoperable electronic health records (EHRs). This movement is driven by the Meaningful Use incentives and efforts to prepare for payment reform, which places a strong emphasis on following the evidence, care coordination and population management.

These systems require significant organizational investments of money, management and clinical time and effort. Moreover, the implementation of an EHR requires that resources be diverted from other worthy initiatives.

Still, implementing an enterprise-wide electronic health record is a critical undertaking for a provider. It will not be possible to effectively create new care models (such as a patient-centered medical home), reduce care variability and respond to new quality-based payment models without an electronic health record. Providers reasonably expect to see improvements—significant improvements—in organizational performance as a result of these investments.

However, we should understand that the implementation of an electronic health record may be necessary, but alone it is insufficient to improve performance. Information technology is not the only factor that leads to IT-enabled performance gains.

Two Studies Worth Noting

Two studies have examined companies in a range of industries that made significant investments in IT—most notably enterprise-wide application systems—to materially improve their performance and competitive position. These studies found that, while many companies implemented fundamentally the same application system, the resulting performance gains were uneven. Some companies saw significant gains in performance while others did not. There were winners and losers.

Companies that outperformed competitors. The first study (McAfee and Brynjolfsson, *Harvard Business Review,* July 2008) examined all publicly traded companies, in all industries, from 1960 to 2005. The authors sought to understand the forces that led to winners and losers over that period of time. Interestingly, the study found that the gap in performance between the top 25 percent performing companies and the bottom 25 percent performing companies widened significantly over the latter half of that time frame, particularly for IT-intense industries. An IT-intense industry is one in which the use of IT can have a major impact on a company's strategy, e.g., telecommunications and manufacturing.

If the technology was available to all (companies might choose enterprise resource planning [ERP] systems from different vendors but they all could implement an ERP system) why did the gap occur? And why did the gap widen?

McAfee and Brynjolfsson found that those companies that outperformed their competitors did three things.

First, they implemented a common IT platform throughout the organization. The system supported critical functions, possessed the right level of features and functions, was well supported internally and by the vendor, and was able to handle needed modifications and enhancements. This factor proved important; however, it did not distinguish winners from losers. Many low-performing companies had implemented a common IT platform, often the same system as a high-performing company.

Second, the winning companies engaged in a series of thoughtful, goal-directed and well-managed innovations using the common platform. They tried new ways to improve customer service, manage inventory, eliminate unnecessary work, and provide new services and products. These innovations taught them ways to improve their performance and hence competitiveness.

Third, having identified innovations that had merit, they propagated them across the organization using the IT platform to implement and "enforce" the innovation. These companies were effective at introducing and managing change and did so repeatedly with many innovations.

Companies that took the first step but not the other two, or did a poor job in any of the three steps, saw their performance suffer.

The above findings explain the gap. As we all know, information technology is a tool. In that regard it is no different from a chain saw or a hammer. And like all tools the possession of a tool does not mean that the owner is effective at using the tool. All of us who are weekend handy persons can relate.

The widening of the gap is attributable to the growing power of information technology: During the span of the study, the Internet, ERP systems and business intelligence all emerged. As the technology becomes more powerful the innovations can become more sophisticated and effective—e.g., today's use of social media to engage customers. Once these innovations become part of the organization's routine way of doing business, the performance gains are that much more dramatic.

The gap results from the second and third factors building on the first factor. The widening of the gap is due to the second and third factors taking advantage of a more powerful first factor.

Companies with "digital maturity." The second study (Capgemini Consulting, 2012) examined digital innovations at 400 large companies. The study examined the "digital maturity" of these companies and compared this maturity with the performance of the companies. Digital maturity is defined according to two variables:

- Digital intensity, or the extent to which the company had invested in technology-enabled initiatives to change how the company operates. Example investments included advanced analytics, social media, digital design of products and real-time monitoring of operations.
- Transformation management intensity, or the extent of the leadership capabilities necessary to drive digital transformation throughout the company. Example capabilities included vision, governance and ability to change culture.

The study examined the degree to which digital intensity and/or transformation management intensity separated those that performed well from those that did not.

The study found that companies that had low scores on both intensity dimensions fared the poorest (24 percent less profitable than their competitors) while companies that had high scores on both intensity dimensions performed the best (26 percent more profitable than their competitors).

However, the study found that transformation management intensity was more important than digital intensity. Companies that had high transformation management intensity but low digital intensity performed 9 percent better than their competitors. And companies that had high digital intensity but low transformation intensity were 11 percent less profitable than competitors.

Ramifications for Health Care

What does this mean to the health care industry as it implements interoperable electronic health records across the health system?

First, investments in EHRs are a necessary foundational step to prepare the organization for the changes of broad health reform efforts. In the Capgemini study those organizations that failed to make the analogous investment fared the worst.

Second, as EHRs evolve to incorporate and complement a broad array of increasingly powerful information technology, their ability to enable gains in performance increases significantly. New technology matters.

Third, the organization's ability to change—to transform itself—is vital. In fact this ability is more important than its ability to "install" an enterprise-wide system. Change management skill (or transformation management intensity) enables the organization to fully realize its information technology investment. At its core, change management involves identifying important small and large innovations and successfully propagating those throughout the organization.

The importance of change management is illustrated by the fact that in the Capgemini study those organizations that had transformation management ability outperformed their competitors even if they had underinvested in information technology. The flip side was not true—organizations that had made significant investments in information technology but lacked transformation management intensity did worse than their competitors.

Fourth, given the third point above, as organizations invest in information technology they should examine whether they need to make investments in their change management ability. Attention to the organization's change management skills may be necessary before leaders shift their focus to IT.

Fifth, those of us who are bona fide members of the health care IT industry should be humbled by these studies. As important and necessary as we are, our talents and offerings are less important than the skilled administrative and clinical leadership of the organizations we serve.

John Glaser, Ph.D., is the CEO of the health services business unit of Siemens Healthcare in Malvern, Pa. He is also a regular contributor to H&HN Daily.

Managing Complexity with Health Care Information Technology

October 8, 2013
By John Glaser

Information technology enables us to master complexity, especially for patient data, medical knowledge and clinical processes.

Health care delivery is arguably the most complex industry in existence.

Multiple factors drive this complexity. Health care delivery is a socio-economic good provided by organizations that have a societal and community mission and traditional business obligations, such as generating a positive operating margin and providing high-quality products and services. As a socio-economic good, however, strategy and investment decisions for health care organizations have a more multifaceted set of decision criteria than for a traditional business.

Medicine, too, is a complex and rapidly evolving knowledge domain. Last year, according to the National Library of Medicine, approximately 800,000 articles were added to the referred biomedical literature. Ten years ago, that number was slightly less than 400,000 A *Learned Publishing* article estimates that 50 million articles have been published since formal research began.

If you view patient care as a manufacturing process, you'll find that a typical hospital carries out hundreds of unique processes that are variably performed. These processes "produce" outputs for which the quality of the output can be difficult to measure. And the processes are performed on "inputs" or patients who exhibit significant variability in symptoms and histories. Therefore, hospitals execute an exceptionally complex manufacturing process that has highly variable inputs, processes and outputs.

Finally, the structure of the health care delivery ecosystem requires coordination among a wide range of types of organizations. These organizations provide acute and/or long-term care services, or serve patients through physician practices, public health agencies, diverse purchasers of care, and government entities.

Given the all of the above, it should not surprise us that Peter Drucker wrote that the hospital is one of the most complex organizations ever created.

The Primary Value Proposition

Information technology (IT) has transformative power. It can accelerate processes, and make them less error prone and more efficient. It can offer new services that overcome distance, time and the need for a physical structure, such as a storefront. It can deliver information instantly and in novel ways to decision makers. And it can run algorithms to monitor equipment and correct minor problems before they become major problems.

Sophisticated analytics have enabled us to predict the weather, launch satellites that visit remote planets, capitalize on split-second opportunities in the financial markets, and model the actions of proteins.

We see this power in all facets of our lives. And yet if you step back and ask, "What is the most fundamental value proposition of information technology?" you could very well answer, "It enables us to conquer complexity."

At times, information technology is used to uncover complexity, such as determining the particle composition of the universe. At other times, information technology is used to create or enable a complexity that is valuable and so user friendly that you can use your smart phone to find the nearest fancy restaurant. And still, at other times the technology is used to master complexity or make complexity more manageable, for example, searching the literature more efficiently.

In health care, electronic health records (EHRs) enable providers to manage the complexity of a patient's care more efficiently over multiple venues, time and conditions. EHRs do so by allowing clinicians to retrieve and exchange their patients' data easily, thereby helping the clinicians to make optimal clinical decisions, providing workflow technologies to monitor and assess care decisions and processes, and capturing data that can be analyzed to assess care patterns.

On the administrative side, revenue cycle systems help a provider manage an increasingly bewildering array of payment schemes, purchaser contracts and medical necessity rules.

Mastering Three Sources of Complexity

The fundamental value of health care information technology is to tame, as well as we can, the complexity that characterizes the delivery system. This "taming" or mastering should enable a reduction in care costs, a more consistent delivery of care according to the medical evidence, a reduction in errors associated with errant clinical processes, and superior service for patients and clinicians.

There are three fundamental sources of complexity in health care: data, processes and medical knowledge. Information technology can reduce or manage complexity in all three sources.

Data. A patient's medical record can contain thousands of different data elements in a wide range of types (such as numbers, text, images and videos). These data may be plagued by different coding schemes, suffer from problems of inaccuracy and incompleteness, and be distributed across dozens of organizations. There is no customer record as complex as the medical record.

Multiple strategies are under way, many of these led by the federal government, to reduce the complexity of patient data. For example, data and transaction standards are under development, and their use is being enforced. In addition, health information exchanges are being introduced to create more complete sets of a patient's data.

New methods are available in which the computer assists the caregiver by highlighting the data that is likely to be relevant, given the patient's history, current complaints, and evidence-based treatment guidelines and protocols. These methods help prevent caregivers from becoming overwhelmed by the sheer volume of data.

Also, we can anticipate advanced techniques that use pattern recognition and machine learning to correct deficiencies in the data, for example, noting that the patient's data indicates that he/she is a diabetic even though a diabetes entry isn't in the problem list. Methods that identify patterns in the data, such as a predictive algorithm that indicates a high readmission risk, are already in use. These methods enable clinicians to focus on the pattern and not the underlying data.

These data efforts fall into two overall approaches:

- reducing data complexity through standardizing data, correcting problems of data inconsistency, and enhancing data completeness through health information exchange; and
- hiding complexity by highlighting relevant patient data and offering algorithms that guide clinical decisions, and by using methods to identify data patterns.

Processes. At times, there isn't adequate clinical evidence to guide the care that a patient receives. At other times, there is evidence but it is not followed. Either way, the result is high variability in care processes.

Care processes invariably traverse departments within a hospital or among specialists in the treatment of a patient with multiple chronic diseases or multiple care venues; this occurs, for example, with surgical procedures that require rehabilitation. Since these nodes do not always operate in the same way, and processes that traverse are often ad-hoc and idiosyncratic, complexity is inevitable.

There are several IT-based strategies for addressing process complexity.

Improving data liquidity through health information exchange enables each node to be aware of the care given and the results obtained by all of the parties involved in a patient's care. A fundamental aspect of good care coordination is that everyone involved in a patient's care is aware of the others' actions.

In addition to data accessibility, someone—often the nurse on an inpatient unit—must choreograph care processes. Information technology can provide orchestration support.

Workflow engines can monitor care processes and alert caregivers if the steps in a process are occurring in a sub-optimal sequence, or if the interval between steps is too long or steps have been skipped. Joint care plan development and documentation can also assist team-based orchestration of care. Personal health records enable the patient to be more effective as a team member and orchestrate aspects of his or her own care.

These efforts help address complexity by informing caregivers when a process has crossed a boundary that is deemed undesirable or unacceptable. For example, a workflow engine can alert caregivers that no one has followed up on an abnormal result. It's like the indicators on your car dashboard that inform you of impending trouble.

In a similar way, IT-based support of care teams does not remove or hide complexity, but it does enable caregivers to identify complex processes that are no longer on track.

Medical knowledge. For the caregiver, there is too much to know, and the body of knowledge changes and expands too frequently. Previous efforts to address this problem, such as creating sub-specialties, have proven unsustainable and often simply move the complexity problem rather than solve it. For example, while sub-specialization may enable a person to master an increasingly narrow body of medical knowledge, the result is increased care fragmentation. The knowledge problem has become a process problem.

There are several strategies that can be applied to address the medical knowledge complexity problem.

Clinical decision support can guide the caregiver's diagnostic and treatment decisions. This support can use computerized provider order entry by, for example, reminding the clinician to perform a genetic test before ordering a particular chemotherapeutic regime. Clinical decision support can guide documentation by highlighting the data that should be gathered to conduct a thorough health maintenance assessment.

Several multifaceted "big data" efforts are under way. Some of these mine EHR data to identify patient characteristics that call for different treatment approaches. Other efforts bring together diverse types of data—EHR, molecular medicine and radiology images—to determine if novel combinations can lead to highly sensitive and specific diagnostic and treatment decision aids.

These efforts generally seek to shift the complex problem of knowledge acquisition, delivery and synthesis from the caregiver to the machine.

Architecture Is Fundamental

Improving the quality, safety and efficiency of health care requires that we address the complexity of care delivery. This complexity has many sources. However, patient data, care processes and medical knowledge are fundamental sources.

Information technology has core capabilities that enable us to uncover, manage and create usable complexity. However, in health care today, our primary interest is in managing existing complexity. This management can take the form of hiding complexity, removing complexity, alerting caregivers if complex processes deviate in unacceptable ways, and shifting complexity management from the person to the machine.

The necessary core capabilities of IT are the exchange of health information; rules and workflow engines; algorithms and decision aids; and the support of team-based care. These capabilities are not specific EHR features and functions. They are capabilities that are present (or not) in EHRs and that form their architectural foundation. Hence, a broad range of application features and functions can make use of these capabilities.

A Caveat for Leaders

While we all recognize the importance of the technology, we cannot achieve the goal of complexity management by implementing health care information technology alone. Multiple other clinical and managerial interventions must accompany the deployment of the technology.

Clinical and operational processes must be re-engineered and standardized so that activities that only make things more complex and have no value are removed. Reward systems (such as reimbursement reform) are needed that provide the incentives and revenue to offset the costs of technology and re-engineering.

Finally, leaders must motivate and guide efforts to change how the organization functions. Complexity management is critical to effecting material improvement in health care. And information technology is an essential contributor to this management.

John Glaser, Ph.D., is the CEO of Siemens Healthcare's Health Services in Malvern, Pa. He is also a regular contributor to H&HN Daily.

Expanding Patients' Role in Their Care

June 11, 2013
By John Glaser

All the good the HITECH legislation is accomplishing in shifting our focus from adoption to meaningful use of information technology will be limited if patients are not engaged in their own care.

While some of us are running around with Fitbit devices, staying active and tracking every step (yes, I'm one of them), there are plenty of us opting not to follow doctor's orders to reduce this or cut that out of our diets. Admittedly, I'm one of them too.

And so it goes with patient engagement. Like that familiar saying, it seems you can engage all of the patients some of the time and some of the patients all the time, but you cannot engage all of the patients all of the time.

Still, the industry continues to retool itself for value-based payment models that emphasize prevention of readmissions and population health—models that will require us to place patients squarely at the center of our collective efforts to bend the health care cost curve and improve patient outcomes.

As we contemplate the benefits that patient engagement and population health will have on the industry, it's unclear if the throngs of patients we're seeking to engage—let alone our nation's health care providers—are ready to play such a starring role in their own care. As we know, the willingness and ability of patients and providers to engage varies depending on a host of socioeconomic, infrastructure and demographic factors—many of which we've only begun to penetrate.

Indeed we are at a critical juncture where patient engagement is concerned. This fall, as the first round of eligible hospitals attest for Meaningful Use Stage 2, they will be required to let patients view, download and transmit their health information within 36 hours of discharge. Eligible professionals are required to do so within four days of the information being available to the provider. Additionally, the minimum threshold for this measure is set at 5 percent of patients—a number some are skeptical is even reasonable.

This step is only a modest contribution in a long journey toward ensuring patients are informed and playing an active role in their health care. It is, nonetheless, an important demonstration that our nation's providers are working to involve patients more in their own care.

Getting There from Here

In large part, the HITECH legislation is shifting our focus from adoption to meaningful use of health care information technology (IT). But we won't get much from our investment without patient engagement.

For example, research tells us that less than half of non-surgical patients follow up with their primary care provider after discharge, one in four chronically ill older adults do not comply with their doctor's recommendations about prescription drug regimens, and less than 50 percent of elderly patients are up to date on clinical preventive services. The costs associated with these dismal statistics cannot be eliminated even if every provider in the nation is fully using the most elegant electronic health record (EHR).

To counter these non-compliance tendencies and transition-of-care issues, a variety of interventions must be employed to stay in constant contact with patients and gently nudge them toward better self-care and prevention. In general we must recognize that patient non-engagement is often not due to patients' lack of willingness: They may not be able to afford their medications. They may not be able to get a ride to their physician's office. They may not be able to read English. Still, many of our interventions will employ electronic tools and patients' personal devices to bridge the gap between hospital and home.

However, despite the benefits of patient-centered technologies, a provider's move toward patient portals, EHRs integrated with personal health records (PHRs) and provider-patient messaging, for example, is often low on the IT priority list.

For instance, when respondents to the 2013 HIMSS Leadership Survey were asked to identify the top IT priorities to be addressed at their organization in the next two years, 28 percent cited implementing the systems needed to achieve Meaningful Use. Another 20 percent indicated their top IT priority was to optimize the effective use of their currently installed systems. A focus on using information housed in data warehouses and business intelligence systems (17 percent) rounded out the top three priorities.

Only 2 percent of the HIMSS respondents indicated that health care consumer issues were a top IT priority or a primary clinical IT focus. In fact, with all that must be accomplished in fairly short order for Meaningful Use Stage 1 and 2 preparations, many organizations are left wondering how to develop a comprehensive patient engagement strategy. Not to mention how to balance the various competing IT initiatives.

Those organizations seeking guidance in launching or strengthening their patient engagement strategies can turn to some excellent work released late last year by the National eHealth Collaborative (NeHC).

Taking into consideration the patient engagement criteria for Meaningful Use Stage 1 and 2, NeHC's Patient Engagement Framework outlines several attributes of organizations that successfully engage and support patients, and ultimately their communities, in their care. The phases of the framework include Inform Me, Engage Me, Empower Me, Partner With Me and Support My e-Community. The framework helps organizations build out their capabilities in providing useful facility information, e-tools, forms and patient education, and patients' access to their information, as well as letting patients help generate their information and be a part of the care team.

Little Things Can Make a Big Impact

In working with dozens of providers over the past few years, I'm frequently introduced to innovative projects that span the breadth of NeHC's Framework. Often, I'm awed by how a seemingly simple initiative can make such a big impact.

For example, understanding that a hospital stay is a confusing and overwhelming time for patients and their families, Main Line Health, in the Philadelphia area, developed a patient-directed daily care plan (Inform Me) to help educate patients and their families on the various tests and treatments they will receive.

Employing its clinical information system's reporting tools, the plan summarizes information for the patient and care team. To ensure the plan was suitable for patient consumption, Main Line Health created a table to translate terms like "antihypertensive" into "used to treat high blood pressure."

Prior to the patient's daily care plan inception, physicians and nurses made up the majority of users for the provider's clinical information system. Now, patients have become users—or consumers—of clinical information system data and participants in the information flow.

In post-visit surveys of patients who received the daily care plan, the majority reported finding the care plan very helpful and wanting themselves or a loved one to receive such a report during a future hospital stay. Additionally, scores increased significantly for things we may take for granted, such as knowing all the names of the doctors treating the patient, knowing the names of medications and understanding why each is prescribed.

Now that patient satisfaction scores literally impact the bottom line, simply providing patients with a comprehensive daily status update can deliver a big impact. After all, being an informed patient is a prerequisite to being an engaged patient.

Portal Power

As the industry progresses through the NeHC Framework, providers will need to determine what patient-centered technologies they will offer to foster increased information sharing and engagement with their organizations.

With Meaningful Use Stage 2 soon to take center stage, many practices and hospitals are relying on portals and remote access systems for patients who can log into a secure, HIPAA-compliant website and get test results, view doctors' notes, schedule appointments, pay bills or refill prescriptions. Some patient portals are integrated into a provider's existing website, while others are extensions of the organization's electronic health record system.

For example, New York-Presbyterian (NYP) Hospital's award-winning patient portal, myNYP.org, was built via a joint, agile development model that expanded on its existing EHR. Rapidly deployed, the portal measurably increased patient engagement and satisfaction.

The project led to a 42 percent increase of appointments scheduled using myNYP. org, and it lowered the no-show rated from 20 percent to 12 percent over a period of six months after it was made available in January 2012. Additional applications of the same appointment-alert technology can provide customized patient education material and/ or personalized reminders to patients who fit a specific clinical profile, such as patients who missed an immunization.

NYP's joint work teams also created a solution for NYP to send reminder messages to patient phones and other mobile devices, and allow for communication from patient devices back into the information infrastructure. In all, 7,000 patient communication preferences (text, phone or email) were collected, helping NYP stay in close contact with its patients.

Technology Is Only Part of the Equation

From the growing trend toward increased provider-patient contact via mobile devices, portals and personal health records, to novel telemedicine approaches, e-visits and self-care technologies for managing chronic conditions like diabetes, an exciting future awaits us. In fact, several global initiatives have already shown that these technologies and practices hold tremendous promise for engaging patients earlier in the disease process, reducing costly readmissions, and caring for cohorts of patients more effectively and efficiently.

What exactly this future will entail remains to be seen. But, no doubt, the growing number of aging baby boomers who will eventually interact with the nation's health care system will play a key role in shaping what the fully engaged patient experience looks like.

As we move forward, we must ensure that the evolution from a provider-centric model to one that is truly patient-centric employs a step-wise approach to technology adoption such as NeHC's Framework suggests. Additionally, we must take great care that we do not ignore the most pressing obstacles to technology-based patient engagement, such as low health literacy or failing to reach key patient groups like the elderly or low-income households. Missteps such as these could have far-reaching consequences for the success or failure of our efforts.

Health reform demands that we keep patients as healthy as possible for as long as possible, thus avoiding expensive hospital stays and excessive readmissions. To remain healthy—or at least to prevent further decline—patients must take an active role in managing their own health, including modifying personal health behaviors. Medical interventions that occur solely through office-based patient/provider interactions will no longer provide the level of monitoring and scrutiny we need on our most challenging populations.

As the industry's focus on patient engagement matures and the body of evidence supporting its efficacy grows, new innovations in tools and care practices will dramatically impact the health care transformation under way in this country. In many ways, the transformation will fall short of expectations if we do not harness the power of technology to help patients help themselves. But, we must also remember that technology is only part of the equation: There can be no patient engagement without the caring and skillful human interactions between caregivers and their patients that remain the hallmark of health care in America.

John Glaser, Ph.D., is the CEO of the Health Services business unit of Siemens Healthcare in Malvern, Pa. He is also a regular contributor to H&HN Daily.

Ready, Set, Go: Performance-Based Reimbursement

April 9, 2013
By John Glaser and Neeraj Chopra

In the evolving health care ecosystem, providers must be prepared to handle a complex mix of both public and private sector payment mechanisms while meeting a diverse set of patient safety and quality goals.

With penalties for Medicare and Medicaid readmissions in effect and the first year of payouts and penalties from the Centers for Medicare & Medicaid Services' (CMS) hospital Value-Based Purchasing (VBP) program distributed for fiscal year 2013, the era of payment and delivery reform has officially arrived. Hospitals across the nation are automatically participating in these new payment models—ready or not.

Money on the Line

The revised payments associated with these programs signal the federal government's most all-encompassing effort so far to distribute risk and hold providers financially accountable for the quality of care they deliver. These pay-for-performance efforts are of course complemented by an array of pilot accountable care organization (ACO) and bundled payment projects.

While we can argue whether the money at stake in the startup phase of these programs is enough to motivate providers, the potential impacts to the health system are worth noting. Take readmissions: The industry data tells us that three-quarters of all hospitals may face some degree of readmissions penalty. It is also estimated that nearly 60 percent of hospitals and health systems will see readmissions payment reduction between $10,000 and $500,000.

Furthermore, although the VBP program was designed so that roughly half of all hospitals will receive a bonus payment while the other half will experience reduced payments, about two-thirds will end up losing money this year after the readmissions penalties are factored in, according to a *Kaiser Health News* analysis of Medicare's VBP payout data for fiscal year 2013.

In all, during the coming years, approximately 5 to 7 percent of a provider's entire Medicare market basket dollars will be at risk based on performance in a variety of patient safety, quality and outcome measures. This impact will be compounded by parallel private sector efforts to improve care through payment changes. Managing the tsunami of reform measures, maintaining the ever changing standards of care, and implementing best practices are key challenges for the industry at large—providers, payers and vendors alike.

In adapting to these new payment models, electronic health records should be viewed not only as a means to earn Meaningful Use dollars, but also as one of the most effective tools for positioning an organization to perform well against VBP and other payment reform metrics.

Game On

As the U.S. health care system moves from a volume-based business model that incentivizes utilization to a value- and outcomes-based model that incentivizes performance and quality, providers will require sophisticated information technology (IT) tools that support care delivery and related operations but also enable increased transparency in real time. Indeed, the need has never been greater to look inward, to ask more of IT and to chart a course for clinical process improvement.

Of course, health care leaders can certainly write off the CMS carrots and sticks as noise among other pressing issues and choose to do nothing. But savvy organizations will use the initial reform rollouts and the lower risk/reward factor as a time to focus on areas needing improvement and allow the organization to gain experience before penalties increase.

For example, Kaweah Delta Medical Center in Visalia, Calif., decided to view the VBP initiative as the next chapter in its clinical and patient satisfaction improvement efforts. The challenge was assessing how it was performing against the VBP measures and, more importantly, how its current technologies could be applied to help meet those standards.

Upon establishing its VBP financial incentive opportunity to be about $800,000, the executive team's discussion of prioritizing areas of focus evolved considerably. The organization's specific focus was on addressing and improving documentation and data collection requirements related to the 12 clinical process of care measures across the conditions: acute myocardial infarction, heart failure, pneumonia and the Surgical Care Improvement Project, as outlined by the VBP legislation.

Securing key stakeholder involvement—led by the CEO—and tapping the expertise of a multidisciplinary clinical, quality, IT and operational team, Kaweah Delta's VBP project established baseline metrics to provide a current-state analysis and a method to analyze how various process changes could help generate the appropriate outcomes. The organization was then able to use its existing workflow-based clinical solution to prospectively automate numerous clinical processes, data collection and reporting.

Today, Kaweah Delta relies on its IT system to be its eyes and ears—continuously monitoring processes throughout the organization and alerting staff when steps are not taken, occur in an incorrect sequence or take too long. System analytics can help managers understand whether the organization is doing a good job of following its re-engineered processes in real time. These analytics can also point out processes that seem to have uneven performance and can suggest additional training or further re-engineering.

Key Considerations

Like Kaweah Delta, a number of providers have established internal programs to prioritize and initiate their payment and delivery reform preparations. Several key suggestions are worth sharing as others get their reform initiatives off the ground:

Put inefficient areas of the hospital under the microscope. The concept of continuous process improvement should be embedded in every provider organization. Look closely at areas of your hospital with the lowest current performance, while highlighting areas of high performance. Look at the data, make changes and work with your quality and clinical staff to adapt your processes accordingly. Keep in mind that positive movement forward will be rewarded. In a VBP model, even low-performing areas can qualify for high payments if they demonstrate strong year-over-year improvement.

Do not underestimate the need to raise performance awareness. While it's nice to think that most U.S. hospitals, with just a few exceptions, uniformly perform well in following basic standards of care, that's simply not the case. What's even more surprising, though, is the lack of awareness that can exist at the highest levels of an organization—right up through the board.

An interesting study a few years back by Ashish Jha and Arnold Epstein of the Harvard School of Public Health found that not one of the board chairmen in the bottom 10 percent of the poorest performing hospitals thought they were below average. In fact, the majority thought they were above average. Very telling indeed.

A great deal of internal education regarding an organization's current performance level, and more importantly, how the organization performs against its peers and nationally, will be needed to mount a successful performance improvement initiative. Plan on a fair amount of meetings in which clinical leaders are educated on performance levels and related impacts in their vernacular, financial heads in their language, and so on. From the very top of the organization on down, the goal is achieving agreement on a strategy for tackling the various payment and delivery reform measures.

Cross-organizational governance is essential. Multidisciplinary participation in payment and delivery reform preparations is critical. Leaders from across the C-suite (including the CEO) are needed to champion the effort. Additionally, the overall project should be viewed as a clinical performance improvement initiative, not an IT project.

IT must prospectively guide care processes and decisions. In a value-based purchasing world where each core measure needs to be associated with what's happening today, performance improvement interventions must occur in real time—that is, while the patient is still in the acute care cycle. Therefore, sophisticated IT tools such as workflow and rules engines that push information to the front lines, guiding decisions at the point of highest possible impact, will be required.

Investment in comprehensive data collection and reporting systems (both prospective and retrospective) is critical. Successfully achieving the objectives of payment and delivery reform does not occur at a single point in time. Therefore, it becomes necessary to implement a suite of dashboards and workflow elements that help providers know they are complying with a certain set of measures today and that they will be able to monitor their continual performance.

Equally important is retrospective monitoring—finding out what didn't happen and why. For example, if a care provider failed to respond to an alert in a timely fashion, or deviated from a given standard of care process, we can use these data to determine if new care interventions are necessary, or if we need to alter an individual's plan of care.

Likewise, knowing that a patient failed to keep an appointment or was unexpectedly seen in the emergency room will let us know if there have been deviations from the expected plan of care. Tracking patient noncompliance will allow us to find opportunities to engage in new ways to manage chronic disease, presumably for the betterment of an individual's health.

With providers facing penalties for readmission, it will be more important to understand if it's the treatment that failed, the discharge plan that failed, or the patient who did not follow through on the post-discharge plan.

Little things can mean a lot. For some of the metrics CMS is using for the VBP program, there is not a large degree of differentiation in performance among providers. For instance, according to the *Kaiser Health News* analysis of the fiscal year 2013 payout data, 97 percent of pneumonia patients in a U.S. emergency room had a blood culture performed before receiving their first dose of antibiotics. Therefore, when just a few patients do not receive a test on time, or they negatively rate the communication and responsiveness of doctors and nurses, or they complain about the cleanliness and quietness of their environment, it can make a notable impact on how a hospital ranks among its peers.

So, if you think that preparing for payment and delivery reform isn't everyone's job—from nursing to dietary to housekeeping—think again.

Patient satisfaction is exponentially more important. As we know, patient satisfaction—as measured by Hospital Consumer Assessment of Healthcare Providers and Systems survey scores—represents 30 percent of the weighted total for VBP reimbursement, with clinical process of care measures making up 20 percent, outcome measures 30 percent, and efficiency measures 20 percent of the total performance calculation score for VBP reimbursement for fiscal year 2015.

Now that a patient's rating of his or her inpatient experience affects CMS reimbursement, providers are wise to take patient feedback more seriously than ever.

Don't wait to get started. As health care leaders begin recognizing the financial impact of payment reforms such as VBP, they often come to two common misconceptions: 1) It's too late to worry about that now (several years in, with regard to performance periods) or 2) That's something that can be worried about next year. Both views stymie progress and can hamper an organization's ability to meet specified performance measures.

The measurement process for fiscal year 2015 is under way today. Measurement and payments have already been determined for fiscal year 2014. What must be acknowledged is that what happens today impacts payments two years from now. The time to get started is now.

Providing Ideal Patient Care

Time will tell if the industry's efforts toward delivery and payment system reform bring about the intended results of improved quality, reduced cost and a health care system re-focused on accountability.

The question remains if the current Medicare and Medicaid revised payments are enough to move the performance needle. Still, for hospitals that treat a significant amount of Medicare patients, hundreds of thousands of dollars are at stake. As such, the nation's providers ought to be taking a serious look at known process inefficiencies and implementing course corrections that maximize existing IT investments.

As we know, many hospitals and health systems do not operate from a position of excess revenue, and as outcomes become increasingly tied to the reimbursement stream, it will become critical that providers can rely on their IT tools to detect and remedy variations in care. By optimizing care environments through a variety of program dashboards and workflows, best practices can be embedded within a health care provider's core clinical processes.

To thrive in the new value-based environment, health care organizations must use decision-making tools that present options and require actions in near-real time. This will aid in not only meeting the requirements of new reimbursement systems, but more importantly, will produce ideal clinical outcomes for patients—a goal the industry should have no mixed feelings about.

John Glaser, Ph.D., is the CEO of the Health Services business unit of Siemens Healthcare in Malvern, Pa. He is also a regular contributor to H&HN Daily. *Neeraj Chopra is the director of Strategic Consulting, Healthcare Reform Practice, Health Services, at Siemens Healthcare.*

Information Technology for Community Hospitals

February 14, 2012
By John Glaser

To weather the shifts in health care funding, smaller providers can take advantage of health care information technology, which is more accessible than ever.

The Supreme Court will be weighing in on health care reform sometime in mid-2012, putting its future into question. However, the health care industry is not holding its breath. Standing still in today's somewhat chaotic environment—reform, economic woes, capital budget pressures, reimbursement cuts and more—is not an option. Budgets and services are being cut, and hospitals that are considered the hubs of communities, such as the venerable St. Vincent's, have shut their doors.

Doing more with less applies to everyone. The larger academic enterprises and the rural, community hospitals all share the same challenges and the same goals, such as performance improvement and attesting to meaningful use requirements. They need the same tools, they have to meet the same requirements, and they must keep pace with rapidly advancing clinical knowledge. But the rural, community provider must do it with tighter budgets and fewer personnel.

Smaller providers, which have fewer resources and feel the impact of payments cuts more acutely, are usually at a disadvantage. Yet their survival is no less important: Academic centers may be the source of innovation for the health care industry, but community hospitals are the backbone of their communities, not just providing health care but often serving broader social needs. Imagine the catastrophic impact if the almost 2,000 rural hospitals listed in *AHA Hospital Statistics* ceased to exist.

Help for Smaller Hospitals

Fortunately, rural and community hospitals are resilient and, where there is challenge, there is also opportunity. Here are some examples of assistance available to smaller providers:

- Many institutions (1,327 as of March 2011) have become certified as critical access hospitals (CAH). By definition, CAH facilities must have 25 or fewer acute-care beds and must be more than 35 miles from another hospital. They are eligible for a more flexible, cost-based reimbursement program from Medicare. The bump in reimbursements is intended to bolster finances and stem the tide of closures.
- The Patient Protection and Affordable Care Act, in its current form, broadens the definition of a low-volume hospital for fiscal years 2011 and 2012. This redefinition makes more rural and community hospitals eligible for special provisions from CMS's prospective payment system.
- Beyond the absolute value of improving patient care and receiving incentives from the American Recovery and Reinvestment Act (ARRA), providers using electronic health records (EHRs) are eligible to participate in a number of programs. The new Partnership for Patients program, intended to improve care quality, focuses on keeping patients from getting injured or sicker and on helping patients heal without complications. The program addresses issues such as adverse drug events and hospital-acquired infections.
- Reporting on outcomes is the next wave of change as the health care system moves from a volume-based system to value-based, pay-for-performance system. Rural and community hospitals with a CAH designation can participate in the Flex Medicare Beneficiary Quality Improvement Project, specifically designed to improve quality outcomes and related reporting. The project focuses initially on care management protocols; later it will look at quality measures and reporting.
- To address the impending care demands and opportunities, many facilities are banding together in loosely defined alliances to take advantage of group purchasing equipment or partnering with larger neighbors to broaden services. Accountable care organizations are still very much in early formation, but they offer some community hospitals the opportunity to join forces with larger facilities in caring for defined populations.

However, many community and rural hospitals will remain largely independent. Regardless of the nature of their alliances and their status under Medicare, as stated earlier, community providers still need to take the same actions as larger hospitals—and under more challenging conditions.

The Necessity of Information Technology

Managing the coming reimbursement cuts, and dealing with limited budgets, means making operations smarter and more efficient. It also means applying measures to improve quality, reduce errors and help patients better manage their health.

In addition, if the reform legislation stands, rural and community providers can expect an increase in patients, taxing their already strained resources. Their patient bases comprise a large number of the uninsured—they also tend to be sicker and older. These providers will need to care for more people, perhaps sicker people, and without a leap in financing and resources.

Community and rural hospitals have been slow to adopt health care information technology (HIT), hampered by budget, staffing and physical infrastructure. Some of these providers will qualify for an approximately 50 percent increase in Medicare reimbursements to cover the costs of EHR implementation—but only after meaningful use thresholds are achieved.

The incentive payments under ARRA do not fully cover the up-front costs of the software and hardware. Purchasing an HIT system, from a pure product perspective, is only one of the burdens facing providers. Implementing a system is a complex and often lengthy project. Many rural and community-based facilities do not have access to qualified IT professionals to install and maintain systems. In the past, this would leave rural and community facilities out of the reward system for meaningful use of electronic health records.

Fortunately, HIT is more accessible today. The costs of technologies are decreasing, and remote management via high performance networks means it is possible for the rural and community hospital to take advantage of enterprise-level HIT for a reasonable cost. Furthermore, the HIT industry is becoming more adept and efficient at implementing these complex systems, leading to significant reductions in implementation costs. This means that HIT is coming within the technical and budget reach of virtually all community hospitals.

HIT Options

Here are some of the advances in HIT now available to rural as well as academic hospitals:

- Applications can be delivered remotely, with the applications and the data housed "in the cloud." Cloud computing is increasingly able to provider secure, relatively inexpensive and robust application delivery support to many locations. Moreover, managing the cloud helps ensure that core computer operations are expertly run, new regulations are quickly adopted and new technologies are introduced.
- Application systems are provided with comprehensive content. In the past, organizations often had to develop content such as order sets, documentation

templates and data entry screens from scratch. Community hospitals often do not have the resources to engage in this development and will question the need to re-invent that which other organizations have already adopted successfully.

• Model implementations have been established. These implementations bring a degree of rigor to the organization. For an organization that may not have deep project management talent and may not desire to engage in lengthy discussions about implementation tactics, these model implementations can lead to quicker and less expensive implementations.

These advances reflect the convergence of new information technology (cloud), a growing base of understanding of what works, and what doesn't work, in systems design (content) and the maturation of the industries thinking about implementation (model implementations).

Regarding the latter, for many years it was believed that buy-in by clinicians and other stakeholders was critical for a successful implementation. And that buy-in was best achieved by stakeholder involvement in all system decisions. Buy-in is still critical. But many stakeholders have evolved; they have bought in enough to the value of electronic health records that they no longer need to weigh in on a very large number of decisions.

While the convergence of these factors have enabled sophisticated health information technology to lie within the reach of the small community hospital, the industry and the hospitals should not believe that this convergence solves all of the challenges an organization faces when it undertakes an IT-based transformation of its clinical, administrative and revenue cycle processes.

Cloud computing is maturing, but it takes great skill to manage a cloud. Moreover, the skill needed will become more extensive over time as the technology continues to become more sophisticated and the industry faces potential additional regulations (such as treating EHRs as a medical device).

Providing content with applications does save the community hospital a lot of work. However, the content changes as payer contracts, optimal treatments, data code sets (e.g., ICD-10), clinical pathways and medical advances (e.g., genomics) occur. The community hospital must ensure that its content stays current, and it must understand changes in content since these often lead to changes in clinical practice and revenue cycle operations.

Model implementations can be, for some organizations, too rigid. The organization may legitimately have processes that are different from other hospitals, and it may have stakeholders who want to be intimately engaged in a wide range of decisions.

And all organizations need to remember that IT is a tool; real transformation requires leadership, thoughtful process change and good management. The electronic health record, cloud-based or not, does not provide these skills. The hard work of making care better, although now using a powerful tool, remains hard work.

Community hospitals are the backbone of care delivery in this country. While various federal programs are intended to help them, they still face significant challenges in responding to imperatives to improve care quality, safety and efficiency. For many years health care information technology has been out of the reach of these organizations and hence was not available to help them address these challenges.

Fortunately, these organizations can now take advantage of the same information technology as their larger cousins. The community hospital still has work to do to ensure that the technology is used effectively, but it is up to the challenge.

The bottom line is that HIT systems are good for providers—large and small. And having HIT is good for patients, too.

John Glaser, Ph.D., *is the CEO of Siemens Health Services in Malvern, Pa. He is also a regular contributor to* H&HN Daily.

Reprinted from H&HN Hospitals & Health Networks, by permission, February 2012, ©2012 by Health Forum, Inc.

Nursing in the New Era of Accountability

July 28, 2011
By John Glaser and Gail Latimer

As the health care system begins a multi-faceted transformation, nurses will make important contributions to our collective success.

Every day, America's nurses bring compassion, leadership, skill and vision to our health care system. They take care of the sick, comfort the dying and serve as the glue that holds the patient experience together.

They are also leading the prevention-focused, quality-oriented paradigm shift associated with the most sweeping changes to the U.S. health care system in more than 40 years.

Indeed, the recently passed Patient Protection and Affordable Care Act (ACA) ushers in an era of broad health insurance coverage and the first wave of substantial health care payment reform. The private sector has also unleashed a complementary wave of changes in provider reimbursement approaches.

While these payment reform efforts are diverse, they share several characteristics:

- Providers will be asked to measure and report the quality, safety and efficiency of care delivered.
- A significant portion of reimbursement will be based on these measures; providers will face material financial risk if their care is deemed to be substandard.
- Reimbursement is evolving to include episodes and bundles: Payment will be based on the holistic care of a patient, be it a single payment for hip replacement

surgery and rehabilitation care, or a single payment for care delivered to a diabetic over the course of a year.

- Regardless of care performance, reimbursements will decrease.
- Greater transparency of provider quality scores and costs will be required, enabling purchasers of care and consumers to make more informed choices as they seek care.
- Efforts will be made to compare the effectiveness of new programs and treatments with that of current programs and treatments; those that fail to demonstrate quality outcomes will not be reimbursed.
- Provider organizations will be made accountable for the care of populations of patients, with these providers establishing new arrangements such as accountable care organizations and patient-centered medical homes.

HITECH Requirements

For providers to achieve the level of care that will become the new standard, they must employ a solid foundation of health information technology. It is not possible to achieve the necessary levels of quality performance, conform to evidence-based medicine or manage increasingly complex reimbursement arrangements without such a foundation.

The federal government understood the need for this foundation when it passed the HITECH Act in 2009, which provides financial incentives for hospitals and eligible professionals that demonstrate they are meaningful users of electronic health records. In effect, the government, as the largest purchaser of health care in the world, was saying clinicians must use the technology to enter orders, document care and exchange data with other providers if they are to effectively address the changes introduced by the ACA.

As providers embark on their journeys to comply with the requirements of HITECH, savvy nurse executives see this as a time for their profession to shine. They understand that nursing will play a key role in determining their organization's success in this era of accountable care.

Nursing at Center Stage

Nurses are at the center of efforts to coordinate patient care. They ensure that care delivery is delivered efficiently, that the care team is informed of the status of a patient and that transitions of care are managed effectively.

Moreover, nurses generate the majority of the documentation that makes up a patient's medical record. These data will be a source for measuring compliance with the law's quality reporting requirements, helping an organization qualify for federal incentive monies or avoid penalties. In fact, many organizations have found themselves in good standing for the meaningful use quality reporting requirements largely because of the data nurses are already capturing electronically in clinical practice.

Of particular importance to the nursing community is avoiding CMS's "never events," a set of hospital-acquired conditions the agency has deemed preventable and thus not reimbursable. Technological tools alert clinicians so they can prevent never events from occurring. Using technology to support clinicians in day-to-day care delivery can make a measureable impact on the outcome of care.

Regardless of where an organization lies along the technology adoption curve, there is reasonable certainty about the major health information system applications our nation's nurses will encounter in the era ahead:

- an integrated electronic health record that spans inpatient, outpatient and emergency department care;
- a revenue cycle system that also spans this care continuum and is well integrated with the electronic health record;
- workflow engines that help improve the performance of core clinical processes, e.g., patient discharge, chronic disease management and infection management;
- rules engines that critique a specific clinician decision, e.g., drug-drug interaction checking after the entry of a medication order;
- business intelligence and analytics technologies that enable providers to measure the quality, safety and efficiency of their care, monitor clinical performance, and understand the resulting reimbursement ramifications;
- interoperability technologies that enable providers to exchange clinical data, such as patient allergies, problems, medications and information on events (such as an unplanned emergency room visit) with other providers as they jointly manage the care of the patient; and
- patient-oriented technologies, such as the personal health record and online patient communities that assist patients in managing their own care.

The Road Ahead

Benefitting from these health care IT investments is as much a function of leadership as it is the right technology and strategic partner. There is no better time for nurses to exert their leadership and become intimately familiar with their organizations' strategic IT vision, especially the implications it will have on the patient care environment.

Successful nurse executives who have anticipated new technologies are positioning their organizations to thrive in the era ahead. In doing so, they should:

Secure a seat on their organizations' IT advisory board or steering committee. Make it a priority to evaluate the IT roadmap and contribute to decisions about which applications will be rolled out and how those tools will integrate into clinical practice.

Assist in completing gap analyses with regard to meeting meaningful use criteria and prioritizing projects.

Seek out opportunities to become an executive champion. Some of the most successful IT initiatives spring from an alignment between the CIO and executive champions such as the CNO and CMO. Each group remembers to "walk in each other's shoes," influencing the project's key stakeholders and bringing their concerns and recommendations to the project leaders.

Foster interdisciplinary collaboration. Be the ambassador who breaks down the typical organizational silos—dietary, laboratory, occupational therapy—that exist in most health care facilities. Help others embrace a shared leadership model that fosters interdisciplinary collaboration throughout the IT implementation.

Be open to the voice of frontline nurses. Bedside nurses are keenly aware of the challenges associated with handoffs of information and care transitions. Provide ample opportunity for nurses to give input into the design of the system.

Create a sense of nursing ownership. Assuming frontline staff have venues for providing input, be sure that when requested changes are made, nurses see them firsthand. Creating this type of feedback loop is empowering for end users.

Contribute to a communication plan that follows the implementation progress. Doing so will help ensure that all stakeholders understand the organization's strategic objectives and each discipline's role in bringing them to fruition. Share implementation highlights so that team members are aware of progress.

Establish a set of guiding principles for end users as they adopt new technologies. Perhaps these will support the culture change the technology is expected to drive; perhaps they outline how the IT staff will work with and solicit feedback from the nursing staff, for example.

Continuously assess readiness for change and adoption. Survey clinicians and understand that lower response scores will come from those who realize the new applications are affecting their workflow. Help staff members move from skepticism to hopeful realism, informed optimism and, eventually, satisfaction with the new technology and processes.

Show other nurses the way by sharing best practices. As technology continues to make it easier to implement evidence-based practice and protocols, take advantage of the many opportunities the industry offers for sharing successes with and learning from others.

Don't underestimate the power of technology in nurse recruitment efforts. There isn't a nurse joining the profession who wouldn't want to use a bar coding solution to help ensure the safety of the patient during medication administration.

Providing Consistency Amid the Chaos

It is difficult to be certain about the impact of the ACA on the nation's health care system in the decade ahead. There are dozens of new approaches to payment, and their effectiveness at a national scale or across all populations is unclear. Moreover, it is not possible to attempt to transform the largest and most complex sector of any economy and have a complete understanding of the mature forms of the new health care system. We are in for a decade of experimentation, chaos and uncertainty.

Through the challenging years ahead, the nursing community must remain the backbone of care delivery. The community must be active, thoughtful and vigorous contributors to reshaping the health care system. They must also be skilled and effective in their application of information technology to improve care. To a large degree, the future of health care depends on nursing and its sophisticated use of information technology.

John Glaser, Ph.D., is the CEO of Siemens Health Services in Malvern, Pa. He is also a regular contributor to H&HN Daily. *Gail E. Latimer, M.S.N., R.N., F.A.C.H.E., F.A.A.N., is the vice president and chief nursing officer of Siemens Health Services.*

A New Era in IT's Strategic Importance

March 23, 2010
By John Glaser

Changes to the payment system and the growing need for electronic records have major ramifications for providers.

The strategic importance of information technology in health care has grown. IT is strategic when the technology becomes an essential contributor to the organization's strategies and its ability to thrive in an environment that brings new opportunities and threats.

IT's strategic importance varies across industries. For example, IT is more important in financial services than in organized religion. Strategic importance often arrives progressively over time rather that appearing in a sudden, dramatic fashion. And strategic importance can be unique to an industry because it results from industry conditions that create the context that make some IT investments more important than others.

While the strategic importance of IT in health care has been growing over the last several years, two factors will accelerate its salience.

Accountability for care: Purchasers of care—both payers and patients—are becoming more interested in understanding the costs and quality of care. Pay-for-performance efforts have had mixed results. The potential value of payment based on bundles of care, episodes or capitation is unclear, and its impact may be uneven, which makes these conceptually appealing ideas difficult to implement.

Regardless of the spotty track record, the direction is clear. Provider reimbursement will be increasingly based on care quality and efficiency, and a variety of stakeholders will demand data on clinical performance. Purchasers and other stakeholders will also push to require that providers follow various evidence-based protocols and decision-support guidelines.

Interoperable electronic health records: The adoption of electronic health records (EHRs) is expected to increase significantly in the coming years. It is driven by several factors, most notably the Medicare and Medicaid meaningful use payments and penalties that are part of the American Recovery and Reinvestment Act (ARRA).

We can't predict the level of EHR adoption or the degree to which health information will be exchanged among providers five years from now. Regardless, the industry can reasonably expect significant increases in both areas.

Impact on Providers

The two factors—accountability for care and interoperable EHR adoption incentives—have several major strategic IT ramifications for provider organizations.

EHRs as an essential investment. EHR adoption is low in this country. There are many explanations for this, but a primary reason is these systems were traditionally not viewed as a strategic necessity. An EHR may not enhance a competitive position nor improve revenue opportunities, and the skill required to implement the technology leaves many organizations doubting that they would achieve the care gains seen by others.

The increasing demands for accountability for the cost, quality and safety of care cannot be met through systems and processes based on paper. The federal and state incentives and penalty programs, which may be paralleled or leveraged by private payers, make the absence of an EHR an increasingly problematic financial issue.

Moreover, as a growing number of providers in a region adopt EHRs and begin to exchange data, those who have not made these investments could find themselves competitively disadvantaged. They will be seen as offering inferior service and possibly sub-standard care. Imagine a similar scenario in the financial services world: No one would place their deposits in a bank that did not offer ATMs or that sent monthly statements written by hand.

Data as a critical organizational asset. Data has always been important to the provider. Managing reimbursement, controlling costs and understanding variation in care practices have become core activities in provider organizations.

Nonetheless, most providers have data fragmented across many systems, differences in data definitions and uneven data quality across these systems, and operational and clinical processes that place insufficient emphasis on ensuring that data capture is comprehensive and well managed.

Reimbursement based on bundles or episodes and demonstrated quality and efficiency of delivery will require very good data. The exchange of data between providers will require developing policies regarding data reuse and the means to assess the quality of incoming data. Fragmented systems that lead to slow and expensive information aggregation will become increasingly intolerable and perilous. Operational processes will need to be examined to ensure that the human and technological means are in place for capturing needed data "at the source."

Ensuring high-quality data is a multifaceted organizational undertaking requiring improved information systems, process changes, data analysis tools and policies regarding data use. Managing data well has often been viewed as a back office function performed in the medical records and finance departments. However, changes to the payment system will promote data management from a secondary consideration to a strategic consideration.

A higher bar for IT execution. Major applications such as the EHR are very difficult to implement. These initiatives are at risk of being over budget, taking longer than planned and delivering results that don't match the description in the brochure. In fact, many organizations have resigned themselves to mediocre execution and results.

As systems become more critical strategically, tolerance for suboptimal execution becomes much lower. The strategic stakes are high, and any initiative that fails to deliver what was intended has consequences that are now much more serious. Moreover, a tightening of capital availability means that organizations are able to fund fewer IT initiatives. Hence those that are funded had better deliver the goods.

The heightened premium on excellent execution will lead to efforts to strengthen project prioritization, project management and change processes. Moreover, the organization may need to address situations in which the individuals involved do not have the necessary skills. And, a status report on the execution of IT strategy will need to become a standing agenda item in senior leadership and board meetings.

The imperative of effective clinician engagement. Many provider organizations have relationships with their medical and other clinical staff that are indifferent or borderline antagonistic. It will be impossible to effectively address the requirements of accountability for care and EHR adoption without a strong working relationship between the organization and its clinicians. An unused or poorly used EHR will not improve care nor will efforts to increase accountability on the part of clinicians who see little reason to be held accountable by "suits."

While strong clinician engagement is not an IT undertaking, it is a predicate to achieving the gains that information technology has to offer.

Looking Forward

IT has become strategically important for provider organizations. This elevation in importance is driven by two factors that are inexorably altering the environment of care delivery. Achieving the strategic yield of EHR is not automatic. It requires investment in the technology, heightened management of data, terrific execution and superior working relationships with clinicians.

John Glaser *is a vice president and the CIO of Partners HealthCare in Boston. He is also a regular contributor to* H&HN Weekly.

Reprinted from H&HN Hospitals & Health Networks, by permission, March 2010, ©2010 by Health Forum, Inc.

IT Strategies for Process Improvement

February 17, 2009
By John Glaser

Four strategies can help you ensure the success of your next IT initiative.

Information technology can make organization processes faster, more accurate, less expensive, more convenient, and more widely available. This is not news to health care providers. Nor is it news that the introduction of a new application should accompany efforts to reengineer current processes. Without associated process change, a new application system speeds up broken practices and procedures and makes them more expensive and harder to fix.

What can surprise providers, however, is the importance of four strategies learned by a wide range of industries over the course of many IT implementations:

- Focus on core processes
- Define the scope of the work
- Adopt an incremental approach
- Enhance processes with intelligence

Focus on Core Processes

Every organization has a small number of core processes that are essential to effective and efficient operations. For a hospital, these processes might include ensuring patient access to care, ordering tests and procedures, and managing the revenue cycle. Core processes define the hospital; remove any one and the organization's identity changes. A hospital with no process for access to patient care is no longer a hospital.

Core processes meet one of two criteria. First, customers evaluate the organization based on these processes. Patients will judge a physician practice based on appointment availability, not on the efficiency of its appointment no-show processing. Second, the process is fundamental to the core performance of the organization. The physician decision-making process is fundamental to a hospital while the process of a month-end close is not.

The majority of a hospital or health care organization's processes and practices contribute to its performance. However, some processes are more essential than others. IT investments are most potent when they are applied to improving the performance of core processes.

Define the Scope of the Work

Hospitals should begin reengineering efforts by questioning whether a process targeted for a technology implementation is correctly defined. Definitions that incorporate the mechanics of the process—its current steps—into the core description can narrow the reexamination effort and the resulting IT initiative.

Defining a process as "obtaining cash from the bank," for example, might lead a reengineering effort to place ATMs only at the bank. These ATMs might shorten the wait for customers on a Saturday morning and be viewed as an improvement. However, defining the process more widely—"obtaining cash"—would instead guide a reengineering team to consider all the places where people need cash—malls, theaters and airports. ATMs would be installed in many and varied locations, leading to a far more powerful improvement. Similarly, Internet-based retailers have understood that the process of buying a book or a shirt did not need to include "at a store" in the definition.

Correctly defining a process is critical to determining appropriate IT needs. "Paying for delivered care" might lead a provider and health plan to develop applications that are different from those based on the definition "developing and adjudicating a claim."

Adopt an Incremental Approach

Organizations often introduce large computer systems and related process changes all at once. While the desire to minimize the time an organization spends straddled between the old and the new is understandable, big-bang implementations are tricky and risky.

These efforts introduce an enormous number of process changes affecting many people. It is exceptionally difficult to understand the ramifications of such sizeable change during the analysis and design stages that precede application implementation.

Indeed, a complete understanding is impossible. As a result, the organization risks damage. For example, a very rapid implementation of computerized provider order entry across the hospital could lead to broad confusion and possible patient harm.

In contrast, IT implementations (and related process changes) that take an incremental and iterative approach reduce risk. The organization and its employees have time to comprehend the impact of one phase and can alter the course before embarking on the next one. Moreover, incremental change helps the organization's leaders and staff to understand that change and improvement are a never-ending aspect of organizational life rather than something to be endured every couple of years.

Most of the time, organizations that wind up dominating an industry do so through thoughtful advancements over the course of several years. Persistent improvement by a talented team can result in significant strategic gains. The strategic value of IT investments is a marathon: It is a long race that is run and won one mile at a time.

This incremental approach has ramifications for the sequence and timing of an implementation plan. It also means that the new application must have capabilities that enable the organization to apply its ongoing learning and to change the features and capabilities of the system.

Enhance Processes with Intelligence

Effective process performance is increasingly dependent on knowledgeable clinicians and staff. Staff must understand the specifics of a patient's insurance during registration, the physician must know the possible side effects of a prescribed medication and the nurse must know of a patient's medical history.

These demands for knowledge increase the complexity of health care processes. More complexity increases the risk that there will be a failure to follow-up on abnormal test results or that care won't fully comply with payment requirements, regulations and guidelines.

Improving processes means adding intelligence to them. Applications will need to ensure that appropriate information is delivered to process participants at the right time. These applications will also need to monitor and direct processes, and identify inappropriate sequences of steps, such as a delay between actions or the assignment of a task to the wrong person. Improved processes need robust rules and workflow-engine technologies.

The primary value of information technology is the improvement of organizational processes. Reengineering is just the first step. Health care organizations should also incorporate strategies derived from IT-enabled process change across several industries.

John Glaser is vice president and CIO of Partners HealthCare in Boston, senior advisor, Deloitte Center for Health Solutions, and a regular contributor to H&HN Weekly.

What Happens After EHR Implementation Is Done?

July 11, 2007
By John Glaser

A survey (*Continued Progress: Hospital Use of Information Technology,* American Hospital Association, 2007) found 11 percent of US hospitals reporting that they had fully implemented an electronic health record (EHR). In addition, using a measure of the range and depth of EHR capabilities that had been implemented, 16 percent of hospitals had a high level of EHR use in 2006. In 2005, 11 percent of hospitals were at this level.

In the health care industry, most of our discussion and focus centers on encouraging adoption. This focus is appropriate. The percentages above indicate that adoption remains a challenge for a significant majority of hospitals. However, the percentages also indicate that a growing number of hospitals are "done." EHR implementation is complete, and they have put in place a broad range of information technology capabilities such as CPOE, the outpatient medical record, documentation and decision support.

To be fair, most of those who are done are not really done. There are invariably applications that remain to be implemented and new technologies, such as wireless networks, that may still be in the rollout phase. However, the long, expensive and difficult task of implementing an electronic health record may be largely behind them.

If they are done, what do they do now?

It is hard to believe that these hospitals have arrived at the peak of health care information technology existence. They can go no further. The can lay off all of their IT staff except the data center staff. The organization need merely apply application upgrades from time to time.

However, if the implementation of the electronic health record can be considered Phase I, then there must be a new phase—a Phase II. It is likely that Phase II has three major classes of activity.

Continuous Improvement of Processes. The organizational imperative to relentlessly and continuously improve core processes of care, operations and the revenue cycle never ends. Process change is not only an important component of EHR implementation, but it is also an important activity after EHR implementation. With the EHR in place, the organization can now apply the technology to facilitate change.

Moreover, implementation does not mean that problem lists are complete, all medications are written using order entry, or health maintenance reminders are being followed. Adoption does not mean that care has been improved.

Phase II will involve ongoing efforts, now EHR enabled, to improve core processes. The organization must have mechanisms to identify process improvement opportunities, teams that can effect needed changes and the means to measure the results.

Phase II will require efforts to ensure that the implemented EHR is being used effectively. The organization will need to provide ongoing training, approaches to integrating EHR use into the workflow and data to measure the effectiveness of use—e.g., the percent of radiology orders written electronically.

Leveraging of Data. The implementation of the EHR will result in the steady accumulation of potentially large amounts of patient data. This data can be leveraged. Potential leverage opportunities include:

- Support of analyses needed by continuous process improvement efforts
- Development or extension of pay for performance contracts—e.g., contracts can change from incentives that reward an appropriate number of visits by a diabetic to incentives that reward achievement of hemoglobin a1c targets
- Pharmacovigilance
- Industry comparison of differences in outcomes between competitive medical products and medications
- Support of clinical research, perhaps through the integration of genomic and phenotypic data

Phase II will require mechanisms to identify and assess data leverage opportunities, staff skilled in data and care/operations analyses, information technology to support business intelligence activities and feedback loops into applications and workflow improvement efforts to increase the quality and completeness of data capture.

System Extensions. The EHR can be extended outside of the walls of the organization. There are three major types of extension.

First, the EHR can be extended to patients. Personal health records and remote monitoring of the chronically ill can be implemented. Second, the organization's EHR can be integrated to varying degrees with the EHRs of other organizations to support clinical affiliations. This extension might involve the electronic exchange of clinical data or the use of one organization's EHR by the other. Third, the EHR can be utilized to support very specific workflows such as eprescribing transaction integration with pharmacies and pharmacy benefits managers.

Phase II means that the organization has developed interoperability strategies, understands how to manage information technology infrastructure that is shared with other organizations and has identified the best approaches to using the EHR to involve patients more directly in their care.

Observations. There are three observations that can be made about Phase II.

First, planning for Phase II must start while the organization is in Phase I, and aspects of Phase II need not wait for Phase I to be completed.

If continuous process improvement is a key activity of Phase II, then the EHR technology being implemented in Phase I must be chosen such that it provides the rules and workflow engines needed in Phase II. The leveraging of the data and EHR implementation can begin well before every outpatient clinic and physician office has an electronic medical record.

Second, there are parallels to these phases in other industries. The airline industry initially focused on online reservation systems. Once that was done, the industry began to appreciate the ability to leverage data (frequent flier programs and yield management systems) and the value of system extension (systems to manage baggage movement between carriers and the ability to check-in to a flight from home).

Third, the mature forms of Phase II are generally not well understood. For example, organizations often embark upon a program of "clinical transformation" and implement EHRs as a foundational element of that transformation. Unfortunately, the "transformation" term implies that, once transformed, you cannot be any better. The transformation orientation can be an incomplete understanding of process change—an orientation to change that knows that it can never end.

Significant aspects of data leverage are not well understood. While there may be impressive clinical research and pharmacovigilance opportunities, these opportunities are largely hypothetical. EHR data can have a myriad of problems that make such leverage opportunities problematic. Many of the leverage opportunities today are visions rather than proven realities.

While there is much discussion of personal health records, there is not a mature understanding of their value. Similarly, the country is struggling to find models that enable the widespread sustainability of regional health information organizations.

Conclusion. There is a long organizational life after EHR implementation has been completed. The phase that follows adoption can be outlined, and some organizations have begun to confront this phase. However, there is much to be learned about how to effect sustained process improvement, data leverage opportunities and systems extensions.

John Glaser *is vice president and CIO of Partners HealthCare in Boston, senior advisor, Deloitte Center for Health Solutions, and a regular contributor to* Most Wired Online.

Reprinted from H&HN Hospitals & Health Networks, by permission, July 2007, © 2007 by Health Forum, Inc.

The Myth of IT's Competitive Advantage

March 22, 2006
By John Glaser

The national health care information technology (IT) discussion is centered on furthering the adoption of interoperable electronic health records (EHRs). At times, this discussion is viewed with suspicion by those provider organizations that have made significant investments in clinical information systems. The board and the leadership of those organizations may believe that widespread adoption of interoperable EHRs will remove a competitive advantage that they have achieved through their own IT investments. For example, local physicians can access test results and images electronically from the hospital's systems, but a rival hospital cannot offer the same capabilities.

Organizations holding this belief should remind themselves of the lessons learned by many organizations in various industries over many years as a result of the pursuit of IT as a source of competitive advantage.

IT can enable a significant improvement in organizational performance and assist in achieving an advantage when it is utilized to leverage core organizational processes, support the collection of critical data, and/or differentiate organizational products and services.

Leverage Organizational Processes. Information technology can be applied in an effort to improve organizational processes by making them faster, less error prone, less expensive, and more convenient. However, improved organizational performance through process gains is not an automatic result of IT implementation.

The right processes must be chosen. The leverage of processes is most effective when the processes being addressed are critical, core processes that customers use to judge the performance of the organization and/or define the core business of the organization.

For example, patients are more likely to judge a provider organization on the basis of its ambulatory scheduling processes and billing processes than they are on its accounts payable and human resources processes. Making diagnostic and therapeutic decisions is a core provider organization process—a process that is the backbone of its business.

Organizations must also examine and redesign processes. If underlying problems with processes are not remedied, the IT investment can be wasted or diluted. IT applications can result in existing processes continuing to perform poorly only faster. Moreover, it can be harder to fix flawed processes after the application of IT since the "new" IT-supported process now has an additional source of complexity, cost and ossification to address—the "new computer system."

IT can be applied to effect significant process improvements if processes are chosen wisely and they are re-engineered skillfully.

Rapid and Accurate Provision of Critical Data. Organizations define critical elements of their plans, operations and environment. These elements must be monitored to ensure that the plan is working, service and care quality are high, the organization's fiscal situation is sound and the environment is behaving as anticipated. Clearly, data is required to perform such monitoring.

In addition to monitoring, data can be used to guide management actions. Airlines use data on passenger utilization to effect real-time adjustment of fares. Internet-based retailers use purchase data to target their advertisements.

However, obtaining and reporting critical data is not easy.

Data quality may be limited and incomplete. For example, while physicians are using an EMR, they are not recording all of a patient's problems, and many of their entries are free text. There may be confusion about which patients belong on specific physician panels. There can be significant disagreements about the definition of "a visit."

Using IT to improve performance through the capture of critical data requires addressing process problems that hinder data capture, developing user incentives to record good data and engaging in difficult conversations about data meaning.

Product and Service Differentiation. IT can be used to differentiate and customize products and services. For example, supermarkets send information to customers about upcoming sales. This information is often based on knowledge of prior customer purchases. Hence, a family that has purchased diapers and baby food will be seen as a household with young children. Information on sales of products directed to young parents will be sent to that household and not to households in which the purchase patterns indicate a single male. The supermarket is attempting to differentiate its service by helping the household plan its purchases around "specials."

Customization and differentiation often rely upon data. Effective customization presumes that we know something about the customer. Differentiation assumes that we know something about the customer's criteria for evaluating our organization so that we can differentiate our processes, products and services in ways that are deemed to have value.

Customization and differentiation often center on organizational processes. These processes can be made distinctive, but this requires a solid understanding of the needs of patients, providers and other customers.

Leveraging IT to differentiate products and services requires that organizations address process and data issues and have insight into customer needs and desires.

Obtaining and Sustaining an Advantage. It is very difficult to obtain an IT-based competitive advantage. Any advantage results from skilled process changes, tackling complex problems with data and thoughtfully understanding how to differentiate oneself.

The advantage does not come from the application system. In an industry where most applications can be purchased from a vendor, it is almost impossible for the application to provide an advantage. If you can buy an EHR from vendor X, so can your competitor, and any advantage becomes short lived.

Moreover, the fact that an organization has implemented an EHR does not mean that it has achieved a competitive advantage over a rival that has not implemented one. In fact, it may have hurt itself relative to its competitor. Its performance may be no better, but it has reduced its operating margin and shrunk its capital because of the costs of the EHR.

Some organizations can achieve an advantage that persists because they leverage some other assets that are quite difficult for their competitors to also garner. Such assets can include market share, access to capital, brand name recognition and proprietary know-how. However, few provider organizations have such differential assets.

Lacking these assets, any sustained IT-enabled advantage occurs because the organization is continuously more effective at process change and gathering critical data than its competitors and because an organization is able to effect performance improvements faster and more efficiently than its competitors.

IT is incapable of providing an advantage by itself. Value, including competitive advantage, occurs when IT is applied by intelligent and experienced leadership in the pursuit of well-conceived strategies and plans that are directed to continuously improving core processes, acquiring and providing critical data and differentiating service.

Provider organizations should worry less about whether others in its region are adopting interoperable EHRs. They should worry more about whether they are effective at achieving gains from their own IT investments.

John Glaser is vice president and CIO of Partners HealthCare in Boston, senior advisor, Deloitte Center for Health Solutions, and a regular contributor to Most Wired Online.

Reprinted from H&HN Hospitals & Health Networks, by permission, March 2006, ©2006 by Health Forum, Inc.

The Fundamentals of Sustained Collaboration

January 25, 2006
By John Glaser

© Health Forum, Inc.

The development of community clinical data exchanges requires the collaboration of various stakeholders. Moreover, it requires that this collaboration is sustained—it occurs year after year.

What fundamental factors enable these collaborations to be sustainable?

Individual Gain Is Apparent

Sometimes the binding "glue" of a collaboration is altruism. The collaboration participants work together for a common good, such as improving the health status of a community.

However, the most powerful "glue" for sustaining a collaborative clinical data exchange is the self-interests of the participants. They are working together because there is something in it for them. This "something" may be difficult to measure and not well understood. But they must at least believe that there is potential gain that is sufficient enough to justify the expense, time commitment and hassle of collaboration.

This something may be different for each of the stakeholders—e.g., a provider may see the opportunity to reduce the difficulty of obtaining needed clinical information while the payer may see the opportunity to reduce unnecessary testing. And not everyone at the table will achieve the same amount of gain. Some may perceive greater value than others.

Nonetheless, all participants must see some gain for themselves and their organization.

High Degrees of Interdependency in Achieving Gain

Each exchange participant must believe that they cannot achieve their gain unless the others are also participants. In effect, no participant can achieve their gain unless the others achieve their gain. The situation is akin to being the first owner of a fax machine or telephone. To achieve your value from your new fax machine, you need to have others using a fax machine and to derive their own value.

If there is no interdependence of gain, many of the participants will not bother with the collaboration. They will go after their gain themselves—it is easier and they have more control.

Moreover, each participant's gain must increase as the number of participants grows. The value of email increases to an individual as the number of people using email grows. There is value from scale.

If the collaboration is to be sustainable, the participants need as many other participants as possible in order to achieve their maximum value.

Clinical Data Exchange as a Commodity

The participants usually include competitors and antagonists. Invariably, a room full of stakeholders will include organizations and individuals who have egos, don't like each other, have sued each other and have worked very hard to get an advantage over "the other guy."

The formation of an exchange does not change this history and recognizes that competition will go on and uncivil behavior will not vanish from the landscape.

If the collaboration is to be sustainable, the participants have to believe that data exchange is a commodity capability and not a basis of competition. As an analogy, the participants do not compete on the basis that they have a dial tone or email and their competitor does not. They do and will continue to compete on service quality, pricing and marketing.

Several industries have discovered that their efforts to create a competitive advantage through information technology that connects them to customers and suppliers have turned into the redundant industry development of commodity capabilities (e.g., automated teller machines and credit card swipe boxes). The result is a capability that distinguished no participant but, because of redundant development, is unnecessarily expensive to support.

The participants must believe that clinical data exchange capability provides no more of a competitive advantage than automated teller machines provide a competitive advantage to a bank.

Collaboration Efficiencies

Collaboration provides several advantages in the development of a commodity capability.

The cost of developing implementation guides and policies could be incurred once rather than redundantly by each organization.

Exchange technologies can be acquired once, with the costs shared, rather than be redundantly acquired.

Managing a regional implementation schedule can be done by one organization, rather than by each of the participants trying to assemble its own version of a master schedule.

Implementation lessons learned (technical and operational) could be gathered by one organization and broadly shared across the exchange membership.

The core strategy behind the creation of any commodity capability is to spend as little as possible while achieving a specified outcome.

Minimally Invasive Approach

The participants must see the exchange is being minimally invasive. The exchange should be able to connect to a wide range of participant technologies. And participants should be able to effect a connection to the exchange at a time that makes the most business sense to them.

To the degree that the exchange forces the premature obsolescence of participant information technology investments and/or forces a participant to materially alter its information technology strategy and plans, then the gain has been decreased. Possibly decreased to a point at which a participant's interest in participating disappears.

A clinical data exchange should be be implemented in a manner that requires minimal diversion of participant's strategies, technology commitments and plans.

Summary

For a clinical data exchange to be sustainable, many factors, in addition to those discussed above, must be present. Well-conceived governance must be established. The methods for covering exchange expenses must be seen as fair. Business partner agreements must be created.

However, fundamental factors must be in place. If the participants are unable to see individual gain. Or if the gain is viewed as achievable without involving the other participants. Or if the exchange is regarded as a competitive weapon. Or if the exchange is too intrusive on the participants' information technology agenda.

Then the exchange is unlikely to survive infancy.

John Glaser is vice president and CIO of Partners HealthCare in Boston, senior advisor, Deloitte Center for Health Solutions, and a regular contributor to Most Wired Online.

Reprinted from H&HN Hospitals & Health Networks, by permission, January 2006, ©2006 by Health Forum, Inc.

Success Factors for Clinical Information System Implementation

July 13, 2005
By John Glaser

The implementation of systems such as the Electronic Medical Record and Computerized Provider Order Entry is a very complex and difficult organizational undertaking. These implementations require the political mobilization of the medical and nursing staffs, reengineering of clinical processes, significant capital commitments, management of large scale projects and major changes to the information technology infrastructure.

The magnitude of this undertaking leads to a high failure rate, estimated by some to be as high as 50%.

Despite this failure rate some organizations have been successful. What factors contributed to their success?

Strong Organizational Vision and Strategy. Successful organizations have developed a vision of patient care, and a strategy to achieve that vision, that is compelling, clear and understood by the members of the organization. This vision describes the critical need for excellence in care delivery and points to clinical systems as an essential strategic contributor to the vision.

Most information systems do not require the bedrock of a compelling organizational vision. Clinical information systems do. These systems require the commitment and efforts of virtually all staff. These systems require deep change in operational and clinical processes. These systems require that other investment opportunities be put off, often for several years.

For information system implementations of this significance to succeed, the organization must understand why it is doing so and believe that success is essential.

Talented and Committed Leadership. Clinical information systems implementation, and the related changes in the organization, must be led by senior leadership. This leadership must come from the Board and all of the senior members of the administrative and medical staffs.

These leaders must have the ability to inspire and mobilize others to get things done. They must actively engage in changing the organization. Once committed to the course, they must have the strength to thoughtfully stay the course. These leaders must ask hard questions about the systems and their implementation. And these leaders must be pragmatic—superb practitioners of the art of the possible.

A Partnership between the Clinical, Administrative and Information Technology Staffs. Across the strata of the organization, many effective, multidisciplinary teams will be needed. These teams will design information systems, develop new ways to do the work, revise policies and procedures, craft implementation steps, develop training materials and create approaches to resolving inevitable problems.

Team members must view their efforts as a partnership. They must illustrate the attributes of high-performance teams—skilled, honest, dedicated, willing to compromise and focused on the overall goal.

Thoughtful Redesign of Clinical Processes. The implementation of a clinical information system should be accompanied by an examination of care processes and efforts to redesign them to reduce steps, errors and inefficiencies. Often, the desire to make such changes leads to the decision to pursue the clinical information system.

Effecting significant changes in care processes is difficult. Staff and departments can lose power, behavior change is hard and process designers often have a limited ability to accurately envision a world that is much different from the one that they inhabit.

Nonetheless, it does not serve an organization well to automate ineffective and inefficient processes.

Excellent System Implementation Skills. The implementation of complex information systems requires deep skill. These skills are needed in a small number of critical areas.

Project management is needed to define, manage and monitor the large number of tasks, staff and resources that are being brought to the implementation. Good project management requires clear definitions of scope, well-reasoned delineation of tasks, astute assignment of accountability for task performance, flexibility in addressing problems and necessary modest changes in direction, and the excellent ability to identify and resolve problems.

Support is the set of activities that causes an application to "stick," to become an integral part of the fabric of practice. Support includes training, responsive enhancements, ongoing communication and discussion of status and problems, and the evolution of work and clinical policies and procedures.

Good to Excellent Information Technology. No information system is perfect, and users will find limitations in any clinical information system. Nonetheless, the applications need to be good enough to support the work that needs to be done. These systems must be able to handle critical changes in features that are required to address desired workflow and reporting needs. These systems should improve the work lives of providers rather than hinder them.

The information technology infrastructure needs to be well designed and supported. Slow response time and uneven reliability can cripple a clinical information system implementation in a remarkably short period of time. There are few things as damaging to the credibility of an IS organization as a wounded infrastructure.

In many ways, these success factors seem like slogans. Perhaps trite. In an analogous fashion, a parent might be told that the keys to raising healthy and happy children are to love them, feed them, teach them and protect them. Such advice masks the true challenge of raising a child.

However, these factors have been demonstrated to be critical to the successful implementation of clinical information systems. They serve as a roadmap for the leadership of the organization. The organization would be well served, as it contemplates embarking on this journey, to look at itself in the mirror and ask questions such as, "Do we have a strong vision and strategy? Is it well understood and embraced by the organization? Do we need to take steps to strengthen this factor?"

Many organizations would be better off taking time to strengthen these factors before they plunge head first into a complex and difficult implementation. And once strengthened, these factors must be continuously strengthened. The success factors need to be present throughout the implementation.

John Glaser *is vice president and CIO of Partners HealthCare in Boston and a regular contributor to* Most Wired Online.

Reprinted from H&HN Hospitals & Health Networks, by permission, July 2005, ©2005 by Health Forum, Inc.

Managing Threats to Large IT Projects

June 1, 2005
By John Glaser

Sooner or later most organizations decide to embark on a large IT implementation. These implementations could involve a comprehensive clinical information system suite or the replacement of all applications involved in the revenue cycle.

The decision to undertake such an initiative invariably results from careful assessment of the organization's strategy or a desire to effect a significant improvement in organizational performance. Clearly, senior management plays an essential role in the steps that lead to an organization deciding to commit to an undertaking of this scale. They must ensure that a thoughtful organization strategy has been developed and that the IT implementation is a clear and compelling contributor to that strategy. They must engage in the communication and politics necessary to "sell" the IT initiative; there will be detractors and the opportunity costs are significant.

And although commitment to the initiative may have been obtained, the senior leadership may be (and should be) nervous. The failure rate of large IT projects is surprisingly high. Failure can be defined as a project that is significantly over budget, taking much longer than its project timeline estimates or terminated because so many problems have occurred that proceeding is no longer judged to be viable. Some sources estimate that one third of all IT projects are cancelled before completion, and only 10 percent achieve their original plan.

Senior management plays a vital role in managing the threats, to large project success, that can lead to failure.

There are three major senior management threat management roles: addressing major project risk factors, ensuring excellent project management and reducing the counterproductive management behaviors that can undermine the project.

Addressing Major Project Risk Factors. Large projects may face three major risks.

First, the project may involve information technology that is new to the organization or the vendor. Even if that technology is well understood by the industry, organizational/vendor inexperience with the technology will lead to periods of instability and poor performance. Ill-behaving applications can threaten organizational support, damage operations and dramatically prolong the project timeline and increase its costs. Unless this technology is critical to the achievement of organizational goals, senior management should strive to base the application on technology that is mature and well understood.

Second, the project may involve broad and deep process changes to the organization. Change of this magnitude is exceptionally difficult. Organizational staff will struggle with the required behavior changes. Knowledge of how new processes should work will be imperfect, and the newly implemented processes won't initially work very well. The organization may inflict a form of chaos upon itself. While the old processes needed to be changed, at least they worked. Senior management should ensure that change is well paced and incrementally introduced, enabling the organization to have the opportunity to learn what works and what doesn't work about the new processes.

Third, the size of the project may be much larger than any project that the organization has ever undertaken. While the organization may be generally competent at projects that are $500,000 or 4 person years in size, it is not inherent that it will be competent at projects that are $10,000,000 or 30 person years in size. The organization may not know how to manage undertakings that large, and its inexperience will be evident. Senior management must make sure that large projects are broken down into pieces—pieces that are the size that it can master.

Ensuring Excellent Project Management. Project management is a set of management disciplines and practices that raise the likelihood that a project will deliver the desired results. Project management has several objectives:

- Describe the scope and intended results of the project
- Identify accountability for the successful completion of the project and associated project tasks
- Define the processes for making project-related decisions
- Identify the project's tasks and task sequence and interdependencies
- Determine the resource and time requirements of the project
- Ensure appropriate communication with relevant stakeholders regarding project status and issues

Project management requires the definition of business sponsors (managers who are accountable for project success), business owners (managers whose departments are major contributors to the project) and project managers. Project Steering Committees and project teams must be thoughtfully populated and resourced and given crisp charges.

Clear project charters must be developed. Well-conceived project plans must be created and maintained. And regular communication mechanisms are needed to convey project accomplishments and discuss project problems.

Senior management may play a role as a business sponsor. However, its major role is ensuring that strong project management is brought to the project.

Reducing Counterproductive Management Behaviors. Through their actions over the life of the project, senior management can inadvertently undermine the project.

Senior management's actions may be seen as failing to demonstrate commitment to the projects. Subordinates may be sent to critical meetings. This broadcasts a signal to the organization that the leadership has other "more important" things to do. Senior management may "cave in" when tough project decisions are needed, leading the organization to doubt the rhetoric surrounding the importance of the initiative.

The leadership may not be skilled at handling conflict. And they may be intolerant of bad news. Large projects create a lot of conflict, which must be addressed effectively or the initiative becomes crippled. All large projects will experience rough times and setbacks. Failure to tolerate bad news can lead to project teams hiding the difficulties, which exacerbates the problems.

All major change results in short-term disruptions. Senior management must be tolerant of these disruptions. And they must listen to those who are waist-deep in the change. These staff will know what steps need to be taken to remove the problems. As good listeners, senior management must not cling to ideas that, while they seemed to be good ones at the time, have since proven to be not useful. Intolerant and deaf senior management hinders project success.

Being successful in large IT projects requires that you don't fail. A critical senior management role is managing the threats faced by all large projects that can result in failure.

John Glaser is vice president and CIO of Partners HealthCare in Boston and a regular contributor to Most Wired Online.

The Board's Role in the IT Discussion

April 6, 2005
By John Glaser

© Health Forum, Inc.

For several reasons, the Board may conclude that it can no longer view the IT agenda and IT issues as tangential to its charge.

Investments in information technology (IT) can be an increasingly critical element of organizational strategies and plans. Plans to advance patient safety, revenue cycle and operational efficiency strategies may include the acquisition of new and expensive information systems.

IT investments may be placing significant demands on the organization's capital and operating budgets. The IT operating budget may be growing faster than almost all other budget line items. Large IT capital demands may require hard tradeoffs with investments in buildings and equipment.

Problems with IT security or the controls in financial systems pose a growing risk for organizations.

Despite these realizations, the Board may be unsure how best to perform their responsibilities and assist the organization's management team. IT has never been on the Board agenda, and the Board does not know what questions it should ask. Unlike other topics, such as finance or medical staff relationships, the Board has not developed an understanding of the small number of critical issues that should form the focus of their discussions. The Board may look at its composition and find that no members have any background or experience in IT.

Board Roles

The Board has four core IT responsibilities:

- Ensuring that the IT strategy and plan have been well developed and are tightly integrated with the overall organizational strategy and plan
- Monitoring the organization's progress in implementing its strategy, including its IT strategy
- Ensuring that the IT capital budget demands are understood and have been accounted for in the organization's multi-year capital plan
- Ensuring that risk factors associated with application systems and infrastructure, e.g., security, have been addressed

Committees and Members

The Board can take several steps to ensure that it has access to the expertise and committee structures, necessary to perform these roles.

- Appoint new Board members who have IT backgrounds. These members could be current or former CIOs, executives from IT consultant or vendor organizations, or IT academics from a local business school.
- Establish an IT subcommittee of the Board. This committee could be composed of several trustees and outside members with IT experience. The Committee would undertake the responsibilities described above. However, the Board may decide that IT capital discussions should occur in the Finance Committee and IT risk factors should be addressed in the Audit Committee. Or the Board may request that these topics be addressed in joint committee meetings.
- Instead of an IT subcommittee, the Board may form an external advisory committee that would meet a couple of times a year, with several trustees and management, to comment on the organization's IT strategy and its progress.
- Request a regular update from the CIO on the status of the IT agenda and the performance of the IT group.
- Convene a special Board meeting or a retreat dedicated to a discussion of the IT strategy, plans and performance.

These steps are not mutually exclusive. For example, the Board may add members with IT backgrounds, request a regular update from the CIO and form an IT subcommittee.

What Should Board Members Look For?

Appointing new board members or establishing an IT subcommittee does not relieve the rest of the Board from its obligation to be engaged in the discussion of IT strategy and challenges. During these discussions, a Board member can make an informed assessment of the IT strategy and performance by looking for:

A clear and thoughtful linkage between the organization's strategy and the IT strategy. For example, if the organization has a strategy of improving operational efficiency, what are the associated IT initiatives? This linkage can take the form of a simple two-column table—strategy in one column and IT initiatives in the other column.

A CIO who communicates clearly and in business terms. If the CIO can explain new technologies and application capabilities to the Board, then it is quite likely that they were able to explain them to the organization's management team and medical staff leadership. Hence, the organization's leadership is likely to have made informed decisions.

A track record of success by the IT organization. The CIO (and CEO, COO and CFO) ought to be able to elucidate the IT successes of the organization and describe how they have assessed success. If the CEO can describe the successes, then it is likely that the business or clinical side of the organization believes that it has received value from its IT investments and that the IT organization is competent at execution.

A good understanding of the health care IT industry and the efforts of peer organizations. The CIO should be able to describe the status of the industry and any major forces that influence it. Examples could include HIPAA, the federal health care IT agenda and new technologies that have promise. In addition to understanding the industry, the CIO should be able to discuss the plans of peer organizations, e.g., to what extent other organizations are implementing the electronic medical record and what their experience has been. No health care executive, including the CIO, can be effective if they are ignorant of the industry around them.

A well-reasoned budget. The IT capital budget can be large and mysterious. To a Board that is new to the topic of IT, these costs can seem breathtaking. There may be no way around these expenses. However, IT capital proposals, like all capital proposals, should be explainable in clear business terms. And these budgets should reflect significant diligence, e.g., review by external consultants, to ensure that the budget is comprehensive and reasonable.

Solid controls and plans to address any weaknesses defined by the audit. The IT infrastructure and financial systems must not expose the organization to any material weaknesses. If deficiencies have been identified, there must be evidence that remediation plans are underway.

Summary

The Board can fulfill its IT obligations through some changes in membership and committee structure. Moreover, the Board should focus on a small number of critical areas as it discusses IT.

Perhaps the most important thing that a Board can do is to do what it always does: Ask good questions and continue to ask them until it is satisfied with the answer. And make sure that the management team is strong and supported, as necessary.

John Glaser *is vice president and CIO of Partners HealthCare in Boston and a regular contributor to* Most Wired Online.

The Challenge of IT Value

March 9, 2005
By John Glaser

Organizations invest in IT in an effort to improve performance. Patient care is safer. The revenue cycle is more efficient. Service to referring physicians is improved.

Consistently achieving this value is exceptionally difficult. The pursuit of IT-enabled value invariably confronts three areas of significant complexity—the nature of IT value, the "context" of IT value and the dissipation of value.

The Nature of IT Value

IT value is multifaceted. The value can be tangible, e.g., reduced costs, and intangible, e.g., improved communication. The value can be amenable to financial assessment, e.g., increases in revenue and defy the assignment of a dollar value, e.g., reduced mortality. The value proposition of a single IT project proposal may include multiple types of value—service improvements, cost reductions and productivity gains.

This diverse nature makes it difficult to choose between IT project proposals. For example, it is hard to compare a proposal that addresses a regulatory need with a proposal that improves decision-making with a proposal that reduces labor costs.

Techniques exist that help to distill diverse proposals to a common metric. For example, all IT proposals can be scored against a set of organizational value criteria, such as cost reduction, service improvement and patient care improvement. Each project's criteria scores are summed, and the total score ranks the projects. In theory, projects with high scores are funded, whereas projects with low scores are not. In practice, this method (and all others like it) supplements judgments, political considerations, biases and vision.

The diversity of value also hinders the discussion of a return on investment. How much is improved decision making worth? How would one measure the improvement?

IT did not introduce the management challenge of messy value. Senior leadership has long had to grapple with initiatives with diverse value propositions, e.g., comparing capital proposals with outcomes as diverse as improving the attractiveness of the physical plant versus reducing supply expenses versus introducing a new care model to improve care quality.

The IT Value Context

IT value has a context.

The first context requires that one not forget that IT is only a tool. The question, "What is the ROI of an information system?" can make as much sense as "What is the ROI of a chain saw?"

The value of any tool depends on whether the tool is appropriate given a particular goal. A chain saw is a poor tool if one is trying to scramble eggs. The value of a tool is very dependent upon the skill of the tool user. A chain saw in the hands of a ten-year-old boy is a disaster in the making.

In assessing any IT proposal, one should ask a series of questions that put the tool in context:

- Is it clear how the plan advances the organization's strategy?
- Is it clear how care will improve, costs will be reduced or service will be improved? Are the measures of current performance and expected improvement well researched and realistic? Have the related changes in operations, workflow and organization been defined?
- Are the resource requirements well understood and convincingly presented? Have these requirements been compared to those experienced by other organizations undertaking similar initiatives?
- Have the investment risks been identified and is there an approach to addressing these risks?
- Do we have the right people assigned to the project, have we freed up their time and are they well organized?

The second context notes that IT investments have fundamentally one of two major objectives—improve organizational processes and enhance decision making.

IT investments can be leveraged to reduce the costs, improve the quality, increase the speed and reduce the errors of critical organizational processes. Such processes include patients accessing care, processing a claim and ordering a test, procedure or medication.

Improving a process requires that processes be analyzed and redesigned, if necessary. Improving a process requires change in the way that the organization works and change in the behavior of organizational members. This change is much harder and more complex than the implementation of a tool.

IT investments can be leveraged to provide critical data to decision makers. These data include information on specialist referral patterns, clinical orders guided by decision support and access to a patient's medical history.

At times, the use of IT to improve decision making is straightforward. There is generally little argument about the utility of having a patient's medication history available to providers. At other times, efforts to improve decision making encounter very difficult terrain. Developing the metrics for a Balanced Score Card or computer-generated health maintenance reminders can be non-trivial undertakings. Using IT to improve decision making will often require that the organization agree on how it assesses its success and what constitutes good practice.

Achieving IT value often requires significant skill in organizational change.

The Dissipation of Value

Despite the best of intentions of the organization, the intended value of an IT initiative seems to have evaporated. Promised staff reductions never occurred. Patient service metrics only improved slightly. Nursing staff are still harried.

Where did the value go?

IT value can dissipate for many reasons:

- The IT initiative was intended to support a strategy that was flawed; no IT initiative can overcome ill-conceived strategy
- Inadequate homework or unwarranted optimism by project proponents overstated the value and underestimated the costs of the initiative
- Organizational change encountered too much turbulence, causing the project leaders to scale back their ambitions or make compromises that kept the peace but diluted the promise
- The technology that seemed so alluring turns out to have major limitations and problems
- The organization forgot to make someone accountable for realizing the value and relearns that someone has to manage value into existence
- The project team makes several major mistakes, leading to cost and timetable overruns

Steps can be taken that help to mitigate value dissipation factors. Project proposals can be subjected to very rigorous review. Post-implementation audits can be conducted. Technology can be soberly assessed.

Reducing dissipation risk requires skilled and focused management action.

Summary

IT investments can be leveraged to achieve significant organizational value. However, IT-enabled value is complex and difficult to achieve. Realizing value requires management that knows how to address complex value propositions, lead organizational change and manage the risk factors associated with any major organizational undertaking.

John Glaser *is vice president and CIO of Partners HealthCare in Boston and a regular contributor to* Most Wired Online.

Section Three – IT Management Challenges

The Risky Business of Information Security

August 12, 2014
By John Glaser

With growing threats to patient privacy and increasing sanctions by regulators, make data security central to your business.

Because of the mandatory breach notification requirements of the Health Information Technology for Economic and Clinical Health (HITECH) Act, reports of material data breaches have become somewhat commonplace. While each incident is a serious matter and the penalties can be significant, unless the breach involves a famous person or a record-breaking fine, these stories rarely raise an eyebrow. However, as an industry, we must not let the frequency of such incidents lull us into complacency.

In fact, we know the common causes all too well: the lost or stolen unencrypted laptop, endpoints left unsecure in a bring-your-own-device environment, lack of enforced policies and procedures, and unintentional human error or employee negligence. Additionally, many information technology (IT) departments trying to keep their proverbial heads above water might view safeguard investments in electronic protected health information (ePHI) as low priority. This is especially true when other high visibility projects demand their attention. As we know, making information more secure simply does not bring in revenue, and, frankly, can make the system harder for harried clinicians to use.

Yet, the growth of health care data from electronic health records (EHRs), patient portals, mobile devices and other technologies has led to the accumulation of more sensitive electronic information. It has also spawned the distribution of that information throughout the enterprise and across the community, thereby creating new risks to ePHI.

As ePHI becomes more ubiquitous, it becomes exponentially more difficult to control and audit access. It's no longer reasonable and appropriate to rely solely on the EHR system to manage the access to ePHI. Furthermore, the control structures outside of the EHR can be antiquated, raising the possibility of security breaches.

Against this backdrop, several industry influences are shaping security and privacy. Regulatory enforcement is strengthening, and it's creating a higher likelihood of financial sanctions for those organizations that do not mitigate risks. Industry competition has also raised a business interest in managing the patient perception of securing data, which is significantly impacted by sensationalized events and high-profile data breaches. Moreover, Meaningful Use incentive dollars and eventual penalties are tied to the completion of risk management activities, such as performing a security risk analysis and implementing reasonable and appropriate security measures.

Numbers Don't Lie

Given these pressures—and with some 30 million patients having been affected by data breaches involving 500 or more individuals since 2009, when large breach reporting requirements went into effect—one would assume the time has come for the industry to step up its information security game. But the statistics tell a different a story.

A 2014 study by the Ponemon Institute found that 90 percent of health care organizations have experienced at least one data breach within the past two years, with 38 percent reporting they had more than five. The multiple offenses suggest the importance of performing thorough and frequent risk analyses to identify and address vulnerabilities. Even more disturbing, this same study reports that criminal attacks on health care systems have risen a startling 100 percent since 2010.

Another study of all data breaches in 2013 by the Identity Theft Resource Center found that the health care sector suffered the highest amount of attacks last year, outscoring the business sector for the first time in nearly a decade. Granted, the health care number may be distorted due to industry regulations that call for public disclosure of large breaches, but this is surely not a list one ought to feel comfortable topping.

Also troubling, a 2012 Ponemon Institute study on patient privacy and data security suggested that 69 percent of respondents' IT security and/or data protection activities did not include the security of FDA-approved medical devices. This mirrors a growing concern our information security and risk management consultants are seeing in their work.

Additionally, while the numbers can vary by study, it appears that upward of 90 percent of health care organizations permit employees and clinicians to use their own mobile devices such as smartphones and tablets to connect to a provider's network or enterprise systems. The bring-your-own-device trend has further complicated the challenges of protecting sensitive ePHI, while increasing the risk quotient for provider IT and compliance departments. With mobile devices continuously blurring the lines between our work and personal lives, all too often we read about the well-intentioned employee who shifts data from a work device to devices or systems outside the safeguards and controls of a secure network. This is the definition of disaster waiting to happen if strict policies and procedures are not in place to govern bring your own device.

Warding Off Danger

As health care organizations face increasingly complex federal, state and regional privacy and security regulations along with corresponding fines, the Department of Health and Human Services doled out penalties ranging from several thousand dollars to well over a million dollars per incident in 2013. And the bucks don't stop there. Given legal and breach investigation fees, costs for providing free credit monitoring services to impacted parties, staffing hotlines to handle inquiries, and a host of other miscellaneous damage control steps, the Ponemon Institute estimates the average economic impact of a data breach in health care to be about $2 million.

Providers that do not have their privacy and security house in order can also get tagged with Meaningful Use non-compliance violations resulting in reduced reimbursements and lost incentive payments. And perhaps more difficult to quantify is the diminished patient loyalty and poor public image that can result from high-profile cases.

Our organization, like others, provides security consulting services. With so much at stake and new information security threats constantly evolving, a key piece of advice our privacy and security consultants offer providers is this: "If you are engaging our services as only a function of 'checking the box,' you will remain at risk." Compliant is not always secure.

Indeed, safeguarding ePHI against unauthorized use and disclosure requires constant vigilance and a comprehensive, enterprise-aligned program for information security risk management. This includes a collaborative and integrated security technology framework, experienced and credentialed resources to operate that framework, and adherence to formal procedures and established best practices to ensure the efficacy of operations. If you want to enhance your information security posture, consider the following actions:

Developing a comprehensive risk management program and executing against it. In a security consulting methodology such as ours, a three-step process can metaphorically create a shield of protection for providers. The first step is to design the shield by performing a series of risk and threat assessments—a starting point for developing a broader, long-term security and privacy program. Next, thicken the shield by implementing administrative, physical and technical safeguards across the IT enterprise to mitigate the risks associated with maintaining ePHI. Ultimately, the goal is to preserve the shield through continuous formal risk management efforts, supported by the appropriate level of governance, documentation and ongoing remediation of security weaknesses.

Naming a dedicated information security executive. With many CIOs already wearing multiple hats and reaching their workload limit, the burden of maintaining sole responsibility for a comprehensive enterprise security program can often be too much. Relying on an ace network guy to take on the task, but giving him little to no authority to drive substantive change, will not work either. Hence, there is a trend toward naming a chief information security officer, or CISO, to lead this very key operational function. We are seeing this empowerment of a dedicated security executive in health care and across other industries. In fact, retail giant Target recently named its first CISO in the wake of its data breach last year.

Conducting regular risk analyses and following through on findings. Increased enforcement efforts by the Office of Civil Rights under the Health Insurance Portability and Accountability Act, as well as new sanction guidelines under HITECH and significant Meaningful Use dollars at risk, have coalesced to spur many organizations to conduct the required risk analysis activities. But as mentioned earlier, avoid bringing a check-the-box mentality to the table, and instead, truly invest in these activities. Re-evaluate and re-architect when the findings call for it. Use the regulations to not only compel consistency of action, but also to earn the trust of patients and staff by demonstrating a committed and focused stance on ensuring patient privacy and information security.

Getting prescriptive with security controls. A key difference between approaches to privacy and to security is that the guidelines for disclosing a potential breach of sensitive information are much more prescriptive. In fact, the industry has become quite good at handling such matters. However, in security, there is constant inherent risk in the acquisition and transfer of data and a vast array of options for safeguarding it. Aside from encryption, few security controls are prescribed. Often we find an organization is taking a particular security measure simply because that ace network guy happens to know they should, or because the CIO read an article about a fellow provider's incident and saw his own organization's shortcomings in the media report.

As most who have been forced to overhaul their information security and compliance practices can attest to, taking a much more prescriptive approach to applying security controls at both the industry and provider levels can go a long way toward reducing the loss or theft of ePHI.

Not overlooking medical device security. Advances in electronic documentation, automation of clinical workflow, and increased network integration have prompted providers to assimilate biomedical devices into their organizations' complex health care

IT infrastructure. In fact, newer medical device technology often takes advantage of the same operating systems and protocols favored by mainstream IT developers. As such, these devices and platforms are susceptible to viruses and other threats that must be protected with diligence, given a device's critical function in the delivery of patient care, whether diagnostic or life sustaining.

For example, medical devices using wireless networks can be especially vulnerable to attackers who monitor the network to obtain passwords. Perhaps most worrisome is the denial-of-service attack in which a device is taken offline or prevented from functioning as required. As a baseline safeguard, establish an inventory of devices connected to the hospital's network and catalog who has access to those devices. Furthermore, when performing a risk analysis, be sure to identify the effects of a security breach on each networked medical device.

Not If but When

Few hospitals will be the place where a star-struck staff member sneaks a peak at the next Kardashian baby's birth record. But for the majority of providers, it is entirely possible that an unencrypted device takes a walk, an e-mail containing ePHI accidently travels to the wrong recipient at the hands of a harried nurse, or a malicious attack strikes a vulnerable network. These are very real threats that will not disappear even for the Fort Knox of all health systems.

With the exchange of ePHI among providers increasing through participation in accountable care organizations and health information exchanges, and more and more care being delivered outside the acute care environment, make data security a central component to how you manage your overall operations.

While it may feel like an uphill battle, you can easily find that the cost of *not* investing in improving your information security posture can far outweigh the costs of doing so.

John Glaser, Ph.D., is the CEO of the Health Services business unit of Siemens Healthcare in Malvern, Pa. He is also a regular contributor to H&HN Daily. **Andrew Frazier,** lead for information security risk management consulting, and **Shawn Burgess**, information security risk management consultant, Siemens Healthcare, contributed to this article.

Hitting the Restart Button: We've All Been There

February 6, 2014
By John Glaser

The flawed launch of HealthCare.gov's online insurance exchange reminds us of the tremendous risk inherent in every information technology undertaking. It also offers an opportunity to reflect on our own project preparations as the industry continues to reinvent itself.

As I began thinking about this article last fall, the clock was ticking for officials charged with overhauling the much-maligned HealthCare.gov insurance marketplace. They needed the site functioning smoothly for the vast majority of users before a self-imposed Nov. 30, 2013, deadline.

Since the portal's fateful launch, the Obama administration has been under fire from the American public and congressional lawmakers in both parties—not to mention at the mercy of the late night talk shows—as error rates, slow response times and repeated system outages made it difficult for many new consumers to complete an application for health coverage.

While we have been witness to everything from public testimony about what went wrong, to press briefings detailing the progress on fixing the issues list, to acceptance of full responsibility from the commander in chief, I suspect that by the time you are reading this in February, the site will be stable and operating at its intended capacity with greatly improved performance.

However, if there was ever a need to hit a magic "restart" button for a high-profile technology project, this surely would have been it.

Having spent my entire career in information technology (IT), both as a health care chief information officer and on the vendor side, I've wanted to reach for that restart button a time or two myself. Like many in the industry, I have witnessed a few technology projects get into some serious trouble. Of course, this can happen in a few different ways:

- a meltdown—the system is fundamentally unstable, nonfunctional or both;
- a timetable or budget overrun—the scope and cost are severely off or underestimated; and
- a feature/function that does not meet expectations—it missed the mark on what was needed by a mile.

While none of the above scenarios is particularly pleasant, they serve an important purpose. As Oscar Wilde once said, "Experience is simply the name we give our mistakes."

Indeed, battling technology troubles can help us acquire the key knowledge that can be gained only from the heads-down, 24/7 war room work that is usually required to get a wayward project back on track. No doubt those in charge of HealthCare.gov will emerge from the experience a little worse for the wear, but also a whole lot wiser.

Doomed from the Start?

Now, to be fair, unlike the private sector, the government faces special challenges when it comes to technology undertakings. For one, there is a tremendous amount of political oversight and transparency on these projects. This is of course good for all the obvious reasons, but it is trying in the same way that too many cooks in the kitchen can produce a less than appealing dish. As we know, this administration faces no shortage of competing agendas and dueling priorities.

The government's cumbersome procurement process may also put it at a disadvantage, as a cry for help or extra resources are not simply a phone call away. Moreover, the best vendor for the job, which could be a small startup with novel ideas and innovative technology, may not have what it takes to make it through the arduous procurement process, which typically favors large, established vendors.

Additionally, a government-run IT project can face a complex and shifting set of requirements as well as compressed timelines to get the work done. Often times the ink is barely dry on the legislation when the deadline for the needed technology is established. Furthermore, the regulation writing process can be influenced by the election process; promises made on the campaign trail need to appear in regulation shortly thereafter. Tight timelines and volatile requirements can lead to a project coming off the rails in fairly short order.

Failure to Launch

Despite the fact that many industries have been trying to improve their project management prowess for decades, IT project troubles are not unusual; nor are they confined to a particular industry. In fact, the failure rate for technology projects is sobering—anywhere from 37 to 75 percent, according to the multitude of studies available.

Consider a 2012 McKinsey & Company survey on large-scale IT projects (those with initial budgets greater than $15 million) which found that half of all large IT projects blow their budgets in grand fashion, running 45 percent over budget and 7 percent over time. Moreover, they found that 17 percent of large IT projects go so badly they can threaten the very existence of the company.

Or, in the case of the federal government, a project stumble with the eyes of the nation watching (and waiting to log on) only exacerbates the nation's already heated political divide, particularly over the Affordable Care Act.

Now, we in the health care IT industry may question why it appears the government failed to employ the R&D best practices many of us have come to know so well. These include using an iterative development and delivery approach, establishing betas or pilots, and forgoing the risk of a big bang rollout. And we may wonder which of the most common causes of IT project failures—lack of clear governance or sponsorship, ambiguous requirements, insufficient resources, poor design, or inadequate testing to name just a few—plagued the portal's initial rollout.

Since it was likely a confluence of many of these factors, a refresher on the steps that can be taken to help minimize the risk of failure might be useful for those about to embark on a new IT initiative. Consider the following:

Good project plans. There are several cues that a project plan is as solid as one can make it at the inception of the project. For example, the project charter is clear and explicit, project timelines and staffing needs have been reviewed by multiple parties for reasonableness, and task timelines have some "slack" built into them. Furthermore, needed resources and budget have been committed, and accountabilities for each plan phase and task are explicit.

Great project managers. A great project manager is exceptionally valuable. To a large degree, the reputations of project managers precede them. If project managers have proven themselves over the course of many projects, then their plans are likely to be generally sound. If project managers are novices or have an uneven track record, their plans may require greater scrutiny. First and foremost, a great project manager must have the interpersonal and organizational skills to bring people together and make things happen.

Tight interaction with users and lots of feedback. Failure to view an IT project through the eyes of the users and stakeholders often leads to failing to get their buy-in as well as designing systems that appear, to the user, to be from Mars. Therefore, it's critical to involve users in every phase of the project and as early and often as possible. As we know in health care IT, users may not know what they want until they see a particular feature or function, or try to incorporate it in their daily workflow. Waiting until a project has gone live to obtain stakeholder feedback is nothing short of asking for trouble.

Solid governance. Without the appropriate level of oversight, projects can quickly head off track. The key role of a governance structure is to enable, facilitate, manage and direct the successful implementation of the project's changes and impact into a well-prepared and informed organization (or public) in order to maximize the potential benefits. A solid governance structure also provides clarity on the various levels where decisions are escalated and assigns accountability to the decision makers.

Great project management discipline. In any well-run project, there is strict adherence to a set of management disciplines and processes developed over time. While skilled project management does not provide a guarantee for project success, it can certainly reduce the risk of failure, particularly for large, complex IT implementations.

Well-conceived phases. A large-scale master project plan must be divided into more manageable pieces that can be delivered incrementally. Thinking in terms of phases helps ensure that the deliverables produced at the end of each phase meet their purpose, and that the project team is properly prepared for the next phase. While project teams must have the wherewithal to keep the big picture end game in sight, they must also possess the discipline to successfully execute the myriad tasks that make up each phase of a project.

Thoughtful and appropriate risk management. Projects are full of uncertainties, and failure to identify or manage those uncertainties appropriately can turn them into serious problems. Some examples of project risks include unproven information technology, a deterioration in the organization's financial condition and turnover of project staff. A thorough assessment of risks related to the technology and its impact, the organization's ability to absorb change, project scope and size, schedule, and cost can provide a good starting point for developing a comprehensive risk management and mitigation plan.

Solid project monitoring and openness to candid feedback. Being closely involved in a project day to day makes it difficult to step back and critically reflect on progress. Yet, such reflection is crucial to success. Regular and frequent project review meetings provide the ability to discuss overall project goals and objectives, as well as to assess progress toward specific milestones. Additionally, implementing a continuous feedback loop between project managers and stakeholders can help identify actual or potential problems as early as possible to facilitate timely adjustments to the project plan.

No Guarantees

Even with a sizeable collection of best practices and defined procedures and methodology applied in project management—not to mention ongoing advancements in the field—the risk of getting into IT project trouble is sizeable.

But the way an organization responds when it finds itself in a compromised position can vary based on the nature of the problem. For example, if operations are paralyzed through a complete technology failure, this may elicit a crisis mode response; whereas encountering a substantial budget overrun would not typically throw an organization into a crisis management situation.

Nonetheless, any project setback requires swift and efficient management to contain the situation and minimize the negative impact. As such, the following tips offer practical guidance for managing technology troubles large and small:

- Keep cool; emotions are generally not helpful.
- Make sure that you really know what is wrong and why; at times the hysteria surrounding a rocky project distorts the understanding of the nature of the problems.
- Perform a quick assessment of whether you have the right people on the bus to drive toward a resolution.
- Protect those who have to repair the damage, providing them with resources, time and political air cover.
- Provide lots of communication and transparency to organization, particularly those feeling the daily reality of a troubled undertaking.
- Engage stakeholders in diagnosis and remedy plans.
- Insist on very disciplined management of the "get out of here plan."
- Ensure accountability, but make liberal use of the pronoun *we*.
- Exude strength and confidence even if your anxiety causes your intestines to shrink to the size of a golf ball.

Always a Lesson to Be Learned

As bad as the launch of the federal online insurance marketplace was, there are numerous examples, both in the public and private sector, of similar situations. Indeed, every IT implementation is fraught with risk and presents a genuinely difficult undertaking.

We are wise to treat these projects with respect and humbleness. We are also wise to know that with every misstep, true leaders will rise to the occasion from all levels within the project. This is something to behold.

Despite every organization's best efforts to be prepared and minimize risk, the odds of success may not always be in one's favor. The key for all those involved in such misfortunes is to learn from past failures and to put those lessons learned into action on future projects.

John Glaser, Ph.D., is the CEO of the Health Services business unit of Siemens Healthcare in Malvern, Pa. He is also a regular contributor to H&HN Daily.

Organizational Effectiveness in Implementing IT

December 13, 2011
By John Glaser

Today's health care administrators may feel as if they are in a perpetual state of information technology implementation. Careful self-examination can help determine a provider's ability to effectively manage the change process and ensure that the IT investment continues to bring value.

Whether it's the quest to achieve ACO status, the financial allure of meeting HITECH meaningful use criteria, the must-do ICD-10 conversion, or preparing for evolving pay-for-performance and value-based purchasing initiatives, today's health care organizations face a dizzying array of information technology (IT) priorities. As a result, providers must not only carefully consider their spending allocation for health care information technology, but also their own organizational effectiveness in implementing IT.

A variety of studies have identified organizational attributes that appear to have a significant influence on the effectiveness of an organization in applying IT. These factors include the following:

- the relationship between the IT group and the rest of the organization;
- top managers' support for IT and the quality of the leadership;
- organizational comfort with "visionary" IT applications and ability to experiment with new technologies; and
- organizational experience with IT.

If the IT department has a poor working relationship with the clinical staff, it is hard to imagine that the organization would be effective in implementing an electronic health record. If leaders believe that IT is a necessary but barely tolerated expense, it will be difficult for the organization to invest in IT initiatives that push a strategic envelope. If the organization has a troubled history with IT implementations, it will hesitate to take on another "strategic IT initiative" that suggests another expensive disappointment.

Critical Factors

Two other key characteristics influence the effectiveness of an organization in applying IT: change management and IT governance.

Change management skills enable the organization to direct its identity, processes and structures according to its strategy. An IT initiative is often used as a catalyst for change just as it is used to enable and support change. Even if material change is not envisioned, the implementation of an application system will require some change in workflow and information provision. Organizations that are poor at managing change will be less effective in applying IT.

IT governance consists of the organizational mechanisms by which IT priorities are set, IT policies and procedures are developed, and IT management responsibility is distributed. The effectiveness, transparency and inclusiveness of governance can give IT a boost.

These factors, which are different from the applications being implemented, can be created or changed. The IT strategy development must encompass both the application agenda and improvement in these characteristics and capabilities.

Managing Change

A majority of IT initiatives require organizational change—change in processes or structure, change in the roles of individuals, or the change in the services provided by the organization. IT-enabled or IT-driven organizational change has several possible origins:

- The new IT system has capabilities different from those of the previous system, and hence workflow has to change and the tasks that staff perform have to change.
- The discussion about the desired capabilities of a new application can lead to a reassessment of current processes, workflow and distribution of tasks among staff and a decision to make changes that extend well beyond the computer system.
- The organization decides to engage in substantial change in its functions and operations. For example, the organization may decide to move aggressively to protocol-driven care.

Change management, an essential skill for leaders of health care organizations, is a facet of virtually all implementations of such applications.

The management strategies and skills required to manage change depend on the type of change. As one moves from modest to transformative, the magnitude and risk of the change increases enormously, as does the uncertainty about the form and success of the outcome.

IT Governance

IT governance strategies must address several governance questions, which can be a complex exercise:

- Who sets priorities for IT, and how are those priorities set?
- Who is responsible for implementing information systems plans, and what principles will guide the implementation process?
- What organizational structures are needed to support the connection between IT and the rest of the organization?
- How are IT responsibilities distributed between IT and the rest of the organization, and between central and "local" IT groups?
- How is the IT budget developed?

Problematic governance confuses the organization and creates the risk that the IT department—as well meaning and competent as it might be—will make decisions that are not aligned with the organization's direction.

Good IT governance matters. Peter Weill and Jeanne Ross conducted research comparing organizations with similar strategies. Their study showed that organizations with superior IT governance mechanisms had more than 25 percent higher profitability than those organizations with poor mechanisms. (See *IT Governance: How Top Performers Manage IT Decision Rights for Superior Results* [Harvard Business Press Books, 2004].) The study found that just as corporate governance aims to ensure quality decisions about all corporate assets, IT governance links IT decisions with company objectives and monitors performance and accountability.

Strategy Considerations

Perhaps you've heard the adage, "Effective implementation of an average strategy beats mediocre implementation of a great strategy every time." Organizations nonetheless often fail to operationalize their IT strategies in ways that improve the likelihood of success.

Now more than ever, when a failed IT initiative is no more an option than standing still, the experiences of several industries over many years provide considerations that can help guide IT strategy development. Consider the following:

The realization of IT-enabled value. As the organization develops its IT strategy, it must understand that the acquisition and implementation of an application does not per se lead to value—i.e., streamlined processes, improved decision making capabilities or reduced medical errors. This is evident in the wide variety of health care experiences with IT: At times the implementation of an electronic health record clearly improves care, and at other times it has resulted in no significant improvements. For value to result, IT must be well managed, change in processes must be thoughtfully considered, and ongoing efforts to benefit from the IT investment must be put in place. If value is desired, approaches that manage value into existence need to be developed.

The recognition that IT strategies evolve. IT strategies must evolve. An application system that provides a competitive advantage today becomes an industry commodity tomorrow. The use of ATMs by banks is an example. At one time ATMs provided a bank an advantage. Today ATMs are a "stay in business" expense borne by all banks and distinguishing none of them. In health care an organization that is in the process of implementing an electronic health record must understand that there will be a day when that implementation is done and when most organizations have an electronic health record. What then?

An organization could argue that it will worry about evolution when the day comes that it needs to do so. However, it is useful to anticipate evolution so steps can be taken to enhance the organization's ability to capitalize on that future.

IT as a way to enhance a competitive position. The organization may need to determine if an IT investment provides a strategic or competitive advantage. An important aspect of competitive strategy is identifying goals and ways (1) to achieve those goals that are materially superior to the way that a competitor has defined them and (2) to develop organizational capabilities that are materially superior to the capabilities of a competitor. For example, we and our competitors may both decide that we need to implement an electronic health record. However, we might believe that we can move faster and be more effective at managing process change, arriving at a superior outcome earlier.

Competitive strategy should attempt to define superiority that can be sustained. For example, we may believe that if our organization moves quickly, we can extend the reach of our electronic health record to affiliated providers, making it difficult for a competitor to do the same. "First to market" can provide a sustainable advantage, although very few IT-enabled advantages are sustainable for long periods of time.

Bringing It All Together

As the industry continues to ready itself for the significant changes expected in the years ahead, we must remember that an IT implementation is not simply about technology. It's about equipping organizations to achieve strategic business gains by providing the tools that make organizational improvements possible. With thoughtful consideration given to strategy, IT governance, and the ability to successfully engage staff members in changing processes to effectively use new technological capabilities, today's health care providers will be well equipped to face an ever more daunting IT implementation agenda.

John Glaser, Ph.D., *is the CEO of Siemens Health Services in Malvern, Pa. He is also a regular contributor to* H&HN Daily.

The Scope of an IT Strategy

April 14, 2011
By John Glaser

© Health Forum, Inc.

An information technology strategy requires careful examination of both the assets to be implemented and the organization's ability to use IT effectively.

As with any organizational undertaking, information technology (IT) initiatives should be directed toward supporting and advancing the organization's goals and plans.

But often, providers view the IT strategy as simply identifying a list of applications to be implemented and creating a timeline for their implementation. While identifying the list is essential, the scope of the IT strategy is much broader than developing a program evaluation and review technique (PERT) chart of applications to be installed.

The IT strategy should encompass the following:

- An IT agenda that is connected to organizational goals and initiatives. This agenda will define needs in four areas: applications; technical infrastructure; data; and IT staff, processes and organization. These four areas are collectively referred to as the IT asset.
- Initiatives designed to improve internal organizational attributes that enhance the overall ability to apply IT effectively—for example, improving change management competencies.

The IT Asset

An organization can develop its IT agenda through the following pathways:

Understanding organizational strategies. For example, efforts to improve patient safety can lead to an IT strategy to implement CPOE and medication administration record applications.

Continuously improving core operational processes and information management. For example, efforts to continuously improve productivity can lead to the implementation of data warehouses that enable the labor cost analysis.

Reviewing new information technologies. A review can identify opportunities to advance strategies and improve operations. For example, smart phones can enable patients to better manage a chronic disease.

Assessing strategic trajectories. An assessment can point out the need to take some preliminary strategic steps. For example, the organization may decide that accountable care organizations (ACO) will be a strategic centerpiece but it is unsure of the mature form or importance of the ACO. Hence it decides to take some initial steps and begin the learning process. These initial steps may point out some IT needs such as interoperability with affiliated physician practices.

IT Strategy Elements

Most organizations focus on an inventory of application systems, such as the electronic health record, as the centerpiece of the IT strategy. However, the strategy should be more diverse than applications; it should also include:

- technical infrastructure consisting of the base technologies—for example, networks, operating systems and workstations—that are needed to ensure that the organization's systems are reliable, secure and agile and support features such as extending the reach of applications into a patient's home;
- data—all the organization's data and analysis and access technologies; and
- IT staff—the analysts, programmers and computer operators who, day in and day out, manage and advance information systems in an organization, along with the IT organization structure, core competencies and IT organization characteristics, such as innovation ability.

Each element of the organization's overall strategy may call for new applications, extensions of the infrastructure or creation of new IT departments such as quality analysis. In addition, there is often a need to develop strategies for the IT asset that cut across several organizational activities. For example, strategies may be developed as a response to questions such as:

- What is our approach to ensuring that our infrastructure is more agile?
- What is our approach to attracting and retaining superb IT talent?

- Is there a way we can significantly improve the impact of our clinical information systems on our care processes?

IT-Centric Organizational Attributes

A variety of studies have identified IT-centric organizational attributes that appear to have a significant influence on the effectiveness of an organization in applying IT. These factors include the following:

- the relationship between the IT group and the rest of the organization;
- the presence of top managers' support for IT and the quality of the leadership;
- organizational comfort with "visionary" IT applications and ability to experiment with new technologies; and
- organizational experience with IT.

If the IT department has a poor working relationship with the clinical staff, it is hard to imagine that the organization would be effective in implementing an electronic health record. If organization leaders believe that IT is a necessary but barely tolerated expense, it will be difficult for the organization to invest in IT initiatives that push a strategic envelope. If the organization has a troubled history with IT implementations, it will hesitate to take on another "strategic IT initiative" that suggests another expensive disappointment.

Two other characteristics of the organization impact its effectiveness: IT governance and change management. IT governance consists of the organizational mechanisms by which IT priorities are set, IT policies and procedures are developed, and IT management responsibility is distributed. The effectiveness, transparency and inclusive of governance can make a material contribution to the ability of IT to support organizational goals.

Change management skills enable the organization to evolve its direction, identity, processes and structures as required by its strategy. An IT initiative is often used as a catalyst for change just as it is used to enable and support change. Even if material change is not envisioned, the implementation of an application system will require some change in workflow and information provision. Organizations that are poor at managing change will be less effective in applying IT.

These attributes, which are different from the IT asset, can be created or changed. The IT strategy development must encompass both the IT asset and these attributes.

IT Strategy Considerations

While changes to the IT asset and IT-centric organizational attributes are the result of an IT strategy development process, experiences by several industries over many years have led to considerations or conclusions that should guide strategy development:

Complementary strategies. It may be necessary to devise complementary strategies—organizational initiatives that do not involve IT per se but are needed for the IT strategy to succeed. For example, the federal government goal of accelerating the adoption of electronic health records is greatly facilitated by the complementary strategy of meaningful use financial incentives.

The realization of IT-enabled value. As the organization develops its IT strategy, it must understand that the acquisition and implementation of an application does not necessarily lead to value, streamlined processes, improved decision making capabilities or reduced medical errors. This is evident in the wide variety of health care experiences with IT; at times the implementation of an electronic health record clearly improves care, and at other times it has resulted in no significant improvements. Application implementation must be well managed, changes in processes must be thoughtfully considered, and ongoing efforts to leverage the IT investment must be put in place.

The necessity for IT strategies to evolve. IT strategies must evolve. An application system that provides a competitive advantage today becomes an industry commodity tomorrow. The use of ATMs by banks is an example. At one time ATMs provided a bank an advantage. Today ATMs are a "stay in business" expense borne by all banks and distinguishing none of them. In health care an organization that is in the process of implementing an electronic health record must understand that there will be a day when that implementation is done and when most organizations have an electronic health record. What then?

More Than a List

The scope of an IT strategy is much broader than a list of applications to be implemented. The IT strategy must also examine the IT asset, which includes applications and data, technical infrastructure, and the IT staff. In addition, the strategy may need to identify improvements to IT-centric organizational attributes that support the organization's ability to be effective in IT. Finally, as the IT strategy is developed, provider organizations should consider lessons learned over the years by organizations striving to advance their strategies through the use of IT.

John Glaser, Ph.D., is the CEO of Siemens Healthcare Health Services in Malvern, Pa. He is also a regular contributor to H&HN Daily.

Thinking Strategically about New Information Technology

December 14, 2009
By John Glaser

© Health Forum, Inc.

Some new technologies profoundly alter our organizations; others fail to register a blip on the radar screen. Five questions will help you determine which course the next new thing will take.

From time to time, we are presented with information technologies—the Web, bar codes and MRIs—that significantly influence our organizations' strategies and plans. But we also encounter information technologies, such as artificial intelligence, that failed to have a widespread impact on organizations.

In developing an information technology strategy, we need to accurately predict whether a new technology belongs in the first cohort or the second, and why. An organization that miscategorizes technology runs the risk of investing heavily in a technology that does not help the organization, or, conversely, of failing to use a technology that could be a major benefit.

Five Questions to Evaluate Technology

In analyzing the potency of new technologies, leaders of an organization need to answer five primary questions:

- What are the core capabilities of the new technology?
- How might the technology generally be applied in the organization?
- Given these general application potentials, does the technology provide specific opportunities to solve problems or advance strategies? Are these opportunities important?
- What have the early uses of the technology taught us?
- Given the discussion of all of the above questions, should the organization pursue the technology?

What are the core capabilities of the new technology? This is an easy question to state and a complicated one to answer. For example, the core capabilities of an airplane are that (1) it allows you to go from point A to point B in less time that other modes of transportation, and (2) it costs less to achieve scope (roads or track are not required) and can achieve greater range (that is, it can go to places where roads or track are not practical).

The core capabilities of the mobile phone are that it transports applications and communication directly to you (rather than to a fixed workstation). As another example, the global positioning satellite infrastructure lets you know where something is anywhere on the globe.

Be sure you understand the core capabilities of the technology so you can assess how the technology might contribute and if the contribution will be significant.

How might the technology generally be applied in the organization? A new technology can fill several roles. Bar codes, for example, can track an object as it moves from place to place, identify an object and link it to other data (e.g., the bar code on a can of soup can be linked to current price information) and serve as a "permanent" storage information device that can be applied to irregularly shaped objects.

Use the bar code as a framework for identifying applications of the technology. For example, an organization could use a mobile phone to deliver reminders to patients, support communication between the patient and her care team, or capture data necessary for managing a patient's chronic disease.

Given these general application potentials, does the technology provide specific opportunities to solve problems or advance strategies? Are these opportunities important? Global positioning capabilities might enable the organization to identify the location of equipment. This could reduce the time clinicians spend looking for equipment and reduce the capital budget devoted to replacing "lost" equipment.

In efforts to improve disease management, the mobile phone can be used to remind patients to take their medications, record blood pressure and document food intake.

The Web and videoconferencing could extend the reach of the organization's specialists to anywhere in the world.

Depending upon an organization's strategy and operational needs, these opportunities could be important or irrelevant.

What have the early uses of the technology taught us? Have other organizations been successful in applying the technology to achieve objectives that might be similar? If they have been successful, what gains have they seen, and what steps did they take to achieve those gains? If success has been elusive, to what degree was that due to immature technology or a poor implementation of the technology?

Developing an assessment of a technology's potential based on early experiences can be difficult. Pioneers often overstate their success and minimize their headaches. On the other hand, early efforts to fly were plagued with frequent crashes and pilots that got lost. These problems were a sign of technology immaturity rather than flight being a poor idea.

Given the discussion of all of the above questions, should the organization pursue the technology? This pursuit could be aggressive, with a broad commitment to adopt, or it might be in the form of small-scale projects that let the organization further its knowledge about the technology. The pursuit is goal directed; it is based on a reasoned understanding of the potential value of the technology.

Why Answer These Questions?

In answering such questions, the organization frames its understanding of a particular technology and the role it might play in advancing its strategies. It forms an understanding of the power of the technology, which can range from strategically disruptive (or enabling), to operationally important, to marginally significant.

It is important that an organization address the earlier questions and not leap immediately to later questions. If an organization had based its assessment of the Web on the early efforts to provide access to information, it might have missed the core capabilities that enabled that technology to have a massive impact on our society. These capabilities include:

- the ability to deliver a service to millions of devices at zero incremental cost;
- the trivial effort required to add a new service to the Web; and
- delivered service that can be a rich, multimedia experience.

Using these core capabilities, the retail, travel and financial services industries, among others, have forever been altered. Because of these capabilities, for example, the need to establish well-placed chains of stores or branch offices effectively disappeared for many organizations. Competitors that did not have the capital to create stores could enter the market, and they could enter it quickly because they did not need to take the time required to put stores in place.

If the core capability concepts are powerful, the technology is likely to be powerful. Concepts that appear to shrink distance, collapse time, add intelligence to processes and reduce costs have particular promise.

At times the power of the technology will rapidly become apparent (such as the mobile phone). At other times, the power will evolve more slowly (such as clinical decision support). And sometimes the power is not completely clear (such as Web 2.0 communities of patients that may alter the trust relationship between providers and patients). But thoughtful assessment of new information technologies can always be a critically important strategy discussion.

John Glaser is a vice president and the CIO of Partners HealthCare in Boston. He is also a regular contributor to H&HN Weekly.

Reprinted from H&HN Hospitals & Health Networks, by permission, December 2009, ©2009 by Health Forum, Inc.

Data Challenges on the EHR Agenda

June 10, 2009
By John Glaser

While preparing to adopt or expand electronic records, providers shouldn't overlook the quality of the data these systems will contain.

The health care information technology portions of the American Recovery and Reinvestment Act (ARRA) have led to heightened interest in the adoption and effective use of electronic health records. Given the importance of improving many facets of care and the magnitude of the stimulus funds, this attention is appropriate.

Most of the discussion about advancing EHRs centers on areas such as meaningful use, certification, interoperability and regional extension centers. Underneath these topics is the industry's focus on the *software application* called the electronic health record. For example, when the industry talks about adoption and effective use, it is referring to the EHR software application. And when the industry discusses interoperability, it is focusing on EHR applications being interoperable with each other.

This focus on the EHR software application should not distract us from also concentrating on the data in the EHR. Both the near and intermediate terms of the national EHR agenda pose several data challenges:

- The Office of the National Coordinator and the Department of Health & Human Services may define "meaningful use" of health IT to include the electronic transmission of quality and cost data to Medicare and the exchange of data to support care coordination and quality. In fact, meaningful use may even involve more than reporting and exchanging data—it may include using it to demonstrate clear improvements in care.

- Large-scale information exchange among health care entities raises data management questions for both the senders and recipients of data. For example, under which conditions can data from one organization be used for clinical research by another organization? And if one organization needs to amend data it has exchanged with others, how is that amendment propagated?
- Changes in privacy regulations will require improvements in data access controls and tracking data movement within and between organizations.
- Broad EHR adoption will open the door to a diverse set of secondary uses of data for clinical research, care improvement, population health and post-market medication surveillance. Early efforts to leverage EHR-based data to accelerate clinical research, and to dramatically improve the efficiency of post-market surveillance, show promise but have also exposed data quality problems.
- Widespread EHR adoption may accelerate use of personal health records. Patients using PHRs will likely increase their contributions of data, such as measurements from home monitoring equipment, to their EHRs.
- Federal efforts to improve safety and quality will increase the use of clinical decision support. This, in turn, will heighten the focus on data that drives support algorithms and rules. For example, if the problem and medication lists are incomplete, the potency of drug-drug interaction warnings in the EHR can be seriously diluted.

This is not an exhaustive list of the issues that we will confront in the years ahead. Nor is ARRA the only reason to focus on data; ICD-10 implementation and private payer pay-for-performance initiatives are also factors.

New Considerations

The industry's understanding of these looming issues and challenges—and how best to address them—is imperfect. Despite this, the following ramifications are clear.

The breadth and depth of provider data quality management efforts must increase. In general, most providers focus on the quality of a very narrow subset of data required for reimbursement, targeted care improvement initiatives and external reporting.

In the years ahead, quality management efforts will need to encompass a broader range of data, including data from patients and from other organizations via a health information exchange. Providers will also need to consider applying quality management processes to more unusual forms of data, such as the knowledge assets of EHR templates, computerized provider order entry order sets and clinical decision support rules.

In addition to expanding the breadth of data management activities, providers' data quality management activities will need to be more rigorous. Today's approaches to ensure that the meaning of a particular data element is unambiguous, to document consistency of source application systems and to monitor data quality may no longer be adequate. The degree of data management prowess that is adequate for reimbursement may not be adequate for effective use of clinical decision support. Problems with clinical data quality will severely hinder the value of a health information exchange; receiving providers may not use data from other organizations if they don't trust its comprehensiveness.

Provider organizations have to amend data use and management policies and procedures. Virtually all providers have developed policies and procedures that govern internal and external use of patient data. They cover territory as diverse as approving new clinical forms, defining time frames for completing documentation and determining conditions for release of information.

These policies and procedures will need to be adjusted to reflect changes in privacy law, the specifics of meaningful use and the growth in co-mingled data that will come from health information exchange use. For example, if a provider's clinical data repository contains data that originated from dozens of other providers, policies governing secondary uses, such as improving care operations or conducting clinical research involving anonymized patient data for genome association studies, will be needed.

The definition of the medical record will become more fluid. To the degree that the medical record is defined as data that a provider accessed or had access to during the course of providing care, its boundaries will expand. The definition will grow to include data received from other providers, patient-contributed data and computer-generated clinical decision support warnings, alerts and reminders.

This broader definition has malpractice and care implications. The industry will need to reach consensus on a definition of the medical record that is no longer rooted in a paper chart and confined by the provider's organization. In many ways, this new definition is long overdue.

The Years Ahead

To improve care through the broad adoption and effective use of EHRs, we must focus on the EHR application software. Applications impact workflow, possess features that support documentation and e-prescribing, and must be installed on hardware and software platforms.

We must also have a parallel data focus. Data will be exchanged and used to assess care performance. Privacy protections are centered on data.

The years ahead will require that providers review and significantly change their internal data management functions to encompass broader scope, increased rigor, and a new definition of the electronic health record. Ensuring that we address data centricity well will require a collective, multistakeholder discussion.

John Glaser *is vice president and CIO of Partners HealthCare in Boston and a regular contributor to* H&HN Weekly.

Reprinted from H&HN Hospitals & Health Networks, by permission, June 2009, ©2009 by Health Forum, Inc.

Are They Using IT? Effectively?

November 19, 2008
By John Glaser

Provider organizations commit to the investment of significant resources when they pursue the implementation of electronic health records (EHRs). This investment is seen as necessary to further goals such as improving the management of patients with chronic diseases, controlling the costs of care, reducing medication errors and streamlining care operations.

These organizations understand that providers must use the EHR for these goals to be achieved. The problem list must be complete. Medication lists need to be up to date. Decision support guidance should be followed. As a result, some of the resources invested are directed to training, process reengineering, design of screens and post-implementation support.

How does an organization determine if use is occurring? Most organizations gauge use by surveying their providers and asking if the system improves care, reduces administrative tasks and helps them manage patients. The organization assumes that if providers like the system, they will use it. And if they don't like the system, they won't use it.

Clearly providers (or any one) are unlikely to use a system or use it well if they find it takes too many steps to complete a transaction, the navigation is incomprehensible or availability seems to be under the control of a random number algorithm. However, satisfied users are not necessarily effective users.

The structured problem list may be incomplete, with some problems being buried in progress notes. The medication list may include antibiotics prescribed five years ago. Decision support may be ignored.

I had the following conversation with one of our physicians:

Him: I love the new EHR. It's terrific! It's so easy for me to find my notes and those of other doctors.

Me: That's great. How do you like the medication and problem list features?

Him: I don't use those. I don't have time for that. But I love the new EHR!

There can be many reasons why EHR use is less than fully effective:

- The application is poorly designed: look and feel is inconsistent, data presentation is confusing or too many clicks are required to do a frequently occurring transaction
- The clinical decision support warnings, alerts and reminders are not well placed in the workflow, are not tiered according to importance or do not quickly take the user to remedial actions
- The fit between the EHR and the clinical workflow was not well conceived, resulting in additional tasks and organizational confusion
- Use of the application takes more time than the paper alternative, leading harried clinicians to skip use or take shortcuts

Ineffective or suboptimal use can significantly diminish the ability of the organization to achieve its goals. It may be difficult to analyze care costs and quality if 40 percent of the problems and 25 percent of the radiology orders are missing. Achieving pay for performance chronic care management goals is hindered if providers ignore diabetes or smoking cessation reminders because they feel pressed for time or believe that the guidance is unnecessary. Regional interoperability value can be reduced if health information exchange participants become concerned that the data being exchanged is incomplete.

Achieving effective use is critical. It is also very difficult to achieve and is never fully achieved.

Several steps can be taken to improve the effectiveness of use:

Appreciate the importance of use. Those who are implementing an EHR must understand the importance of use. Satisfied users are important, but they are not equivalent to effective users. Knowing that this is important will lead to efforts to improve use.

Define and measure effective use. What does effective use mean to an organization? How should they measure it? A complete and accurate medication list is a result of effective use. The completeness of the medication list can be determined by comparing the EHR list with medication claims from the patient's health plan. Following health maintenance reminders to schedule a mammogram is a result of effective use. Reminder compliance can be determined by comparing the number of reminders generated to the number of mammogram procedures ordered.

There are some measures of use that are basic—undoubtedly important to all organizations. An example is following clinical decision support warnings about potentially lethal medication interactions. However, many measures will reflect the specific organizational goals and tactics.

Develop strategies for increasing the effectiveness of use. Improving use requires a mixture of broad and specific strategies. Broad strategies can include:

- Providing ongoing training on key features of the EHR. Often, effective use problems are the result of clinicians not knowing that there are easier ways to accomplish a task. The irritating "long way" leads them to bypass steps in a process. Getting clinicians to attend training can be a challenge, but continuing education credits and payment can increase class attendance.
- Structuring pay for performance contracts to include incentives for effective use. The completeness of a medication list can, for example, be one of the criteria that determines the ability of the physician to receive the at risk portion of reimbursement.
- Engaging clinicians in discussion and education regarding the importance of effective use. This discussion centers not only on the linkage between use and organizational goals but also understanding the problems that interfere with use. These discussions can be supplemented by physician-specific reports on use measures.

Specific strategies center on instances of use that are disappointing. If the completeness of the medication list is an issue, some improvement approaches could be:

- Examining if changes can be made to the ePrescribing screens and navigation to reduce the time required to prescribe and populate the medication list
- Reviewing other potential changes to the application, such as using natural language processing to identify medications in the note that are not on the list or comparing the problem list to the medication list to identify the potential absence of medications
- Exploring the leverage of the SureScripts-RxHub medication transaction infrastructure to determine if medication histories from the pharmacy benefits managers and retail pharmacies can be used to suggest entries into the EHR medication list
- Exploring the use of the personal health record to engage patients in ensuring the accuracy of the list
- Assessing practice workflow to see if efficiencies can be made in the internal medication management processes that free up provider time

Regardless of the steps taken, the organization should appreciate that improving the effectiveness of use is a never-ending task. The strategies may move from one area to another as progress is made and new issues and opportunities arise, but there will always be a need to pay attention to use.

In addition, the organization should understand that use will never be perfect. There will always be reasons outside of the control of the provider (such as DEA limitations on prescribing narcotics) and imperfect human behavior that will thwart the ability to achieve 100 percent.

However, the difference between a 75 percent use grade and a 95 percent use grade is very significant and worthy of pursuit. Such a difference may determine whether the goals of the EHR are achieved or not.

John Glaser is vice president and CIO of Partners HealthCare in Boston, senior advisor, Deloitte Center for Health Solutions, and a regular contributor to Most Wired Online.

Necessary Downtime

August 6, 2008
By John Glaser

One of our very senior IS executives was on vacation last week. During that week, I did not receive a single email from her.

I am a huge fan of this person. I have worked with her for a very long time, and she and I have an exceptionally effective working relationship. She has very significant responsibility and accountability for managing the Partners IS organization.

This relationship and her responsibilities usually result in us having several conversations and multiple emails during the course of a week.

And last week there were no conversations and no emails.

Best I can tell, project executions continued, support went on, decisions were made, issues were addressed and the work got done.

The IS organization was quite capable of carrying on for a week without her. And it would carry on for a week without me. And your organization will carry on for a week without you. Our organizations would feel her, my and your absence if we were to be gone for many weeks. But one week—no problem.

At times, folks take time off, but they don't really take time off. They check their email. They return phone calls. They might go to a meeting. They keep their Blackberry/ Treo on their person.

Why?

It's clear to me that the work is not requiring this (OK sometimes it does). It seems to me that we can't let go. We do this for ourselves rather than for our work colleagues.

We decide to take precious and fleeting time that we have with our family, our friends and ourselves, and we decide to spend part of that time with work colleagues who probably don't need us. And we divert time away from those who probably do need us.

We take time that could be spent swimming in a lake or playing mini-golf or reading a racy spy novel or riding a bike and divert it to worrying about a project or an issue or a budget. We take time that could have been spent holding hands with a child or hugging a spouse or watching the sunset and divert it to work stuff.

We have decided that work is more important. We are wrong.

And I think we actually know that we are wrong.

What's not right with these pictures. You are standing in line for a roller coaster ride with a five-year-old who is squirming with excitement, but rather than bask in their exuberance, you are on your cell phone talking about who misbehaved at a meeting. You could be sitting back and just enjoying being with your kids as you eat some really bad for you fried shrimp and french fries. But instead of really being with them, you are wondering if one of your managers is making the right decisions. Your wife whispers that she loves you as you walk along the beach at sunset, but you don't hear her because you are troubled by an email you just read.

Your body needs downtime. Your heart and soul need time with friends and family. Your psyche needs time to enjoy the world and become immersed in activities that you find fun. Family and friends need you.

And you need them. You need to be part of their lives and they need to be part of your life—a deep, profound part of your life. Viewing them as background activity as you continue to work while sitting around a campfire is a pale and hollow bonding with those who matter.

Your work colleagues need you. But for one week or two weeks they don't need you.

If you don't take vacation time, I am ordering you to do so. And when you do take vacation time, you have my permission and encouragement to not check email or voicemail and to leave your cell phone and Blackberry/Treo in the bottom drawer of your bedroom dresser. I'll write to your boss if that helps.

Enjoy the summer. Do send me a postcard if you take a trip to a neat place.

John Glaser *is vice president and CIO of Partners HealthCare in Boston, senior advisor, Deloitte Center for Health Solutions, and a regular contributor to* Most Wired Online.

The Legacy of Leadership

April 2, 2008
By John Glaser

Over the last several decades, I have had the honor of being taught and molded by some great mentors. They have made me a different, better person because of what I have learned from them.

I learned that however one goes about it, one should leave the world a better place. I am the beneficiary of the accomplishments of millions of people who, in small and large ways, advanced medicine, technology, democracy, economics, the arts and many other aspects of my life. It is unlikely that history will remember me. But we should hope that our time on this planet will add something to the efforts of those who went before us. I owe future generations that which has been given to me.

I learned about the meaning behind the words "patient care." I learned that it is the bedrock, has to be the bedrock, behind all that we do in this field. I learned that it is more than making the physicians the best that they can be. It is making the nurse, social worker, pharmacists, and all of the other participants as good as they can be. It means reaching out to those who are poor. It means remembering that the patient is a human being not a broken mechanical system. It means that the preservation of the patient's dignity should govern all that we do.

I learned that caring for the people who work with you and for you matters. It matters because they are people and that's what people do: They care for each other. It also matters because it builds incredible loyalty. Loyalty that keeps talent and deters their leaving for other opportunities. Loyalty that causes them to want to give more of themselves to pursue the goals and work that needs to be done. I learned that caring is not a set of actions, although those happen, but rather it is an attitude. An orientation. A principle that guides actions.

I learned that accomplishing things that matter requires teams of people. There is no question that great things can be accomplished by individuals. This is true in sports, science and international affairs. However, there is no question that teams account for the vast majority of progress in this world and their accomplishments are more significant than those of individuals.

I learned about taking enormous risks. I learned that we are in a position to take those, and that, at times, we must take those if we are to lead. I learned about managing risk. I learned about supporting, helping those who are in the middle of a risky venture and standing by them, running interference for them, when the inevitable turbulence sets in.

I learned how to manage very talented people. Point them in a broad direction. Support them with resources, political help, and picking them up when they stumble. I learned to cherish talent and nurture it. I learned to let them grab center stage when it all goes well. I learned to step in and take the flack for them when things aren't going well.

I learned what it means to be tough. That it isn't about growling or clobbering people. It is about conviction. About being persistent, stubborn. It is about making hard decisions and sticking with them. It is very much about having core values and principles that guide everything. It means never acting in a way that is not consistent with those values.

I knew, but learned more, about the treasure that is created by deep love and commitment to one's family.

I learned that it is important to know your strengths and weaknesses. I have gifts, and I have flaws. It is important to understand and accept both. You can't give yourself gifts that you do not have—I will never be a professional athlete. And you usually cannot correct your flaws. Self-awareness of who you are—the good and the bad—is essential if you are to lead.

And, to the degree that I lead or am a good leader, I learned that from my mentors. It is all of the above rolled into a complicated mixture of skills, talents, emotions, beliefs and experiences that guide what you say and do every day. I learned that leading happens every time you say something, do something, are present or don't say something, don't do something or are absent. Leadership is no single thing. No single attribute. No single skill. It is the accumulation of everything that you are and your actions. And within that, it is nobility and constancy of purpose and strength.

I have been molded, changed by them significantly over the years. I bear their imprint and always will. They have made sure, to the degree that I was capable of it, that much of what they are, I have become. And I hope that I, in turn, teach and mold others.

John Glaser is vice president and CIO of Partners HealthCare in Boston, senior advisor, Deloitte Center for Health Solutions, and a regular contributor to Most Wired Online.

IT Effectiveness, Part 1— The Fundamentals

January 12, 2005
By John Glaser

American Airlines. Amazon.com. Dell. Federal Express. Bank of America. These organizations, and others, are often cited as examples of exceptional effectiveness in applying information technology (IT) to improve organizational performance and, at times, achieving a significant competitive advantage. These organizations are more than one hit wonders. They have been exceptional over very long periods of time and seem to have one IT success after another.

What is it that these organizations have done to achieve such IT excellence? What makes them different?

Several researchers have pursued answers to these questions. The have identified a series of factors that lead to organizational IT excellence.

Leadership was critical. The leadership in these organizations was smart, honest, seasoned, committed and valued the healthy exchange of ideas. They were individually excellent and a great team. This leadership understood the strategy, communicated the vision, was able to recruit and motivate a team and had the staying power to see the organization's strategies through several years of hard work. The American Airlines SABRE system, the first computerized airline reservation system, was crafted by a core team of the airline CEO, the manager of customer service, and staff from IBM.

Strong, sustained and clear themes provided the basis for IT strategy decisions. Organizations often develop themes or strategic imperatives such as "we must continuously improve the care we deliver" or "we must relentlessly focus on efficiency." If there is sustained commitment to pursuing these themes, organizations become increasingly competent at addressing them. This competency extends to IT. In effect, organizations, year in and year out, get better and better at improving care and get better and better at applying IT to improve care. Dell's unwavering focus on reducing the costs of its personal computers led to IT-based continuous flow manufacturing and customer ordering systems.

The evaluation of IT opportunities was thoughtful and rigorous. IT initiatives that involve major commitments of resources and significant organizational change must be analyzed and studied thoroughly. However, these organizations also understood that a large element of vision, management instinct and "feel" often guided the decision to initiate investment and continue investment. These organizations were careful to ensure that IT initiatives were strongly linked to key organizational strategies and plans. USAA instinctively believed that growth in its insurance business would occur if it concentrated its applications on addressing the needs of customers, providing courteous service and expanding its services.

Extracting value from IT required innovation in business practices. If an organization "merely" computerizes existing processes without rectifying (or at times eliminating) process problems it may have merely made process problems occur faster. In addition those processes are now more expensive since there is a computer system to support. All IT initiatives must be accompanied by efforts to materially improve the processes that the system is designed to improve. Federal Express rethought the package tracking process and developed handheld devices that enabled its truck drivers to track packages as they moved from receipt to delivery.

The economic improvement of IT came from incremental innovations rather than "big bang" initiatives. Organizations will often introduce very expensive application systems and process change "all at once." Big bang implementations are very tricky and highly risky.

It is exceptionally difficult to understand the ramifications of such change during the analysis and design stages that precede implementation. In fact, it is impossible to fully understand the consequences. As a result, organizations risk material damage. It may set the organization back, and, even if the organization grinds its way through the disruption, the resulting trauma may make the organization unwilling to engage in future ambitious IT initiatives.

On the other hand, IT implementations (and related process changes) that are more incremental and iterative reduce the risk of organizational damage and permit the organization to learn. Incremental change helps the organization's members understand that change, and performance improvement, are never-ending aspects of organizational life rather than something to be endured every couple of years. Amazon.com has progressively developed approaches to inform customers of purchase opportunities that are based on prior purchase patterns.

The strategic impact of IT investments came from the cumulative effect of sustained near-term initiatives to innovate business practices. If economic value is derived from a series of thoughtful, incremental steps, then the aggregate effect of those steps leads to a competitive advantage. Organizations often took five to seven years for major initiatives to fully mature and the results to be seen. Persistent improvements by a talented team, over the course of years and across many initiatives, will result in significant strategic gains. These organizations had learned how to improve themselves, year in and year out.

The American Hospital Supply ASAP system evolved, over the course of several years, from supply ordering to suggestions for supply substitution to inventory management to automatic supply order generation when par levels were low.

Exceptional effectiveness is a marathon. It is a long race that is run and won one mile at a time.

Innovation was encouraged. These organizations were comfortable and competent at innovation. This innovation was not confined to IT. They knew that innovation had to be practical and goal directed. Innovation had to focus on a real business problem, crisis or opportunity, and the project needed budgets, political protection and deliverables. Bank of America, recognizing the cost of manual sorting of checks, developed the magnetic ink check number enabling automatic sorting of checks by account.

Well-architected technology was the great enabler. Information systems that are difficult to change, unreliable, overly costly, functionally weak and impossible to integrate can severely hinder an organization's strategies. The organizations studied had taken the time to develop approaches and policies needed to ensure that desired levels of integration or reliability were achieved. These organizations knew what to look for during IT purchasing decisions as they assessed the degree to which new applications could provide necessary levels of flexibility. Their CIO had, and shared with the leadership team, a strategic understanding of information technology architecture. American Hospital Supply's architecture enabled it to migrate its systems gracefully from dumb terminals to personal computers to the Web.

Summary. Achieving organizational excellence in IT requires much more than great information systems and a great IT staff (although these are important). Excellence requires talented people, great working relationships, organizational thoughtfulness and dogged, year in and year out, pursuit of performance improvements. These factors are probably not materially different from the factors that determine organizational excellence in general.

It is more important for an organization to focus on addressing these factors than it is to work on any specific IT application.

John Glaser *is vice president and CIO of Partners HealthCare in Boston and a regular contributor to* Most Wired Online.

Reprinted from H&HN Hospitals & Health Networks, by permission, January 2005, ©2005 by Health Forum, Inc.

IT Effectiveness, Part 2— Evaluating the IT Department

January 12, 2005
By John Glaser

The leadership of an organization may wonder if their Information Technology (IT) department is world class or something other than that. The leadership might believe that other organizations have IT departments that seem to accomplish more or spend less. Management and physicians may express dissatisfaction with IT; nothing is getting done or projects cost too much or take too long.

There can be a large number of reasons for dissatisfaction: poor expectation setting, unclear priorities, limited funding, and inadequate IT leadership. How does one assess the effectiveness and efficiency of the IT department? A thoughtful assessment is an essential step in correcting any problems or deficiencies.

An IT assessment needs to cover several areas.

Linkage of the IT Agenda to the Organization's Agenda

Organizations develop strategies. They develop plans to improve organizational performance. The IT agenda (application acquisition and implementation and infrastructure improvements) must be well linked to the organization's strategies and plans. If not, the

IT folks may be executing well but they are working on the wrong things. Answers to a few questions can indicate whether linkage is occurring or not:

- Can we take each item in our strategy and performance improvement plans and point to the IT initiatives that support these undertakings?
- If there are IT initiatives that cannot be mapped to the strategy and plans, do we know why we approved these initiatives?
- Is there a regular senior leadership discussion of the IT agenda, and does the leadership take responsibility for making decisions about which IT initiatives to fund?
- Does our CIO take the lead in bringing new information technologies to the attention of the management team? Does our CIO help them understand the potential contribution of these technologies?

Governance

Governance refers to the organization's structures and processes for assigning responsibilities, making decisions and defining policies and procedures. Governance can be assessed by asking:

- Is it clear how we set the IT agenda? What processes and committees do we use?
- Is the process for setting the IT budget well understood, efficient, sufficiently rigorous and perceived as fair?
- Can we articulate how standards are set for information technology?
- Do we have a well-accepted approach for acquiring new applications?
- Do the IT project teams have well-defined roles and methods for implementing new systems?

System Implementation

The implementation of new applications is where "the rubber meets the road." The objective of any implementation is that the organization is better off as a result. Implementation can be critiqued by asking:

- How well do we do in implementing systems on time and on budget? If our experience is uneven, do we review the problems that occurred and attempt to improve our processes?
- Do we follow up after implementations to assess the degree to which the desired outcomes, e.g., reduce denials, actually occurred?
- Are the key users and constituencies well represented in the implementation? Do we have them assume overall responsibility for managing the implementation?

IT Service Levels

IT staff deliver service every day, e.g., manage system reliability and response time and respond to Help Desk calls. The quality of these services has a significant impact on organizational perception of the IT group and the ability of the organization's staff to do their work. IT service levels can be gauged by posing several questions:

- Does the IT organization measure its service? For example, do they measure the percent of Help Desk calls "closed" within 48 hours? Do they communicate these measures to the organization?
- Has the IT organization established service goals? Was the organization's management involved in setting those goals?
- Does the IT organization engage the leadership in discussions of steps and investments that can be taken to improve service levels? Does the IT organization have plans for improving service levels?
- Does the IT organization regularly solicit feedback on its service?

IT Staff

No IT organization can be excellent unless it has great staff that are well managed. The IT staff and management can be reviewed by asking:

- Are IT staff and management articulate, smart, thorough and responsive?
- Do they manage their budget? Are they on top of the status of IT projects?
- Are the turnover rates within industry norms? Is there a staff development plan in place?
- Does our administrative and medical staff generally like working with IT staff?
- Does morale seem good?

Summary

Assessing the efficiency and effectiveness of the IT department requires that a series of questions are posed and that there are thoughtful discussions of the answers. All IT groups have areas where performance can be improved. The organization may decide to accept current levels of performance but at least it has made a well-reasoned decision.

There is no set of well-accepted, unambiguous measures that can be used to definitively assess an IT organization. The answers to the questions above come in shades of gray, and it can be impossible to aggregate the answers into an overall score. This makes assessing the IT organization no different from assessing the overall organization.

Benchmarks with other organizations and the use of industry metrics, e.g., the percent of the organization's budget devoted to IT, can help the organization identify areas that may need particular scrutiny. However, benchmarks and industry data are, at best, suggestive and should never be regarded as providing absolute guidance.

Establishing a terrific IT organization is a responsibility shared between IT leadership and the rest of the management team. Linkage problems may be due to overall deficiencies in the organization's strategies. Ineffective governance mechanisms may be due to management inattention. Poor implementation outcomes can be attributed to inadequate user management. An assessment of the IT organization requires that the leadership also look at itself in the mirror. And the correction of any problems requires a joint effort between IT and the rest of the organization.

John Glaser *is vice president and CIO of Partners HealthCare in Boston and a regular contributor to* Most Wired Online.

Section Four – HIT Industry Observations

Why We Do What We Do

October 12, 2015
By John Glaser

The reason for health care information technology is that it allows clinicians to focus more on the human aspects of care.

We know why we devote our careers to the implementation and effective use of health care information technology.

Care quality is too variable. Medical costs are too high. Many people cannot get access to the care they need. There are too many medical errors. Patient service in some of our organizations is appalling.

We believe, and rightfully so, that information technology can help solve many of these problems. Computerized physician order entry, the electronic health record, mobile technologies and health information exchanges can make a difference.

When we talk about these problems in health care and the role of information technology, we usually talk in the abstract. We talk about processes, organizational change, advances in technology and application capabilities. We observe with alarm the growing burden of chronic disease. We discuss challenges in engaging physicians. We assess a vendor's solutions.

This abstract discussion can lead us to forget that there are real people who deliver care.

My Father

My father, George Glaser, was a very bright, engaging, accomplished and witty man. He had an exceptional sense of humor.

He died recently.

He had a form of dementia (Lewy body disease) that results from a combination of Alzheimer's and Parkinson's symptoms. On top of this he had a series of other medical maladies such as kidney stones, spinal cord degeneration and a broken wrist from a recent fall.

The loss of those you love is inevitable. I know that. You know that. My dad knew that. Sometimes the loss is sudden. And sometimes, as is the case with my father, the loss occurs over years. The father I knew slowly vanished. While we all know that it is inevitable, loss is filled with sadness and grief and renewed desire to love those who are close to us because we will, some day, lose many of them, too.

During his last year I had many encounters with the health care delivery system. I took my father to get a CT scan of his lower abdomen. MRI films of his back were fetched from a local hospital. We took him to an orthopedic surgeon's office to assess the mending of his wrist. There were meetings with physical and occupational therapists to discuss his care needs. I sat with him and a physician assistant to review his overall care plan.

I have lost track of the number of health care tests, discussions and visits that filled his final months.

I met many exceptional people. The physician assistant, a former corpsman with the Marines, had superb assessment skills; he also called every night to check in on my father. The physical and occupational therapists demonstrated an impressive set of skills and empathy. The orderly who helped me lift my father into the CT scan showed genuine kindness and gentleness. The receptionist at the neurology clinic had become a friend of my father's and was delighted to see him when we dropped off his MRI films. The orthopedic surgeon, who seemed to be one of those surgeons to the stars, was patient in his explanation of the X-ray results that showed good progress in the healing of my father's wrist.

I have lost track of the number of health care professionals I met. But all of them were superb.

The Foundation of Medical Care

These professionals reminded me that great medical care sits on a foundation of great professionals who are real people. Medical care is not like buying groceries or going to the dry cleaners. Medical care is a very human undertaking. Medical care often brings with it deep emotions of love, loss and duty. And while the technical performance of medicine is very important (I want the best physical therapist and I want efficient care processes), perhaps equally important is the human performance of medicine—being gentle, interested, patient, respectful and empathetic.

Our job in the health care information technology field is often directed to improving the ability of health care professionals to enhance the technical performance of medicine. We implement systems that track health maintenance tasks, suggest which medications to order or improve the accessibility of test results. But our job is also to enhance the human performance of medicine. To the degree that we help remove the hassle from health care delivery and reduce the difficulty of getting basic operations to work well, we help those professionals devote more time to the human performance of medicine and be less frazzled as they do so.

In the months and years ahead, as I sit in meetings about product plans and the status of implementations, I will have in the back of my mind the images of those people who took care of my father. And I will be asking myself if this work, and the way we are doing it, is likely to help those who are caring for people like my father be better at both the technical and human performance of care.

We should always remind ourselves that we provide systems for real people, not "users." We should take a day or an afternoon and shadow a physician, nurse or therapist and really see and feel the technical and human performance of medicine. We should close our eyes and remember the health care received by someone close to us and the terrific health care professionals whom we met.

I love you, Dad.

And I do what I do to help those who provide care to people like you.

John Glaser, Ph.D., is a senior vice president of Cerner Corporation, headquartered in Kansas City, Missouri. He is also a regular contributor to H&HN Daily.

Health Care IT Innovation: The Best Is Yet to Come

February 12, 2015
By John Glaser

© Health Forum, Inc.

The convergence of several factors is leading to an era of accelerated innovation in health care information technology.

"It's just a painful business to be in. I think the regulatory burden in the U.S. is so high that it would dissuade a lot of entrepreneurs."

Indeed, Google co-founder Sergey Brin, speaking at a venture capital conference last summer, hints at the sentiment shared by many—that the intense regulation surrounding the health care industry has the potential to stifle innovation, particularly from a health care information technology (HIT) perspective.

On the contrary, regulatory policy can actually help spur innovation—regulation and innovation can and do co-exist. For the last several years, HIT adoption in the United States has been driven by regulation—the Meaningful Use incentives. At the same time, the industry has experienced unprecedented growth in HIT innovation.

An Era of Accelerated Innovation

While the pace of Meaningful Use needs to be moderated, and many of the electronic health record (EHR) requirements seem to verge on micro-management, there's no denying that the significant expansion of the industry's HIT foundation—EHRs, analytics, electronic prescribing and health information exchange—can be attributed to the 2009 HIT legislation known as the HITECH Act. Consider the following:

- Hospital adoption of EHR systems has increased more than fivefold since 2008.
- In 2013, nearly 78 percent of office-based physicians had adopted some type of EHR system. About half of all physicians (48 percent) adopted a basic EHR system with select features in 2013, more than doubling the basic system adoption rate in 2009.
- Electronic health information exchange among hospital and outside providers grew 51 percent from 2008 to 2013.
- Experts predict that advanced health data analytics will continue to grow significantly, from a 10 percent adoption rate in 2011 to 50 percent by 2016.
- Seventy percent of providers nationwide are now using electronic prescribing through their EHRs, a tenfold increase since 2008.

This level of IT use creates a context that accelerates innovation. Innovation occurs within EHR and health information exchange products, for example, and the adoption levels provide a sizable IT foundation upon which other innovations can take place. For instance, with a large base of EHRs, the innovation of personal health records can be accelerated.

A Societal Shift

The Meaningful Use program is not the only factor providing a supportive context for HIT innovation.

Health provider leaders have become progressively aware of the need for substantial investments in HIT if their organizations are to address the challenges presented by material changes in payment strategies and tactics. Moreover, these leaders are part of a generation that grew up with computers—they played Pong, wrote high school papers on personal computers and saw the introduction of minicomputers enabling departmental systems. This generation is more comfortable with HIT than their predecessors.

But perhaps the most important factor influencing HIT innovation is the relentless IT product, service and business-model innovation we experience in all facets of life.

Our world has been fundamentally transformed by the influx of digital devices into our daily lives. Technology has democratized and consumerized nearly every major industry, from retail to banking to air (and even city) travel, within the past few decades.

Want to avoid the hassle of hailing a taxi and instead sip a latte while you track your driver's whereabouts on your phone? Simple: Download the Uber app.

Although there's nothing particularly novel about consumer preference toward a shiny black car over a yellow cab—or the use of GPS to track a vehicle's location, paying for a service directly on your phone (tip included), or providing instant feedback on said service—Uber's founders creatively combined these features to the delight of its customers. With a throng of early adopters in tow, Uber literally drove full steam ahead into another heavily regulated industry, disrupting entrenched incumbents and mature supply chains in major cities across the country and around the world.

And while Uber's success has also come with its share of challenges and growing pains—including court battles with regulators and city councils, PR crises, lawsuits and international bans—we are wise to remember that some battles are worth fighting, especially when the potential exists to enable dramatic improvements in service quality.

Uber is one of many examples of information technology permeating our lives, and is a terrific example of IT innovation. This extraordinary overall IT innovation phenomenon has strengthened the innovation context in health care. Not only can we import these advances into health care, but we also have a deeper understanding of IT's potential.

Playing to Win

The collective impact of federal actions, IT-savvy leadership and the dynamic IT marketplace has led to a significant increase in the level of HIT innovation. A scan of the current landscape shows that HIT innovation is coming primarily from five main sources:

HIT startups/entrepreneurs. According to StartUp Health, just over a billion dollars was invested in HIT startups in 2010. By 2013, investments rose to $2.9 billion via 590 deals. And in 2014, approximately $6.5 billion went into HIT startups, more than doubling the 2013 funding. Furthermore, top incubators such as Rock Health, DreamIT and Blueprint Health are funding and supporting anywhere from 50 to 100-plus startups at any given time.

Traditional HIT companies. From a traditional HIT company's standpoint, patents are often a telling metric for innovation. In the last five years, Siemens, Microsoft, Cerner, McKesson, Optum, Epic and Allscripts have been responsible for a combined total of 526 patents granted in HIT. Prior to 2009, the combined total of the same group of vendors stood at 150.

Additionally, today we see more and more HIT vendors opening up their software for innovation by others. Cerner, Allscripts and Athenahealth have opened up their platforms, enabling third-party developers to integrate their technology with the EHR vendor platform.

Athenahealth aims to further encourage entrepreneurship through its HIT accelerator program. Complementing its own development efforts with a network collaboration approach, the company actively recruits and fosters startups to expand its range of services for physicians.

New and interesting collaborations among the leading HIT vendors and forward-thinking providers are also yielding impressive early results. For example, the Healthcare Services Platform Consortium has its eye on advanced interoperability as well as sharing more complex processes, such as clinical workflows and clinical decision support logic among different EHR vendors' platforms. The group's work thus far is both impressive and tangible.

Traditional IT companies. They've become global household names to just about everyone from grade schoolers to senior citizens, and they have recently set their sights on health care. Companies such as Apple, Google and Facebook are poised to grab significant health care market share as the industry continues to digitize and shift more power into the hands of health care consumers.

For example, Apple's Healthkit platform debuted with its iOS 8 release and offers the ability to track and share a vast array of health, fitness and medical data points through multiple apps and devices, essentially turning your iPhone into both a fitness/wellness tool and a personal health care assistant complete with a medical ID feature.

Samsung, which rivals Apple in the smartphone market, continues to tweak its Simband health tracker, which uses a variety of sensors to measure biometric data such as blood flow, EKG levels and skin temperature.

Not to be outdone, Google unveiled its wearable technology platform known as Google Fit last year. The company's health care strategy also includes smart contact lenses that monitor bodily functions such as blood sugar levels detected in human tears by minuscule sensors. Less invasive than the traditional finger stick method, Google's approach may resonate well with the millions of diabetes sufferers.

Joining its Silicon Valley neighbors Apple and Google, Facebook also appears to "like" the health care space. Although Facebook's intentions are less well defined, app and content development, as well as online support communities, would be a natural fit for the social networking giant.

Whether or not these Silicon Valley giants' efforts take hold in health care, their presence in the market should make the established players—traditional HIT vendors, payers and providers alike—step up our collective innovation games in patient engagement, usability and design of systems, and in delivering a more personalized health care experience.

Medical informatics/academia. Organizations like the American Medical Informatics Association (AMIA) and its members fuel the science of informatics, which in turn drives innovation. Naturally, there are reasonable connections between the vendor community and the medical informatics community.

For example, AMIA corporate members include many of the large HIT vendors and traditional IT vendors such as Oracle and IBM. Likewise, many AMIA members are employed within the vendor community. In fact, approximately 13 percent of AMIA's members work in industry.

Also demonstrating academia's ties to innovation, of those startups funded from November 2013 through November 2014, 20 percent include a co-founder who is an academic or licensed from an academic institution.

Adjacent players (e.g., drug stores, payers, life sciences). Large retail pharmacy chains like Walgreens and CVS have been taking dramatic steps to expand their business models and services, emphasizing tools and partnerships to improve care coordination and help consumers better manage chronic diseases.

While CVS has gone as far as opening a technology development center that will focus on building customer-centric experiences in health care, Walgreens is actively pursuing its telemedicine strategy.

Payers are also busy making moves in the HIT space. For example, focusing on the consumer, Cigna now offers a digital coaching program and ecosystem of mobile tools, social media engagement, gamification and Web-based incentives to help its members meet their health goals.

UnitedHealth Group's Optum unit is seeing good traction among providers using its cloud-based population health analytics capabilities and decision support solutions. And for its part, Aetna invests in acquiring or building a variety of solutions so accountable care organizations can deliver more efficient patient care and better outcomes.

Pharmaceutical and life sciences companies such as Pfizer and Merck are also responding to the digital enablement of health care through investments in new technologies and partnerships that help identify the right treatment for the right patient at the right time.

Living in Harmony

In our ongoing quest to improve care quality and reduce its cost, innovation has long been the hallmark of American health care. With new challenges mounting as we move from a volume- to value-based system and progress further into Meaningful Use requirements, we must make certain that innovation continues to be the driving force behind our nation's health care system—and that we strike the right balance between product, process and business model innovation.

Growth in IT innovation from both established health care players and new entrants is welcome and important. However, it will place additional stress on providers. Which innovations are mature and potent? How does the organization adopt and use these new technologies well? How is my vendor handling this? And so on.

Stress of this nature adds to the stress of delivering superior patient care while responding to payment pressures, new regulations and IT demands such as ICD-10 and further Meaningful Use stages. While deciding which HIT innovations are sufficiently potent and mature to adopt at scale is difficult, there is no doubt that these innovations will accelerate our collective efforts toward improving how care is delivered and managed.

John Glaser, Ph.D., is a senior vice president with Cerner in Kansas City, Mo. He is also a regular contributor to H&HN Daily.

Of Guns and EHRs

August 13, 2013
By John Glaser

There is nothing inherently good or bad about technology; there is no technology determinism. Guns can be used to protect us and they can be used to harm us. Similarly, health information technology can be used to improve care, but it can also be used to inappropriately take advantage of the health care system.

It's been nearly a year since electronic health records (EHRs) first came under fire for their potential connection to medical billing fraud and rising hospital Medicare costs. The widely publicized studies and subsequent allegations that some providers were using their EHRs to "game the system" by upcoding services such as emergency care—or cutting and pasting their way to assigning more costly billing codes through a practice called cloning—set off an industry firestorm.

As someone who has devoted his professional life to espousing the myriad benefits of health care information technology (IT), I was troubled by this industry black eye. Moreover, I was discouraged by the "one step forward, two steps back" impact the controversy might ultimately have on the positive strides made through the Meaningful Use program.

After all, here was a golden opportunity to cry foul for those who have long questioned the value of health IT or those opposed to the EHR incentive program for a variety of reasons. And many did.

Some even criticized the Office of the National Coordinator's investigation of the issue, suggesting the experts involved were too closely tied to the industry to be objective—likening the situation to asking the National Rifle Association to investigate gun violence.

An Odd Parallel

Comparing the ONC with the NRA is neither particularly illuminating nor fair. However, there is a comparison that can be made between guns and EHRs.

If we allow the very tools designed to protect us and keep us safe to find their way into the hands of those with mal intent, the consequences can be devastating. Likewise, tools designed to ensure that better care is delivered and accounted for can be used to harm the industry and its participants.

If the intent to harm or cheat is there, technology can amplify our ability to perform such dubious acts. Sadly, health care technology joins guns, automobiles and the Internet in being applicable to a wide range of motivations.

While the billing fraud concern is certainly a legitimate one—well worth efforts by the government to investigate, audit and eradicate—we must not lose sight of the critical role information technology, specifically revenue cycle software, plays in the delivery and financing of care. And, ultimately, in supporting the overall well-being of our health care systems.

In fact, if we were to examine the other side of the fraud debate, we may see that the rise in billing is rather a result of providers getting better at documenting care and capturing their costs more accurately through the use of EHRs and revenue cycle technology.

In Praise of Revenue Cycle Systems

As we know, the contractual agreements and reimbursement terms involved in managed care in the United States are complicated and becoming exceedingly difficult to manage for both care providers and payers. In reality, it is not uncommon for some providers to routinely deal with several hundred different health plans and arrangements. Without the appropriate tools to manage the billing and reimbursement terms of these agreements, providers can easily fall short of realizing expected net revenues and cash and place their continued existence in peril.

For example, underpayments cost physicians and hospitals millions of dollars each year—either because the underpayments are difficult to identify or the effort and cost to recover them exceeds the gain. Likewise, industry data suggests that many health care providers are writing off up to 4 percent of net patient revenues because of payer denials. For a median-size hospital (358 beds) with annual net patient revenues of $370 million, this is more than $14 million in lost revenues and operating margin.

Additionally, government claims review programs such as recovery audit contractors have made claims management practices increasingly complex and burdensome for health care providers. As private payers adopt similar practices, it will become ever more critical for providers to expand accountability for effective claims management throughout the revenue cycle—from point of scheduling and patient access to care delivery, documentation, charging, coding, claims submission and payment reconciliation.

Clearly, in today's challenging financial environment, adopting a more coordinated, efficient and cost-effective approach to revenue cycle management, enabled by sophisticated IT tools, has become a strategic priority for many health care providers. In addition, it will not be possible to manage care in an era that rewards those that provide high-quality and efficient care without the ability to analyze integrated care quality, cost and reimbursement data.

And while these very same IT tools can threaten the integrity of our industry through isolated instances of abuse, we must not overlook their many potent benefits. Consider the following ways information technology supports the revenue cycle and can position an organization to provide ongoing care for its community:

Make a good first impression. The consumerization of health care is compelling providers to look for opportunities to differentiate themselves by improving the patient experience—beginning with the first point of contact.

As a patient's first encounter with the hospital is typically through scheduling or registration, this is a key opportunity for transformation. Not only do these processes impact the patient experience, they can also affect all downstream clinical and financial processes.

To create the best patient experience and improve the quality of patient information throughout the episode of care, providers need technology that automates, standardizes and streamlines user workflow by improving the speed and accuracy of data collection. The right IT system can turn scheduling and registration activities into a seamless, patient-focused business process. Moreover, these systems can reduce the patient headaches and aggravation that occur when problems with claims turn into interminable arguments with the payer and the provider.

Generate cleaner claims. Care providers know effort and costs are wasted when time is spent correcting and not collecting. One of the keys to successful revenue cycle management lies in securing and verifying patients' health care financial information, including payment sources.

Imagine an intelligent system that already knows the billing rules so that patient intake staff can create a proper claim and avoid many of the error corrections that consume precious staff resources and delay reimbursement. Think about the financial and operational benefits of reallocating those resources to more valuable activities, such as customer service, pre-service financial clearance, accounts receivable or cash collections.

A sophisticated revenue cycle system can be driven by provider rules that define the types of activities and information that must be satisfied before a patient encounter can be "cleared" for services and/or billing. Such a system can also prompt the collection of complete and accurate information early in the revenue cycle to help reduce delays and denials. Additionally, office staff can complete tasks like medical necessity and eligibility checking up front, within the preregistration workflow, so they can collect and verify the right information to ensure accurate and quick patient billing.

Improve denial prevention and management. Reducing denied claims is critical to improving operating margins. With provider operating margins reaching unprecedented lows, a focus on denials avoidance and management is necessary for an effective revenue protection strategy.

The risk of lost payment from denied claims is compounded by the burden of administrative expenses and delayed cash flow related to rebilling, appeals, follow-up and denial recovery. However, modern revenue cycle systems can help eliminate the various points of failure that contribute to denials.

Additionally, while optimizing recovery is necessary for a denials management program, preventing denials up front via the right IT tools offers a better long-term strategy for improving revenue capture. In fact, some experts believe an effective denials management program can have a more dramatic impact on the bottom line than any other revenue-generation or cost-reduction initiative.

Prepare for payment reform. Many payment reform models are being tested and proposed. One thing they have in common is the requirement that providers be able to manage the revenue, cost and reimbursement of care across multiple providers and care settings.

A next generation revenue cycle system can support these models because of its inherent ability to aggregate or segregate charges across multiple providers, create receivables and claims, and calculate expected reimbursement based on the payer requirements and payment model that applies. Having the ability to handle traditional billing and reimbursement requirements—along with the agility and flexibility to support accountable care organizations, bundled payments and other future payment reform initiatives—will become the new norm for providers.

Measure and manage better. Today's revenue cycle systems can notify financial executives when a key performance indicator exceeds a preset threshold, enabling timely attention to a negative performance situation. A dashboard of multiple indicators such as expenses, revenue, accounts receivable, charity care and average length of stay can show a complete picture of which metrics are doing well and where improvements are needed.

Much of today's innovative financial software allows finance executives to see top-level information and drill down as deeply as necessary to get to the root of a problem. Moreover, advanced business intelligence tools can keep financial leaders informed of operational performance in real time and without intensive IT involvement, delivering information through easily configurable, browser-based dashboards and reports. These capabilities and analyses will be essential in a health care system that tightly links clinical performance to provider revenue.

The Best Laid Plans

Advanced health care information technology can help organizations remain prosperous in this new era of accountability.

The technology is available today to simplify patient registration, increase staff productivity, improve claims integrity, and enable providers to spend more time collecting cash and less time correcting errors. Additionally, analytics and contract modeling tools can offer greater financial insight and enable near real-time access to information to improve forecasting, payer management, revenue management and contract negotiations.

Yet, despite the efforts and plans of many to improve care through IT there will be those rare few who choose to use the technology with malicious intent—intent to game or cheat the system. But, thanks to the heightened scrutiny now in place on hospital billing and collections practices, those who attempt to do so will suffer the consequences.

It has been said that we should not blame a gun for any act of violence any more than we can blame a pen for misspelling a word—another interesting comparison we might want to ponder, should health care information technology come under fire again because of the actions of a few.

John Glaser, Ph.D., is the CEO of the Health Services business unit of Siemens Healthcare in Malvern, Pa. He is also a regular contributor to H&HN Daily.

More Time Needed for Meaningful Use

February 7, 2013
By John Glaser

The time constraints on Meaningful Use may hinder the program.

In many ways the Meaningful Use program is well conceived.

The focus on use that is meaningful shifted the industry from its prior focus on adoption. The number of hospitals that adopt computerized physician [or provider] order entry (CPOE) is less important than whether those hospitals use CPOE extensively to enter orders.

The focus on meaningful use also stops short of outcomes. This is appropriate. Use must precede outcomes, and while the meaningful use of electronic health records should improve care delivery, major gains in outcomes are likely to be more effectively driven by changes in payment reform than by changes in the degree to which the problem list is maintained. Meaningful Use provides the foundation for improvement in outcomes.

However, using electronic health records to improve care requires more than a shift in focus. It requires implementation assistance to providers, increased numbers of clinical systems professionals, and advancement of standards for interoperability. It also requires quality measures, clear privacy and security requirements, and the furthering of the health information exchange infrastructure. Programs, initiatives, funding and advisory committees have been put in place to ensure that these supporting mechanisms are established.

Reason for Concern

There is no question that the needle has moved as a result of the Meaningful Use program. As of August 2012, almost 4,000 hospitals and 280,000 providers have registered for the program. The percent of physicians who use a basic electronic health record has increased from 48 percent in 2009 to 72 percent in 2012, according to the National Center for Health Statistics.

While acknowledging many of the successes of the Meaningful Use program, there is reason for concern.

As of October 2012, 19 percent of eligible physicians and 29 percent of hospitals have attested for Stage 1 Medicare Meaningful Use. These are significant numbers. But they are a minority of providers.

Stage 2 requirements have been defined. These requirements raise the bar significantly for providers. With the specific testing and certification requirements close to completion, providers and their software vendors will have about 18 months to complete development, testing, upgrading and implementing those electronic health record and clinical process changes necessary to begin attestation for Stage 2.

This is an extraordinary amount of change and work. It also coincides with the implementation of ICD-10 and with providers who are undertaking their own local efforts to improve care quality and efficiency through information technology.

One of the more difficult decisions about implementing change in an organization is determining the appropriation ambition and pace of change. The organization may have aspirations that clearly will require significant increases in performance as well as broad and deep changes in processes. If the aspirations are too modest, the organization could fail to achieve what it could have. If the aspirations are too high, the organization could become dispirited and demotivated. Change that is implemented too slowly places the organization at risk of mediocrity. Change that is implemented too fast risks breaking the organization.

Fundamental Risks

The time frame for the implementation of the Stage 2 is too short, given the aspirations of Stage 2. The requirements pose two fundamental risks for the government's effort to significantly improve care delivery through the meaningful use of electronic health records.

First, providers could blow it off; they could decide not to pursue Stage 2 (and perhaps Stage 3). Hospitals and physician practices can look at the costs and effort required to achieve Stage 2 and decide that it is not worth it. There are too many other things to do, such as the conversion to ICD-10. There are too many other demands on the organization's capital budget. There are too many other tasks claiming managers' and clinical leaders' bandwidth. And Meaningful Use is voluntary, while other demands are not.

One can tell those organizations that penalties—significant penalties—are coming. One can tell them the meaningful use will be a critical capability for addressing the demands of looming payment reform. They will acknowledge all of that. But they face extensive, often crushing demands, today. And to meet the demands of today, they may make a perfectly rational decision to forgo Stage 2.

The percent of providers attesting that we see today may represent the near peak of participation in Meaningful Use. No one would view this as success.

Second, given the tight time frames and high energy demands, many providers may hurriedly slam the system in, forgoing many of the necessary process and care delivery changes as they rush to get the Stage 2 payment. Implementing any major application system should be accompanied by the thoughtful re-engineering of processes and practices to ensure that the information technology investment generates as much organizational gain as possible.

What can result? Several years from now we could step back and ask if we can see material improvements in the efficiency, quality and safety of care delivery that should have resulted from the meaningful use of electronic health records. And we could find that we do not see these improvements or the level of gains that we had expected to see.

Again, no one would view this as success.

Time for a Time Out?

The Meaningful Use program is a critical contributor to our country's efforts to improve care delivery. There are many thoughtful, well-conceived and well-executed aspects of the program.

However, as we implement it, we should be mindful of the need to calibrate the pace and direction of change. A delay in Stage 2 would be well advised. Moreover, we should take time to ensure that, as the program progresses, we are seeing evidence that the desired goal of improved outcomes is being achieved. Hence we should assess the gains in care quality, safety and efficiency by providers that have attested to Meaningful Use. And we should assess provider ability to perform associated process re-engineering and care improvement steps needed to optimize investments in electronic health records.

In a season of many sporting events, we are reminded of the value of a time out to assess the situation. As with any team in the middle of a football or basketball game, we have worked hard to get here, and we have a goal in mind. Let's make sure that we get what we came here to get.

John Glaser, Ph.D., is the CEO of Siemens Healthcare's Health Services in Malvern, Pa. He is also a regular contributor to H&HN *Daily.*

Seeing Health Care from Both the Provider's and the Vendor's Viewpoints

December 6, 2012
By John Glaser

© Health Forum, Inc.

I am fortunate to have viewed this industry from different sides and with different perspectives. But as someone once said, just because everything is different doesn't mean anything has changed.

For over 20 years I was a chief information officer at Partners HealthCare and one of its founders, the Brigham and Women's Hospital. Partners, and its member organizations, is one of the greatest academic health centers in the world and justifiably prides itself on the quality of its patient care, research, education and community service.

For the past two years I have been the CEO of Health Services at Siemens, leading its global health care information technology business. Siemens is one of the greatest companies in world, providing a range of products: trains, power plants and imaging modalities in addition to health care information technology. It too is justifiably proud of its products and services.

I have made the transition from a nonprofit organization to a for-profit organization: From an organization that focuses its care delivery on patients in New England to a company that has a presence in 120 countries. From a health system that has an extraordinary academic core to a company that has an extraordinary engineering core. From an organization that has approximately 60,000 employees to a company that has approximately 360,000 employees.

My former CIO colleagues tease me about joining the "dark side." And they ask me if life on this side is materially different from life on the side of the care provider.

So, with the benefit of two years of dark side experience under my belt, I thought I would share some thoughts about what's different on the vendor side and what remains very much the same.

The More Things Change, the More They Stay the Same

Regardless of which side you sit on, the field and its challenges are still the same. As an industry, we are facing greater challenges in every dimension—from reimbursement changes and shifts in the health care business model to preparing for ICD-10 compliance, multistage meaningful use achievement and evolving the EHR to support the accountable care movement. Indeed, I cannot recall a time in my career when there has been more on our collective plates than we are faced with today. And as the bar on a provider's performance keeps getting raised, so too does the bar on the vendor side.

It is clear that the aspiration to improve all that ails health care and the commitment to get it done is just as strong on the vendor side as it is on the provider side. Yes, a vendor has a profit motive, but people choose to join a health care vendor (versus other options available to them) because it shares the mission of its provider colleagues.

This shared belief in mission among both parties is what drives the industry forward, what leads to terrifically successful vendor-provider partnerships, and what fuels our continued collective dedication to sharing best practices, despite the fierce competitiveness that often exists within this industry.

On both sides of the industry, leadership is needed and the skills needed to be a good leader are the same.

It's time for all of us to step forward and exert as much leadership talent as possible, because our organizations are certainly going to need it. We used to talk in the CIO community about being more strategic and stepping up to the leadership table, that leadership is needed more than ever before. On the vendor side the leadership standard has been raised too; rapidly evolving market demands require enhanced product functionality as well as even more efficient and effective implementation services. We must give more substance to the term "solution."

On both sides the skills, experience and talents that make a leader a good leader are the same. Leaders must help their organizations see a path forward in highly uncertain times. Leaders must have the ability to inspire and mobilize others to get things done. They must actively engage in changing the organization. Once committed to the course, they must have the strength to thoughtfully stay the course. These leaders must ask hard questions about the systems and their implementation and whether value is being delivered. And these leaders must be pragmatic; they must be superb practitioners of the art of the possible.

On both sides it takes talented and committed senior leaders to inspire the troops to successfully execute the organization's plans. In fact, over the course of my career, I've come to appreciate just how much influence CEOs, CIOs and other members of the leadership team have on the tone, values and direction of an organization—whether provider or vendor.

Finally, I've learned that skillfully navigating a matrixed organization and influencing a diverse group of colleagues is certainly a required competency in a large global corporation. But these same leadership attributes were also needed in my former academic health care environment. So, when I'm often asked, "How do you manage the organizational complexity of a huge, global company?" I simply respond, "Years of practice."

Yet, Some Things Are Different

Of course, part of what's different now is being exposed to a much broader, global perspective on health care. While it continues to be really interesting to appreciate the range of providers we have in the United States—big, little, rural, academic, tightly integrated, loosely affiliated, ACO leaning or not—and hence their range of needs, it's equally fascinating to see what's unfolding with health systems in Japan, Germany and China, for instance.

I've come to learn over the past two years that across the globe, the practice of health care is very local from market to market, culture to culture. Clearly, the payment systems are diverse. But often equally diverse are the primary health care challenges faced by the country. For some it is access; for others it is cost; and for yet others, public health challenges are more important than medical care challenges. And you might think that the roles of the physician, nurse and pharmacist are the same across countries; but you would be wrong.

This diversity makes developing a global IT solution very difficult and at times impractical. As a vendor you must not only develop approaches to respond to the diversity of health care in the United States, but also the diversity across the globe; the diversity of the challenge of identifying IT solutions that address care needs is broader on the vendor side. How do you optimize a global product portfolio? What are the keys to success in emerging markets where the main barrier to entry is often a variety of cultural and legal mechanisms that favor local companies over global players? Ideal global markets tend to be those that are mature, sizeable, have few technical or other barriers and consist of health care systems similar to those in the United States.

Another difference that exists on the vendor side is the often much crisper and leaner decision making structure. Health systems generally have a consensus approach to making decisions. In the vendor world you would be wise if you ensured that you had sufficient political support for something significant that you want to do. But at the end of the day, as CEO, I get to decide; there is a strong emphasis on accountability.

Additionally, vendors have a much simpler way of measuring their performance. Order volume, gross margin, profit and customer satisfaction sit at the center of metrics that are used to judge success or failure. Nonprofit providers of care also judge themselves based on metrics: admissions, outpatient volume, margin and quality scores. But health systems have a more complex mission than a vendor. Because of this complexity, health systems must often undertake activities that cause them to lose money or for which the value proposition is expressed in terms of phrases such as "address the care needs of the underserved" or "train tomorrow's care providers." Judging the success or failure of a provider is much harder. That complexity of the mission of a provider makes the identification of priorities much more difficult.

If you join a vendor organization, you will find that your vocabulary changes. Sometimes you use different words to express the same idea. A provider might talk about "increase volume for the oncology service line," while a vendor might talk about "top line growth of orders for a product." Same idea—different phrases.

While at Partners I don't think I ever used the word "customer"; now I use it routinely, and patient satisfaction has been replaced by customer satisfaction. Also, my daily acronym usage has shifted from common medical abbreviations like ICU, CABG and H&P to incorporate a host of "corporate speak" acronyms like M&A, SG&A and EBITDA.

On a more serious note, perhaps one of the most potent differences I've felt on the vendor side is simply being one step removed from the reality of the care process. As a CIO I was able to walk the floors, talk to the unit nurses, and come face to face with patients who were benefitting from our IT efforts. In the provider setting, the reality of health care surrounded me all the time—the good and the bad, the joy and the sorrow.

I no longer have those daily experiences, but I understand their importance. These experiences remind me of why I do what I do and the daily life of caregivers. One of the challenges of being a vendor is helping my staff develop an appreciation of the reality of delivering care and managing operational processes that surround care. All vendors would be better at what they do to the degree that their staff "feel" what it is like to take care of someone who is sick, scared and perhaps dying.

We All Play a Part

No matter which side of the industry you sit on, it's going to take all of our effort and hard work to ensure the health care improvement agenda we've embarked upon delivers the intended results. That care is safer and more efficient because the nation's providers are meaningfully using their investments in health care IT. That we are emphasizing outcomes over volume and keeping populations of patients healthy. And perhaps most importantly, that the country is tremendously better off 10 years from now because of the collective work we've done.

Two years ago I left an organization I treasure, a job I loved and colleagues I care deeply about because I was ready for a change and desired professional growth and learning. I made the transition knowing we were in for a remarkable, tumultuous decade and an incredible amount of change. I arrived at my new place of employment with the same level of passion for this industry and the same depth of commitment to making health care better that I had as a CIO.

Yes, I've gone to the dark side, as they say. But oddly enough, once you arrive there, you find it looks very much like the side you left.

John Glaser, Ph.D., is the CEO of Siemens Health Services in Malvern, Pa. He is also a regular contributor to H&HN Daily.

Getting Ready for the Big Dance

November 23, 2010
By John Glaser and M. Kent Locklear

Computerized provider order entry is a complex, yet tractable undertaking.

A small number of core processes determine an organization's excellence. For a restaurant, these processes include purchasing ingredients, preparing food and waiting tables. A restaurant that fails to perform any of these processes well ceases to be in business.

For a hospital, it's determining the next steps in a patient's care delivery and initiating the activities needed to carry out those steps. In fact, it could be argued that this process, generally referred to as provider order entry, is *the* most important process in an inpatient setting. When performed properly, it drives care quality and efficiency. When flawed, it leads to patient safety problems.

This process is also exceptionally complex. In a typical hospital, a provider must make decisions regarding hundreds of medications, procedures and laboratory tests, sometimes all in the same day. These decisions must occur in the right sequence and be continuously adjusted based on a patient's progress. The execution of this process involves dozens of staff members and intricate workflows.

Given the importance of provider order entry, it is not surprising that the federal government's promotion of health information technology—via the HITECH provision of the American Recovery & Reinvestment Act and related Meaningful Use rules for implementation of an electronic health record—places so much emphasis on using computerized physician order entry (CPOE). However, considering the complexity of adopting CPOE and the challenges any organization faces when changing a core process, it's also not surprising that so few hospitals have taken on CPOE.

Still, many organizations, from large academic medical centers to small safety net hospitals, have implemented CPOE successfully. Those who have succeeded can attest that implementing this holy grail of all clinical information systems requires significant change management expertise, time, patience and good old fashioned thick skin.

HITECH has effectively put CPOE in a prom dress, requiring those who wish to pursue stimulus dollars to get ready for the big dance.

Early Adopters Set the Stage

Information gleaned from early CPOE adopters reveals that successful implementations are a result of strong top-down management support, broad-based multi-disciplinary participation and buy-in, and careful analysis of clinical workflows from the outset.

The managers conducting the workflow analysis must understand and support the nursing- and physician-specific activities that end with writing the order and all the downstream workflows that begin with order entry. The computer will not fix broken or malfunctioning workflows.

CPOE adoption experts also stress the importance of usable, appropriate clinical content, in the form of evidenced-based order sets, robust clinical checking capabilities, and prudent alerts and reminders. Most importantly, those who have completed the CPOE journey are realizing demonstrable improvements in patient care, which is central to the goals of HITECH.

Winning at CPOE

While implementing CPOE is a significant organizational undertaking, the experiences of others provide an inventory of important steps.

1. **Secure managers' engagement early and keep them involved.** Simply put:
   - They must understand the project.
   - They must support the project.
   - They must fund the project.

2. **Recognize that CPOE is a team sport.** Multidisciplinary participation is critical, and everyone has a role—physicians, nurses, pharmacists, lab, radiology and IT. Strong leaders such as a medical information officer or physician champion are needed to captain the effort. And remember, this is a clinical project: The clinical team should own it throughout and celebrate it when it is successful. Last, but not least, listen to the end users.

3. **Craft a game plan that fits the organization's unique characteristics.** Each health care organization comes to the table with unique characteristics and

existing approaches to workflow. CPOE should be introduced as a way to enhance and streamline these processes without disrupting the provider's identity. If this isn't done properly, adoption will suffer. Additionally, order set development is a demanding project and must be started early. This is an opportunity to make CPOE quicker, more usable and more effective. It's also a chance to introduce a healthy dose of evidenced-based standardization.

4. **Employ a realistic, flexible training strategy.** Super users are critical. On-unit, face-to-face, real-time training has a winning record among early adopters, as do online tutorials. However, experience has shown that classroom teaching environments do not work well in most settings.

5. **Understand that the computer will not fix flawed processes.** Use this opportunity to analyze and correct suboptimal processes. Take the time to clean up the vague or confusing orders that, in many cases, have been tolerated for years.

6. **Accept that "go live" is critical but it isn't the end point.** The value of having 24/7 support at the point of "go live" and for several months afterward should not be underestimated. Equally important is having a long-term plan for system review and enhancement after the dust begins to settle.

7. **Show up with the right equipment.** This includes both software and hardware. The solutions must be accessible, usable and reliable. Remote access is a big selling point, and mobile devices are now a permanent fixture of the workplace. From a hardware standpoint, think about location, access and flexibility.

8. **Implement a smart content strategy.** Develop a content strategy early in the process and deploy it in a thoughtful manner with input and buy-in from physicians and nurses. Beware of "alert fatigue"—clinicians' tendency to ignore medical alerts when they become excessive.

9. **Communicate, communicate, communicate.** There is no better way to engage the community than to provide timely updates on project milestones, key successes and even challenges—including what's being done to overcome the obstacles. In addition, as the organization collects pre- and post-metrics, share information.

10. **Allow for mourning.** This is an inevitable consequence that tends to go hand and hand with change. Be supportive, but firm. "No crying over CPOE!"

At its heart, CPOE implementation is a clinical project involving information technology—not the other way around. It is incumbent on vendors to deliver software that supports the clinical workflow and to facilitate implementations that leverage the benefits of the technology. By establishing a true partnership for success between vendors, their customers and consultants alike, we all win, the ultimate goal being safer patient care and improved clinical outcomes.

John Glaser, Ph.D., is the CEO of Siemens Healthcare Health Services in Malvern, Pa. He is also a regular contributor to H&HN Weekly. *Kent Locklear, M.D./M.B.A., is the director of physician strategy for Siemens Healthcare Health Services.*

Reprinted from H&HN Hospitals & Health Networks, by permission, November 2010, ©2010 by Health Forum, Inc.

The Federal Electronic Health Record Strategy

July 6, 2010
By John Glaser

© Health Forum, Inc.

The HITECH Act's financial incentives for EHR implementation will create a challenge for many health care organizations, but will lead to more effective use and better care.

The federal electronic health record strategy will transform health care information technology and profoundly impact the delivery of health care in this country. The strategy, part of the American Recovery and Reinvestment Act (ARRA), provides financial incentives to hospitals based on their use of EHRs.

Four observations can be made about the strategy, which is detailed in the Health Information Technology for Economic and Clinical Health (HITECH) sections of ARRA:

Meaningful Use

For decades the health care information technology industry has tracked the number of hospitals that have adopted applications such as computerized physician order entry systems. But tracking adoption has an obvious flaw: It does not mean that providers are using the technology or that care is being improved. It does not, per se, lead to complete documentation of a patient's problems or cause providers to do a good job of managing the health of their patients.

HITECH provides financial incentives to hospitals and other providers that make "meaningful use" of EHRs. Among other requirements, hospitals and providers must use EHRs to engage patients, improve care coordination, ensure privacy and reduce disparities. This approach says that if our goal is care improvement, adoption is relevant only if the technology is used well. It shifts our attention from adoption to use.

In addition, while providers must report quality data, they do not need to prove in the early phases that specific improvements occur. The writers of the legislation understood that meaningful care improvement will take more time than the initial ARRA timetables allow. And they understood that while EHRs are an essential foundation for care improvement, additional factors must also be present.

Most importantly, to achieve significant gains in care outcomes, providers require reimbursement that explicitly rewards them for improvements in care quality, safety and efficiency. The recently passed Patient Protection and Affordable Care Act initiates payment reform for federal programs.

Meaningful use moves the industry away from a focus on adoption but does not overstep that movement by leaping all the way to outcomes.

Incentives

The federal strategy provides Medicare and Medicaid financial incentives to encourage the meaningful use of EHRs. Initially these incentives take the form of additional reimbursement that can total millions of dollars for hospitals and tens of thousands of dollars for eligible professionals. But after a period of time the hospitals will receive penalties if they don't reach certain goals.

While the additional reimbursement will not necessarily cover the full costs of an EHR, it is substantial. And the industry can expect that the federal incentives will be amplified.

Private sector purchasers of care may target pay-for-performance contracts based on the assumption that the provider is already a meaningful user. The contracts may assume that e-prescribing is being done and quality measures are being reported. Such contracts may compel the provider to go beyond the meaningful use goals.

Once about 40 percent to 50 percent of the providers in a region have adopted an EHR, those who haven't may find they need to adopt in order to compete. Primary care physicians may discover that it is easier to deal with specialists who use EHRs; data exchange is faster and the information exchanged is more complete. At this point, the motives for EHR use change from garnering incentives to ensuring sufficient business.

While the patient protection act focuses on insurance coverage, within that legislation are sections that lay the foundation for payment reform. In the next couple of years providers can reasonably expect that the federal and state governments will base a significant amount of reimbursement on demonstrating care quality, safety and efficiency. In effect, the government is noting that with the broad adoption of electronic health records it can now engage in more ambitious outcomes-based reimbursement.

The ARRA's meaningful use incentives provide a foundation for further incentives that are likely to lead to very high EHR adoption and use.

The Changing Meaning of EHR

In many ways current EHRs are defined according to the functions and content of their paper predecessors and by the clinical operations of providing care. Hence, we understand that the EHR must support access to patient data and allow us to order a radiology procedure. But we will increasingly come to view EHRs as the set of capabilities necessary to achieve meaningful use and support the new reimbursement schemes that result from payment reform.

For example, as a result of meaningful use, EHRs are now expected to include the ability to submit data to public health laboratories. Payment reform will cause us to expect EHRs to include disease registries and software that supports care team collaboration.

Given the magnitude of the incentives, a large portion of the development agenda for EHR vendors will be driven by the need to support meaningful use and the requirements of payment reform. Medicare and Medicaid reimbursement demands will come to dominate EHR development and may crowd out other development requests from customers. Vendors who cannot meet the demands based on government reimbursement may disappear from the market.

The Complexity and Scope of the Federal Strategy

The federal EHR strategy has altered the industry through incentives linked to meaningful use; changes to the EHR certification process; and the identification of EHR data, transaction and privacy standards. However, the strategy goes beyond those changes.

Most of the care in this country is delivered by small physician groups and hospitals that do not have an information technology staff. Regional extension centers have been established to provide necessary IT support to those providers.

A health information exchange infrastructure needs to be in place so individual patient data as well as population data can move securely. Funds have been given to the states to establish this infrastructure, and a plan to establish an over-arching national health information network is being developed.

The country will need to increase the size of the workforce available to support EHR adoption and use. Funds are being awarded to educators to provide necessary training and curricula.

Funding will go to beacon communities, which will help us understand how best to leverage the technology to improve the health of a community. They will also teach us how to address important issues of governance, data use and coordination of care.

Advanced health information technology research centers have been set up to provide ground-breaking research into security, new EHR architectural models, decision support and secondary uses of data.

These federally funded implementation activities are breathtaking in their scope and sophistication. And the activities are the result of an astute assessment of the range of "levers," in addition to incentives, that should be applied to achieve meaningful use.

However, initiating so many diverse initiatives that have a significant impact on multiple parts of the industry comes with some risk.

Bumps in the Road to Universal Adoption

It is not possible to launch this much activity of this scope with this many actors and have great certainty about the outcome. This uncertainty will be magnified by the evolving actions of the private sector—hospitals, health plans, suppliers and others that are engaging in a diverse array of often very imaginative implementation activities.

The implementation plans are good plans. Change of this magnitude will bring very real progress, but it will also bring a period of time that is likely to be bumpy.

The federal electronic health record strategy has been formed and the country is at the start of its implementation. The strategy is ambitious, multifaceted and sophisticated. This journey faces many uncertainties and will not be easy. However, the strategy has a high likelihood of causing many health care organizations to make meaningful use of EHRs and improving the health care delivered in this country.

John Glaser is a vice president and the CIO of Partners HealthCare in Boston. He is also a regular contributor to H&HN Weekly.

Reprinted from H&HN Hospitals & Health Networks, by permission, July 2010, ©2010 by Health Forum, Inc.

Boundary Erosion in Information Technology

January 12, 2010
By John Glaser

Careful planning is needed to ensure rewards outweigh risks as IT moves off-site.

For many years, organizations have talked about their applications using their data running on their infrastructure in their data center supported by their information technology staff and used by their employees and medical staff.

"Their" encompassed management oversight of the direction and use of IT assets, control over organizational capital and operating investments in the assets, ownership of the assets, and the assets being located on site.

But the reality of "their" has been changing.

Minicomputers, followed by personal computers, led to departments and individuals engaging in IT acquisitions and use that were barely or not at all controlled by the organization. Meanwhile, some provider organizations have been running applications on hardware located off site through a shared service arrangement. More recently, software as a service and cloud computing enable organizations to function using someone else's applications and infrastructure.

Outsourcing provides the organization the ability to leverage someone else's IT staff.

Value and Risk

This erosion in the boundaries around the organization's IT assets provides value. Organizations can share capital costs with others and turn over the routine management of infrastructure to vendors that are more efficient and skilled. Individuals using personal computers have been able to improve productivity and data analysis capacity. Obtaining staff through outsourcing has enabled health care organizations to access scarce talent and ease the challenge of flexible staffing needs.

At the same time, this trend has created risks. The use of software as a service potentially exposes the organization to external infrastructure management and application development limitations. Individual use of personal computers can lead to undisciplined and difficult-to-support software development. Outsourcing arrangements can turn sour.

As the boundaries wear away, the pursuit of potential value has had to be accompanied by a mature appreciation of risks and the development of sufficient contractual arrangements, knowledgeable assessment of service or resource provider's capabilities, organizational policies and management mechanisms to assess and enforce controls.

Consumer-Oriented Technologies' Impact

The weakening of IT boundaries is continuing. The two most significant contributors to this erosion are Web 2.0 technologies and consumer computing devices, which are becoming integral components of the organization's IT assets.

Web 2.0 technologies include social networking sites such as Facebook, Sermo and MySpace. They also include sites that support shared knowledge development, such as Wikipedia. Both types of sites have exploded in recent years; there are more than 50,000,000 users of Facebook in the United States, and more than half are older than 25. Wikipedia has more than 3,000,000 articles in English.

Many clinicians and staff use these technologies, which provide personal and professional value. Social networking sites help staff members locate others with common professional interests, engage with communities that are important to the organization and identify professionals or companies that can provide needed information, services or products. Physicians and other clinicians use social networking sites to seek the advice of other clinicians and to learn more about issues and challenges related to living with a chronic disease.

Knowledge sites, such as Wikipedia, are an easy way to access current and accurate information. Clinicians and staff also contribute to these sites, advancing the ability of others to deliver care and manage organizations and departments.

Consumer computing devices, such as the iPhone and the Blackberry, include a range of very potent technologies. These are powerful computers, and they have led to a stunning array of applications that are very inexpensive. Moreover, these devices offer full access to resources available through the Internet. They also support the user's ability to work from almost anywhere and often extend the organization's electronic health record by providing access to knowledge resources, image viewers and integration with medical devices.

As with other boundary-eroding technologies and services, risks are introduced. Staff members may view their contributions to social networking sites as a form of backyard conversation. The informality of these sites may lead a user to forget that he or she may be seen as a representative of the organization rather than a friendly neighbor. Staff members may not understand that a response to one individual may have been seen by many and, unlike a remark over the back fence, remains online long after the conversation ends. Social networking sites often bring a false sense of anonymity, resulting in individuals behaving in ways that they would find embarrassing in a meeting with colleagues.

Consumer computing devices pose a different form of risk. Clinicians and staff members often store patient data or sensitive organization information on these devices, not realizing the increasing legal and regulatory consequences if the device is lost or stolen. Users often will assume that all of the organization's applications should work on the device and that device problems are the IT department's responsibility.

Finding Balance

Health care and other industries are struggling to find the right balance between reaping the benefits of Web 2.0 technologies and consumer computing devices, while protecting the organization from the incipient risks.

This struggle occurs every time a new boundary-eroding technology or service arrives. Decades ago, organizations established "microcomputer" committees to control personal computer acquisition and develop microcomputer use policies. In the last decade, countless articles and conferences were held to help organizations understand the benefits and challenges of outsourcing.

There is no quick and easy path to a mature understanding of the balance. Time is needed to gain experience and perspective. Thoughtful review of early efforts at use and control are needed to separate overly optimistic hype and unnecessarily gloomy projections of grave risk from the realities of use.

Health care organizations also should avoid taking an extreme position on these types of technologies. Boundary erosion is an underlying, unalterable trend in information technology. It will not reverse itself. Neither an unbridled embrace nor blanket dismissal of these technologies has ever been the eventual outcome. A careful balance of risk and reward is far more likely.

John Glaser is a vice president and the CIO of Partners HealthCare in Boston and a regular contributor to H&HN Weekly.

Taking Care in EHR Adoption

October 19, 2009
By John Glaser

As more and more systems take on electronic health records, we need reminders that the EHR is a tool: It can be used well, or it can be used badly.

The number of providers adopting interoperable electronic health records (EHRs) is about to skyrocket. This is due to a number of factors, including federal and state government incentives that have been linked to the effective use of EHRs. These incentives will be complemented by the pay-for-performance programs taken on by a wide range of purchasers of care.

In addition, electronic health records have become part of the mainstream of care delivery organization strategies and plans. EHR adoption is no longer the province of pioneers; increasingly a provider is at risk of looking "out of touch" if he or she has no plans to go online. Indeed, a growing cohort of young and middle-aged physicians, for whom information technology is a given, have come to expect advanced capabilities.

With this impending increase in adoption, we need to keep in mind a few things about EHRs. They're not magic bullets—they require thoughtful implementation and planning if they're going to bring about positive changes. In addition, it will be difficult to predict how quickly and where they will be adopted. Finally, they will likely bring about changes greater than first imagined.

EHRs Are a Tool

We know that EHRs are a necessary foundation for the transformation of health care. However, we must never forget that EHRs are a tool and have no inherent magical properties that can transform care.

Tools can be leveraged thoughtfully and with great skill to achieve desired results. Tools can also be applied in ways that lead to disappointing results or make the situation worse. (Those who have engaged in weekend fix-it projects understand this well.)

Improving care will require the deployment of the appropriate tools *and* require clinical and administrative leadership, careful process redesign, terrific support and ongoing evaluation of impact. Patients and purchasers will care little about possession of the tool; they will care about results.

Moreover, the industry's fixation on adoption metrics will need to shift to an emphasis on effectiveness of use and care outcomes. Outcomes also help assess the ability of a well-implemented tool to be used to deliver value. The tool called the EHR may not always be the right tool—no more than the hammer is the right tool for all fix-it projects.

Adoption Will Be Difficult to Predict

With the increase in adoption will come efforts to predict where we will be some number of years from now. There is some utility to these estimates—they can project purchaser incentive outlays. However, for the most part, the value of these estimation exercises is largely to engender interesting conference-panel discussions and provide fodder for after-conference libations.

It has always been difficult to predict technology adoption. Adoption is driven by the interaction of many complex factors that can generally be understood retrospectively rather than prospectively. One can explain the adoption patterns of the television, the telephone and the automobile after the fact; predicting their absorption into the fabric of society would have been difficult.

The factors influencing EHR adoption today are different now than they were five years ago. The incentives are more significant. The technology is better. The organizational understanding of the importance of information technology is deeper and more sophisticated. The urgency to "fix health care" is much more pronounced.

The difference in the nature and intensity of factors will also result in innovations that will help accelerate the increase. These innovations will occur in technology and business models and will affect EHR usability and features, implementation strategies and support mechanisms. The innovations will not result in EHR-enabled transformation of care being a no-fuss, no-muss proposition, but they will ease the challenge and lead to accelerated adoption.

The Future Must Be Assessed

The industry is very fixated on the near-term challenges of improving care through EHR adoption and effective use. But we must also begin to assess the opportunities, challenges and problems that will result from the broad adoption of interoperable EHRs.

The country will have opportunities to engage in the secondary use of EHR data for comparative effectiveness of medications and treatments, post-market surveillance for medication safety and translational research. These opportunities hold great promise. But they are also poorly understood and prey to wishful thinking.

Interoperable EHRs will improve the ability of a provider to have a complete clinical picture of a patient. But there is a risk that we will overwhelm the provider, who may find himself or herself asking, "Which of these 200 notes contains information about the patient's potential thyroid condition?" We will need to understand the decision support and other strategies that can help the provider take advantage of the data rather than be crushed by it.

The extensive use of wireless networks, personal devices and Web 2.0 patient communities will be leveraged by an extensive base of interoperable EHRs. The combination of these technologies should enable material gains in patient engagement. However, we have limited insight into the most significant leverage opportunities.

These futures (and others) will be upon us shortly (in several ways and cases, these futures are here now). Rather than react when they arrive, we should proactively guide them.

The Impact of EHRs Will Be More Extensive Than Care Improvements

Organization theorists believe that the form of organizations is determined by efforts to design the flow of information within the organization, such as formal hierarchies to filter information to the top and between organizations. When, for example, do you buy a service from another organization, and when do you create your own?

Health care is only one of many fields that grapple with questions of form. The structure of the education system and professions is driven by definitions of core sets of information that must be mastered; those definitions change from time to time. The country's approach to war, for example, was altered by the advent of television, which delivered real-time information from the front line to homes during the Vietnam War. And the Internet has badly damaged traditional distributors of information—newspapers, most notably.

Industries, organizations and society change when the information changes—when it becomes more frictionless, less costly, more accessible and more immediate.

What will this mean to the form, structure and interactions that exist between physician offices, hospitals, patients, regulators and purchasers of care? It's hard to visualize the answer. However, it is difficult to believe that the broad adoption and effective use of EHRs won't result in possible material changes to the structure of the health care industry.

Manage the Change

The acceleration of EHR adoption will change us, in good ways. It is difficult to predict the pace, depth and breadth of impact of this change. However, this change is not automatic; we can assess and manage it.

John Glaser is a vice president and the CIO of Partners HealthCare in Boston and a regular contributor to H&HN Weekly.

Health Care's Progressive Transformation

August 18, 2009
By John Glaser

© Health Forum, Inc.

The pace of IT adoption in health care may trouble outsiders, but leaders and clinicians understand why a more measured approach makes sense.

Health care is often accused of lagging behind other industries in applying information technology (IT). Statistics, such as percentage of revenue spent on IT, are used to justify this indictment. Granted, while health care's annual spend of 2.7 percent is lower than the 5 percent that information-intensive industries such as banking invest, it is the same as the average percentage across all industries.

This is often coupled with charges that health care executives are not as "on top of it" as executives in other industries and that clinicians inherently resist information technology and doggedly embrace paper. In fact, health care's complexity makes it very challenging to implement major IT applications such as the electronic health record (EHR). This does not excuse institutions and clinicians from having to make thoughtful IT investments in EHRs. Instead, we must understand and embrace health care's unique characteristics if we hope to improve care by leveraging the power of IT.

As an industry, health care's key differentiators include the following:

Large Numbers of Small Organizations

Health care is composed of numerous very small organizations. The majority of physicians practice in offices with four or fewer doctors, and thousands of hospitals have fewer than 100 beds.

These organizations' size makes it is difficult for them to fund IT purchases. A $25,000 investment in an EHR may be more than a solo practitioner can manage. Additionally, small practices and hospitals find it difficult to hire and retain IT staff who can assist in implementation and provide ongoing support.

On the other side of the transaction, software and hardware vendors have a hard time making money on these sales—they often can't recover their costs of selling and providing support. As a result, major vendors tend to avoid small organizations.

Incentive Misalignment

Many health IT applications have the potential to improve the quality of care. Computerized provider order entry can reduce adverse drug events, and reminder systems in the EHR can improve the management of the chronically ill patient.

Providers bear the costs of these systems, but they do not always reap the rewards. The insurance payment mechanisms may not provide a financial incentive for the provider that has fewer medical errors or better manages its diabetic patients. Because of this misalignment, providers are rightfully hesitant to fully bear the costs of systems that have quality improvement as their goal. For them, the IT investment reduces their income.

This type of misalignment rarely occurs in other industries. For example, a bank that invests in technology to improve the quality of its service can expect to be rewarded by having more customers and having existing customers do more business.

Fragmented Care

Over the course of their lives, most individuals will seek care in several organizations, often across several regions of the country. A patient may not remember all of the providers he or she has seen. And any one provider may not know which other providers have data about the patient.

It's not uncommon for patients and others outside health care to complain that if they can withdraw money from their bank from anywhere in the world, they ought to be able to access their medical records as easily. This disingenuous statement fails to acknowledge that no one bank has any understanding of an individual's financial holdings in other banks. Moreover, the customer knows exactly which bank has the funds he or she seeks to withdraw. Assembling a complete clinical picture of a patient from an idiosyncratic distribution of data across an unknown set of possibly dozens of organizations is a far more complex undertaking.

Process of Care

If the process of care is viewed through the lens of manufacturing—for example, sick people are inputs, a "bunch of stuff" is done to them and better or well people emerge—it can be argued that medical care is the most complex manufacturing process that exists. This process has three major challenges: defining the best care, care process variability and process volatility.

First, while standards of care exist in some areas, such as with diabetes, there are areas where best care practices have not been broadly accepted or developed.

Second, great variability in treatment can occur. In an academic medical center, a physician may be able to order one of 2,500 medications and 300 radiology procedures. The sequence of these orders, along with patient condition and comorbidity, all determine the relative utility of a particular approach to treatment.

Nonetheless, care guidelines are developed that reduce this variability. However, in an average year, hundreds of thousands of articles are added to the base of refereed medical literature, and new medical technologies are introduced that can lead to a need to continuously revisit guideline consensus.

All application systems are formalisms, meaning they reduce workflow, logic and data to a set of software rules. Designing applications that "structure" the process of care in terms of rules is challenging.

Health and Medical Data

The health status and medical condition of a patient can be difficult to describe using comprehensive, coded data. Structured vocabularies exist for many key sets of medical data, such as diseases, yet clinicians can find these expressions inadequate to describe the patient's condition. Additionally, there are often complex relationships between sets of medical data.

And although research is ongoing, well-accepted methods to formally break down the key components of the patient record into coded concepts have not yet been developed. Even when the data model has been developed and coded terms defined, the entry of coded data rather than ordinary text into the record is cumbersome and constraining for the provider.

The Nature of Provider Organizations

Health care organizations, particularly providers, have attributes that can hinder IT adoption. Among all types of organizations, provider organizations are unusual in that they have two parallel power structures: administration and the medical staff. The medical staff is often loosely organized and does not have clear lines of authority.

This structure requires a very high degree of negotiation and coalition building. This can result in lengthy application acquisition decision-making and protracted discussions on the extent of use of applications.

The Path Ahead

Despite health care's complexity, the industry is making significant progress. Advances are being made in developing inexpensive, very robust EHRs for small provider organizations. The health care IT sections of the American Recovery and Reinvestment Act (ARRA) have taken a significant step in addressing the challenges of misaligned incentives and EHR interoperability. The care process is complex, but the appropriate way to manage many diseases is well understood. There are established data standards for diseases, procedures and laboratory tests.

And there are multiple, notable examples of organizations that have confronted the complexity of health care and demonstrated impressive care quality, safety and efficiency gains.

The application of IT does face daunting challenges of complexity in health care. While these challenges must be understood and respected, they are not insurmountable.

John Glaser is vice president and CIO of Partners HealthCare in Boston and a regular contributor to H&HN Weekly.

Health Care IT Progress Report

April 17, 2009
By John Glaser

Advances in IT adoption during the past four years will help health care leaders to tackle several additional challenges.

Health care information technology (IT) today is in a different place from where it was four years ago. A new president, a new congress and economic stimulus funds for incentives, grants and loans have made the adoption of interoperable electronic health records a priority. While policymakers and health care leaders define the adoption agenda for the next four years, it is an excellent time to consider health IT's progress during the last four years. These reflections reveal both progress and work that remains.

Hard Work Pays Off

Public and private groups led efforts to increase IT adoption and standards development.

EHRs become a national priority. Interoperable electronic health records are now a permanent fixture on federal and state government agendas, and a topic for discussion among senior leadership across all health care stakeholder organizations. This level of interest did not exist four years ago.

IT adoption grows. While health information technology adoption remains low, it has increased. In 2006, 46 percent of community hospitals reported moderate or high use of health IT, compared to 37 percent of community hospitals in 2005. A 2007 survey found that almost 40 percent of physicians use a basic electronic health record, up from 29 percent in 2006.

Incentive programs gain traction. The absence of financial incentives and access to capital has been a major barrier to broad EHR adoption. However, a diverse array of incentive programs has been introduced, including programs from several health plans. Examples include a program to encourage e-prescribing from the Centers for Medicare & Medicaid Services and a Massachusetts law that requires EHR and computerized provider order entry adoption by providers over the next several years.

National groups propel standards development. Several important national bodies have been created to advance the development of interoperability standards and EHR certification.

The Certification Commission for Healthcare Information Technology (CCHIT) has implemented certification standards for outpatient and inpatient electronic health records. Since 2006, CCHIT has certified 136 ambulatory products.

The Healthcare Information Technology Standards Panel (HITSP) has approved interoperability standards in results reporting, public health reporting, genomic/genetic test data and biosurveillance based on input from nearly 400 participating organizations.

Finally, the National eHealth Collaborative (the successor to the American Health Information Community) is focused on developing strategies to further EHR adoption and interoperability, including standards development.

Health information exchanges achieve sustainability. While many health information exchanges (HIEs) struggle to find a sustainable business model, there have been notable successes in Cincinnati (HealthBridge), Indianapolis (IHIE), Massachusetts (MA-SHARE), New York (Bronx RHIO) and Vermont (VITL). These efforts have successfully tackled governance, financial sustainability, exchange implementation and support and can serve as models for other HIEs.

Health IT body of research expands. The federal government has funded demonstrations of aspects of a National Health Information Network (NHIN), studies of EHR adoption progress and evaluations of HIEs' and EHRs' impact on care quality, safety and costs. These efforts have materially advanced our understanding of the architecture, value and challenges of interoperable electronic health records.

Hurdles on the Horizon

While we have made real progress, real challenges remain.

EHR adoption remains low. Only 4 percent of all physicians report using an extensive, fully functional EHR, and the adoption rate in large practices is four times higher than small practices. Five percent of small hospitals have an advanced electronic health record compared to 35 percent in large hospitals.

EHR return on investment is insufficient. While a variety of groups are creating financial incentives for EHR adoption, the current inducements are generally not sufficient or broadly available. For the provider, the implementation of an EHR often represents a commitment to a difficult implementation that results in a financial loss.

Small practices and hospitals lack support. EHR implementation requires technical and training support and guidance on process re-engineering. The means to provide this support for small and rural provider organizations are largely non-existent. These organizations cannot afford—and may not be able to find—the necessary technical expertise.

Interoperability business case is weak. For most providers, the business case to invest in regional or national interoperability is not compelling. Such investments can divert capital from pressing internal needs and may also be viewed as counter to an organization's competitive strategy.

Vendors question standards' value. A large number of application vendors have pursued CCHIT certification. However, market adoption of the interoperability standards developed by HITSP has been low and is related to the weak business case.

Implementation does not guarantee effective use. EHR adoption does not mean that the system is used effectively or will improve patient care. Problem lists can be incomplete, and e-prescribing can be used on occasion rather than consistently by clinicians. Improvements in chronic disease management are not an automatic result of adoption. The national focus on adoption has lost sight of the importance of effective technology use. Mechanisms are needed to work with providers to ensure that the implemented EHRs result in care improvements.

Privacy risks remain. While EHRs can clearly be applied to improve care delivery, they also pose privacy challenges. These challenges will be compounded by the broad availability of interoperability. The country has not achieved a national consensus on how to achieve the balance between improving care, supporting provider workflow and protecting a patient's privacy.

The last four years have seen great progress in the nation's efforts to increase the adoption of interoperable electronic health records and leverage those investments to improve the quality, safety and efficiency of care. However, significant challenges remain. The gains of the last four years should offer momentum as we continue to make progress in the next four years.

John Glaser is vice president and CIO of Partners HealthCare in Boston, senior advisor, Deloitte Center for Health Solutions, and a regular contributor to H&HN Weekly.

Four Challenges in Personalized Medicine

October 1, 2008
By John Glaser

Unraveling the role of our genome will alter medical care in very fundamental and profound ways. Today, genetic tests have become mainstream practice for some cancers in identifying treatment strategies. As an indication of what the future might hold, genetic analyses indicate that asthma, hypertension and Alzheimer's have many genes in common. Will their treatment eventually be similar, as well?

The effective introduction of personalized medicine broadly across medical practice will require that we address four challenges. These challenges are in addition to the medical science progress needed to understand the specifics of the relationships between our genome, the environment and our health.

Electronic Health Record. The EHR will need to be modified to incorporate patient genetic information and decision support. With the rapid decline in the cost of analyzing very large segments of the genome or the entire genome, it is likely that the EHR will need to store the entire genome (and not just the results of specific genetic tests). Methods for identifying how one stores the whole genome and what data and interoperability standards to use must be defined.

The problem list may be altered to store "possible problems" that are identified through the use of disease-predictive algorithms based on genetic test results. In addition, we will also need to store genome-derived information about medication dosage adjustments that may need to be made for certain drugs.

Moreover, we do not know how to present to a provider (or patient) hundreds (perhaps thousands) of genetic test results in a way that is quickly comprehensible.

Reimbursement. Reimbursement for genetic testing is a complex terrain for health insurers. (*Coverage and Reimbursement of Genetic Tests and Services, Secretary's Advisory Committee on Genetics, Health and Society, HHS, 2006*).

- The clinical validity of some tests is uncertain.
- A genetic test of a child may indicate a high probability of a disease much later in life. Remedial and monitoring care could last for decades, e.g., brain imaging to monitor for signs of a potential stroke. How does one cost effectively insure for this potential?
- Health insurers are hesitant to cover new technologies that have an insufficient base of evidence of beneficial care outcomes.
- Genetic tests may also point to potential problems for which there are no therapeutic or treatment options.
- There may be little likelihood that the costs of the tests and treatments will be recovered in the short term.
- The tests may be done for purely informational purposes.

All of these complexities may mean that reimbursement is slow to occur and uneven.

Privacy. The discussion of privacy treats all genetic test results the same. This is not correct. A genetic test that indicates a high probably of early adult dementia should be kept very private. However, a genetic test that indicates the need to adjust a medication dose may be seen as no more private than any other piece of an individual's health record data.

Genetic data has a unique combination of characteristics (*McGuire, A., et al., Confidentiality, Privacy, and Security of Genetic and Genomic Test Information in Electronic Health Records, Genetics in Medicine, 2008*). The data can be used to identify a specific individual. Genetic data can be used to predict the likelihood of a disease or health issue, does not change over the course of a person's life, is easy to obtain (e.g., a discarded coffee cup) and provides information about others (e.g., if I know your genetic test results, I may also have learned about your siblings). While the combination is unique, many specific characteristics are similar to other types of health care data. For example, one can predict that a person with a Body Mass Index of 40 is at high risk of diabetes.

The Genetic Information Nondiscrimination Act (GINA) made it illegal to deny employment and health insurance on the basis of genetic data. GINA eases some of the concerns associated with genetic information privacy, but society and the law have yet to develop a mature approach to handling this data.

Education. In 2005, genetic tests were available for approximately 1,200 diseases (*Hudson, K., et al., Oversight of US Genetic Testing Laboratories, Nature Biotechnology, 2006*), and this number is growing rapidly. Companies such as 23andme offer consumers testing services on large portions of their genome.

Most providers cannot keep up with the growth in genetic tests. They don't know what the tests do, the validity of the tests, the clinical situation that would benefit from the tests and how to interpret the results. Consumers may be very ignorant of the power and the pitfalls of tests of their genome—e.g., they may not appreciate that some genetic test results will be false positives.

Medical professional societies, health care consumer advocacy groups and the general press have a very significant education challenge. This challenge is exacerbated by the very rapid explosion in genetic knowledge, the complexity of the knowledge and the large volume of tests.

Rapid advances in understanding our genome will enable a health care future for our grandchildren that could be very different from the care we receive today. Lethal diseases may become chronic diseases. Life expectancy might increase. Care could be significantly safer, more efficient and more effective. To help ensure that those who follow us see that future, we must address these four challenges.

John Glaser is vice president and CIO of Partners HealthCare in Boston, senior advisor, Deloitte Center for Health Solutions, and a regular contributor to Most Wired Online.

The Tiering of EHR Adoption

May 21, 2008
By John Glaser

A critical objective of the nation's health information technology agenda is accelerating the adoption of the electronic health record (EHR). While uneven, adoption is increasing. However, adoption is leading to tiers or categories of effectiveness of EHR use. In the lowest tier, adoption has not occurred. In the highest tier, the adopting organization has developed the means to leverage the technology to effect ongoing improvements in patient care and operations.

To the degree that organizations are not in the highest tier, the potential of the EHR is diminished. In addition, the challenges associated with moving between tiers are not the same across all tiers.

Tier 1—Non-adoption

The lowest, and largest, tier is occupied by organizations that have not adopted the electronic health record.

In 2006, 34 percent of hospitals with more than 500 beds had high or sophisticated usage of health IT, whereas only 5 percent of hospitals with fewer than 50 beds had such usage (*Continued Progress: Hospital Use of Information Technology, American Hospital Association, 2007*).

A 2006 survey of EHR adoption by physicians (*Health Information Technology in the United States: The Information Base for Progress, Robert Wood Johnson Foundation,*

2006) found that 11 percent of physicians were using a "full" EHR, 13 percent were using a "partial" EHR and 76 percent were using no EHR. In physician practices with 11 or more physicians, 20 percent of physicians reported having an EHR that supported the ordering of prescriptions and tests, capture of physician notes, and ability to retrieve patient results. For solo practitioners, only 4 percent reported having these capabilities.

The barriers to moving to Tier 2 (adoption) are well understood (at least at a high level): insufficient financial incentives, lack of access to capital, limited ability to obtain support for implementation and privacy concerns.

Tier 2—Adoption but Little Value

There are organizations that have adopted the EHR or are well on their way to completing adoption. However, many of these organizations have not obtained the value that EHR's enable or have achieved significantly less than the potential value.

A study of EHR adoption (*Thompson, Healthcare Financial Management, 2007*) found that about 50 percent of organizations were able to reduce costs. A review of 100 studies on the impact of clinical decision support (*Garg, JAMA, 2005*) noted that 64 percent of studies reported improved practitioner performance but only 13 percent observed an improvement in patient outcomes.

Undoubtedly, some of these organizations believe that the act of installing the technology will automatically result in value. Others will rightfully note that their objectives focused on some value goals but not others; their goal was to improve quality but not necessarily to reduce costs. However, most of the organizations in this tier probably do not know how (or are insufficiently skilled) to carry out the process and behavior changes necessary to achieve a healthy amount of value.

The barriers to moving to Tier 3 (High Value Achievement) are well understood. Achieving a significant "ROI" on an information technology investment requires organizational leadership, clear goals and objectives, well managed process and behavior change, skilled and high performance teams, solid project management and capable information technology.

Tier 3—High Value Achievement

Notable examples exist of organizations that have achieved significant and multifaceted returns on their EHR investment. The industry celebrates, as it should, these accomplishments, e.g., the HIMSS Davies Award. These organizations have surmounted the barriers in moving from Tier 2 to Tier 3.

The core risk for organizations in this tier is that they treat value achievement as one large project that has a finite duration. In other words, once desired value is achieved, the project is done and the organization moves on to some other major initiative.

Although value will have been achieved, these providers may fail to understand that achieving value should be a never-ending organizational activity. There is never a time when an organization can say, "Our care and efficiency are so spectacular that there is no way to make ourselves better." During implementation, the organization may not have focused on establishing the organizational ability to continuously achieve value.

The requirements for moving to Tier 4 (Sustained Value Achievement) can be found in a series of studies that have examined organizations that are very effective users of information technology over long periods of time. Sustained value realization requires leadership focus on continuous improvement, very talented individuals in key positions, great relationships between the IT department and the rest of the organization, well-crafted technical architecture, thoughtful approaches to assessing and managing initiatives, prudent experimentation and a strong alignment between the IT agenda and the organization's strategy.

Tier 4—Sustained Value Achievement

A small number of organizations have achieved the status of Tier 4. These organizations are engaged in continuous efforts to improve care and operations through the effective leveraging of their electronic health record investments. And there is substantial evidence that these efforts are delivering the desired returns. Example organizations include Geisinger and the Veterans Health Administration.

A Tier 4 organization has successfully navigated each of the previous tiers and had the organizational skill, commitment and flexibility to address the range of challenges that confront each tier.

Observations

How many of the nation's providers are in each tier? The answer is not clear. EHR adoption is low for hospitals and physician practices, and there is an adoption digital divide. Larger hospitals and physician offices have higher adoption rates, and the rates that are increasing. Small hospitals and physician practices have adoption rates in the single digits, and these rates are not moving quickly.

Of those who have adopted (Tier 2), what percent have moved into Tier 3? An accurate figure does not appear to be available, but it is likely that less than 50 percent of Tier 2 organizations have moved into Tier 3.

The percent of Tier 3 organizations that move into Tier 4 is also not clear. However, the percentage may be higher than 50 percent. Those organizations that have experienced firsthand the power of the technology are likely to continue to pursue improvement opportunities after the EHR implementation has been completed. The effectiveness of these efforts may be uneven, but the desire to pursue is likely.

Regardless of the estimates of the percent of organizations in each tier, it is safe to conclude that the number of provider organizations that are leveraging the technology well is much smaller than the number of organizations that have adopted the technology.

National electronic health record strategies are often centered on furthering adoption. It is important that these strategies continue, given the low adoption rates. However, it is also important that strategies be developed to assist those organizations that have adopted to address the barriers that confront them as they seek to effect ongoing significant improvements in care quality and safety and operational efficiency.

John Glaser is vice president and CIO of Partners HealthCare in Boston, senior advisor, Deloitte Center for Health Solutions, and a regular contributor to Most Wired Online.

The Four Cornerstones of Innovation

February 6, 2008
By John Glaser

Innovation, and the ability of information technology (IT) to further innovation, is a hot topic in management and information technology publications and conferences. Organizations are learning that it takes more than well-engineered and efficient processes to thrive. It takes the development of new and creative ways to deliver care, provide service and run the organization. It takes "innovation."

While this is true, health care organizations can be perplexed by this realization. How do we become more innovative? Should we put a group of our clinicians and administrators in a room and give them the exquisite guidance, "You all should be innovative!" That doesn't seem like a path to success. Does innovation mean that we have to come up with ideas that are patentable and change the direction of civilization? That doesn't seem very realistic.

Practical innovation is based on four cornerstones.

Innovation Is a Property of an Organization

Innovation is a property of an organization just as prowess in service excellence and efficiency can be properties of an organization. For innovation to be an ongoing aspect of organizational life, it must be more than an occasional management exercise. It must be part of the organizational fabric.

Innovation requires leadership that is interested in innovation, understands how innovation happens, knows how to carve out scarce resources to support innovation, is able to move new ideas from trial to broad adoption and establishes reward systems that value innovators. While they treasure innovation, these leaders are very pragmatic. They appreciate that "being innovative" is never a reason to do anything—there must be the prospect of business or clinical value.

Innovation Happens When People Try to Solve Real Problems

Innovation is goal oriented. It arises from efforts to develop answers to four major classes of questions.

Derive from an organizational strategy/goal. What is the most efficient and effective way to achieve a goal such as reducing outpatient medication errors?

Focus on core organizational processes. Why is the process of scheduling in the clinics so error prone and how do we fix it?

Examine new technology. Can this new technology, e.g., RFID, enable us to solve certain problems or capitalize on certain opportunities?

Explore a vision. What do we have to become and what do we have to learn if we are to truly become patient centric in our care?

Innovation happens when teams (or individuals), who preferably have scars from operations and care delivery, come up with answers to questions such as the above. The answer might be a process improvement, the thoughtful application of a new technology or a significantly more efficient way to achieve an organizational goal. The resulting set of answers can be very diverse. And these answers may or may not involve a new application or technology.

Not all answers will pass an innovation test. But that may not matter, if the answer is a good one. In fact, teams may not care if the answer is innovative per se. They just want the best answer. Best answers are often innovative.

Innovation Can Be Managed

A variety of techniques can be employed to help groups develop answers that are more innovative than not. Consulting firms can be skilled at helping an organization design exercises and discussions that encourage the free flow of ideas. These techniques usually do more than simply instructing people to "think outside of the box."

Managing innovation can require that the organization have processes for conducting pilots, assessing the impact of the innovation and determining if the innovation should be terminated, refined or rolled-out broadly across the organization.

Innovation management can seek to solicit ideas from staff and clinicians who are on the front line. This solicitation can be a challenge—not all ideas are good ideas. However, mechanisms for idea review and resource assignment can provide a fertile channel for innovation.

Innovation management also benefits from a portfolio perspective. At its simplest, this perspective asks if the organization is trying innovations in the areas that are the most strategically important and whether a modest portion of the budget, maybe 5 percent, is being devoted to trying out innovative ideas.

Information Technology Can Be an Important Contributor to Innovation

The information technology group can be a major asset in an organization's efforts to innovate. IT leadership can work with other members of the executive team to instill innovation into the fabric of the organization. Members of the IT staff are often members of teams that are grappling with answers to the four major classes of questions. IT management can establish innovation management practices and processes within the group.

Clearly, technology is experiencing relentless and impressive innovation. The cell phone of today is a remarkably different device from the cell phone of 5 years ago. However, these innovations are irrelevant unless they enable materially different answers to the questions above.

The technology has no inherent ability to "cause" innovation. The innovation value of the technology is determined by the context of its potential use. Is the ability to play Tetris on the cell phone a capability that will enable an innovative answer to an organizational challenge? Unlikely. Is the ability to send a message to patients that their physicians are running late a capability that might have value? Quite possibly.

Conclusion

Innovation is important, and information technology can be a critical contributor. In many ways, innovation is quite simple—someone has an insight into a new way to solve a problem. However, in most ways, innovation is complex. It requires that four cornerstones be laid—altering core properties of the organization, ensuring focused efforts to address core questions, establishing an innovation management process and effecting the thoughtful application of the technology.

John Glaser *is vice president and CIO of Partners HealthCare in Boston, senior advisor, Deloitte Center for Health Solutions, and a regular contributor to* Most Wired Online.

Reprinted from H&HN Hospitals & Health Networks, by permission, February 2008, ©2008 by Health Forum, Inc.

Information Technology Is Not an Intervention

November 28, 2007
By John Glaser

More so than perhaps any other industry, health care studies the impact of information technology on its core processes. The medical and health care IT publications and conferences are filled with a steady stream of analyses of the affect of applications such as the electronic health record on processes such as ordering medications, managing chronic disease and documenting care.

This propensity to study is reflective of the broader academic and scientific basis and culture of medical care. Clinical trials involve studies of device and medication efficacy. Evidence-based care relies on the meta-analyses of studies to identify best care practices. Research involving the human genome is often directed to understanding genetic variations that are specific and sensitive predictors of disease.

There is no question that studies of IT impact in health care have been very beneficial to the field. We are smarter about the contribution of clinical decision support to efforts to improve patient safety. We have a deeper understanding of the roles that EHRs can play in health maintenance. And physician willingness to adopt the technology can be enhanced if IT studies are performed with the same degree of scientific rigor that they would expect to see for any change in medical practice.

However, our industry's focus on studies of IT impact exposes a conceptual trap. IT is not an intervention.

What is an intervention? In general, an intervention involves doing something (surgically, chemically, mechanically, etc.) that should result in a predictable and hopefully desirable outcome. Surgery can repair an aneurysm. Medications can lower blood pressure.

The impact of IT on care does not appear to have very predictable outcomes. Some studies have shown a decrease in errors after the implementation of CPOE, whereas others have shown an increase in errors. There are studies that illustrate improvements in care quality following EHR adoption, whereas other research shows no improvements in quality. Analyses have been done that indicate reduced costs operations following EHR implementation, whereas other analyses do not find these reductions.

The implementations of electronic health records have not been shown to predictably lead to consistent outcomes. There is no technology determinism.

Information technology is a tool. Tools are different from interventions.

Given the right objectives, an intervention is usually the only variable. If the objective is to lower blood sugar levels, the injection of insulin may be the intervention of choice. If lower blood sugar levels do not result, then the intervention has failed.

Conversely, if one had an objective of going from New York to California, then an automobile might be proposed. However, for the automobile to be effective, roads are needed, traffic conventions must exist, gas stations must be present, and automobile repair shops are likely to be required. In the absence of these other variables, the likelihood that a person can get from New York to California in the automobile is very low. Any study that found that the automobile failed to transport a person across the country but failed to note the absence of roads would have inappropriately indicted the automobile as a failure.

For the electronic health record to achieve any objectives not only does the organization need the technology but it also needs leadership, an ability to effectively change processes, the means to provide training and ongoing support, and approaches to measuring objectives and engage in ongoing tuning of the application and care processes. Moreover, specific capabilities of the technology are needed, not simply "an EHR."

For tools to be effective, there are a number of factors or variables, including the tool, that must be present, and these variables must "fit" together.

What's the point of this distinction between health care IT as tools versus interventions?

Any organization that treats information technology as an intervention and overlooks the need to establish and manage all of the other variables faces a high likelihood of disappointment and a waste of money and effort. Any statement similar to, "If we implement CPOE we will reduce our medication errors," exhibits limited understanding.

Studies that examine IT as an intervention are at risk of making erroneous conclusions. Such studies need to consider all variables and not just the introduction of a specific application. Should the implementation of a specific application across a wide range of other necessary variables lead to a disappointing outcome, then the study could conclude that the IT application was not an effective way to achieve an objective. If the other variables were not examined, then the study's conclusions may not be conclusions.

For example, if despite the presence of roads and gas stations, the automobile was not able to transport a person across the country, only then could you perhaps conclude that the automobile was incapable of performing the task.

At times, the industry incorrectly reacts to the results of a specific study. A study that shows limited EHR impact on care quality might draw a reaction such as, "We told you so. EHRs are a waste of money." Conversely, a study that showed dramatic quality gains through EHR implementation might lead to the reaction, "We told you so. EHRs are the answer to all that ails health care." Neither reaction is correct. A correct reaction leads to questions such as, "What combination of factors, including the specific capabilities of the EHR, lead to the results that have been documented?"

Our medical heritage of appropriately studying the impact of interventions can lead us to applying that orientation to health care IT. We should know better.

John Glaser *is vice president and CIO of Partners HealthCare in Boston, senior advisor, Deloitte Center for Health Solutions, and a regular contributor to* Most Wired Online.

When Information Hurts

August 22, 2007
By John Glaser

Privacy is an individual's ability to limit the disclosure of personal information. Ensuring privacy may be one of the most important and difficult challenges of our efforts to encourage the adoption of health care information technology and interoperable electronic health records.

Importance

Why is the goal of ensuring privacy so important?

Inappropriate releases of patient information can damage people. People may not be able to be made whole, and they may not be able to recover from the damage. Information about sexually transmitted diseases can destroy a marriage. Information about a chronic condition can mean the loss of health and life insurance. Information about a psychiatric disorder can ruin a career.

If your credit card information is stolen and someone uses that information to purchase a state-of-the-art high-definition television, you can be made whole. Your misappropriated funds can be returned to you.

There may be no way to repair the marriage. Or to replace the lost insurance. Or to reinstate a career.

The inappropriate release of information about your health and medical history is unique in its ability to lead to lasting damage. The public understands the nature of this potential damage and is concerned that health care IT will elevate the risk of damage. A 2006 Harris survey showed that 62 percent of Americans believe that the adoption of

EMRs would make it more difficult to ensure the patients' privacy, and 42 percent felt that the privacy risks of EMRs outweighed the benefits.

Because of concerns about damage, the inappropriate release of information can erode or destroy patients' trust in their health care providers.

When you are ill or in pain or scared, you are vulnerable. You place your life and well being in the hands of your doctor or nurse, and you trust that they will take care of you. You may not really understand whether their diagnosis or suggested therapies are correct. But you trust that they are, and you trust the experience and knowledge of those who are caring for you.

This trust is essential. We need the trust because we will need you to follow the treatment plan that you and your care team develop. We need the trust because we need to have you tell your providers your full medical history, the medications you are taking, the nature of your pain and your treatment preferences. The care team needs for you to tell them information that you might find embarrassing or about which you are ashamed.

If we release your information inappropriately or we are perceived as unable to manage the release of information, then the trust is diminished. If that reduced trust leads you to withhold information, or to doubt the integrity of your providers, then we have hampered our ability to deliver care.

The delivery of medical care is built on a foundation of trust. If we damage that trust, then we damage our ability to deliver care. There are signs that this trust may be in trouble. A 2007 Harris survey found that 17 percent of respondents have withheld information from their providers.

We devote our professional lives to applying information technology to improve care delivery. The inappropriate release of patient information can sabotage these efforts with remarkable effectiveness and speed.

Difficulty

Ensuring privacy is a very difficult challenge.

Privacy is riddled with individual values and beliefs. There can be different opinions about the definition of "inappropriate." All of these opinions can be right, just as they are collectively inconsistent. Privacy may be akin to art; there is no universally correct definition of art, just as there can be reasonable disagreements about the utility of specific steps to protect privacy.

The privacy landscape is fluid. The connected world in which we live is altering our individual and collective concerns about privacy. New concerns have arisen—identity theft is a fairly recent phenomenon. Previous concerns seem to have faded—most individuals have grown to accept the fact that Internet-supplied cookies are monitoring their activity on websites.

Despite being based on diverse values and beliefs and surrounded by a fluid landscape, organizations can take prudent and generally accepted approaches to ensuring privacy. Patients can be notified of the organization's privacy practices. Employees and clinicians can be educated about the importance of privacy. Violations of a patient's privacy can result in memorable discipline. Access restrictions can be implemented in clinical information systems.

But preserving privacy can be a pain. It's easy to not obtain consents or discuss notices in a hectic clinic with a registration line 30 people deep. It can take longer to use an application because of "need to know" checks. Catching up on Blackberry email messages may seem more worthwhile than paying attention to talk about the organization's privacy policies. It can be hard to truly discipline a great employee who has violated a patient's or colleague's privacy.

Worth It

This pain is worth it. It is worth it because we must protect that trust. It is worth it because none of us, or anyone we care about, wants to experience the lasting damage that can result from the inappropriate release of our health care data.

It is worth it because we do want our health care information technology efforts to be materially undermined because we were sloppy with privacy.

John Glaser is vice president and CIO of Partners HealthCare in Boston, senior advisor, Deloitte Center for Health Solutions, and a regular contributor to Most Wired Online.

Index